Sweetwater, Storms, and Spirits

"George B. Carpenter Company on S. Water Street, Chicago." (Courtesy
Ryerson Collection, Chicago Historical Society.)

Sweetwater, Storms, and Spirits

STORIES OF THE GREAT LAKES

Selected and Edited by
Victoria Brehm

Published in cooperation with the
Historical Society of Michigan

Ann Arbor
The University of Michigan Press

In memory of E. R. B., 1905–88

First paperback edition 1991
Copyright © by the University of Michigan 1990
All rights reserved
Published in the United States of America by
The University of Michigan Press
Manufactured in the United States of America

2000   1999   9 8 7

Library of Congress Cataloging-in-Publication Data

Sweetwater, storms, and spirits : stories of the Great Lakes /
  selected and edited by Victoria Brehm.
      p.   cm.
  Includes bibliographical references.
  ISBN 0-472-10144-7 — ISBN 0-472-08151-9 (pbk.)
  1. Great Lakes Region—Fiction.   2. Short stories, American—
Great Lakes Region.   I. Brehm, Victoria, 1947–   .
PS562.S94   1990
813.'01083277—dc20   89-20682
                                                     CIP

The author wishes to thank the following individuals and institutions for their kind permission to reprint copyrighted material: Walter Havighurst for the chapter "A Gold-Headed Cane," from his book *Signature of Time* (copyright © 1949, printed by the Macmillan Company, reprinted with permission); George Vukelich for his story "The Bosun's Chair," and for the chapter "The Sturgeon" from his book *Fisherman's Beach*; the Clarke Historical Library, Central Michigan University, for the use of "Nänabushu Swallowed by the Sturgeon" and "Now Great-Lynx" from their copy of *Ojibwa Texts* by William Jones; the Bentley Historical Library, University of Michigan, for "The Snow Wasset," and for verses from "The Fisherman *Yankee Brown*," and "The Schooner *Thomas Hulme*" (Ivan H. Walton Papers, Michigan Historical Collections, Bentley Historical Library, University of Michigan); Jay McCormick for the excerpt from his novel *November Storm*; D. Ariel Rogers Peart, for verses from the song "Lock-Keeper" (copyright © Stan Rogers 1980, used by permission from Fogarty's Cove and Cole Harbor Music Ltd., Dundas, Canada); Lake Carriers' Association for the map of the Great Lakes; the Prints and Photographs Division of the Chicago Historical Society for the illustration "George B. Carpenter Company on S. Water Street, Chicago" (from the Ryerson collection); Edward Pusick and Frederick Stonehouse of Shipwrecks Unlimited, Marquette, Michigan, for the illustrations "Hanging On" and "The *Edmund Fitzgerald* in Storm, November 10, 1975"; Leo. V. Kuschel, Taylor, Michigan, for the illustration "Bois Blanche Island Light"; the Institute for Great Lakes Research for "'Lifting a Pot' at Kelley's Pound-net, Lake Erie, 1987."

Acknowledgments

THIS BOOK BEGAN as a bet with the late Richard Wright, who declared that finding unknown Great Lakes maritime short stories would be such a monumental task no one in their right mind would attempt it. He may have been right. In the process of compiling this collection I have not only come to doubt my own sanity, but also have driven a number of librarians close to the edge. For their patience and resourcefulness I wish to thank particularly Helen Ryan and Keith Rageth of the University of Iowa Library, Ilene Schechter and Joann Frankena of the State Library of Michigan, Pat Suttor of the University of Windsor Library, and Virginia Schwartz of the Milwaukee Public Library and Suzette Lopez of the Wisconsin Marine Historical Society. I could not have completed the introductions to the stories or the biographical notes without the assistance of the researchers at historical collections around the Great Lakes area: Jay Martin of the Institute for Great Lakes Research in Perrysburg, Ohio; Joanie Kloster of the Manitowoc, Wisconsin, Maritime Museum; Nancy Bartlett of the Michigan Historical Collections in Ann Arbor; the librarians at *Maclean's Magazine* in Toronto; the researchers of the historical societies in Buffalo, New York, and Marquette, Michigan; and the Minnesota Historical Society in St. Paul. All patiently searched their files for the small details I knew had to be there because I needed them. The directors of the Prints and Photographs Department of the Chicago Historical Society, and John Polacsek of the Dossin Great Lakes

Museum, offered cheerful help with the illustrations. I am equally indebted to those Great Lakes maritime aficionados who wrote to acknowledge my queries in journals. Dennis Kubiak checked documentation and photocopied his cherished copy of *Falkner of the Inland Seas* for me, and Captain Carl. A. Norberg answered questions no one else could.

Many maritime professionals freely gave me their time and expertise. Frank Prothero, editor of the *Great Lakes Fisherman*, advised me about turn-of-the-century fishing on Lake Erie. Marvin Weborg of Gills Rock, Wisconsin, took me fishing and was gracious enough not to make me help clean the catch. I could not have edited this book without the technical knowledge I gained sailing the lakes with Captain James M. Scott of Algoma Central Marine's *Algosoo* and Captain Danny Molnar of American Steamship's *Indiana Harbor*. Both they and their crews patiently answered hundreds of questions while I learned what it means to be a professional sailor on the lakes. I thank them for many pleasant hours in the pilot house.

Paul Baender, William Kupersmith, Kathleen Diffley, Dixie Saylor, and Robert Grunst of the University of Iowa gave me practical and scholarly advice on the manuscript for which I am grateful. Finally, I owe my deepest thanks to John Dann, director of the Clements Library at the University of Michigan, whose support and enthusiasm convinced me to make these stories available to those who love the lakes.

Contents

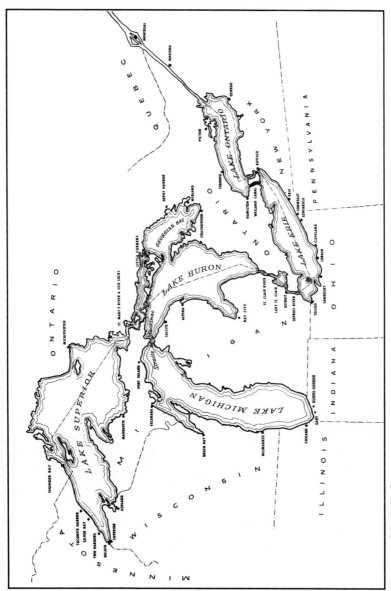

Courtesy of the Lake Carriers' Association

Introduction

The next day we parted, and continued our journey along the shore of this Lake of the Attigouautans [Lake Huron], in which there are a great number of islands; and we made forty-five leagues, keeping along the shore of this lake. It is very large, being nearly four hundred leagues in length, from east to west, and fifty leagues wide, and in view of its great size I named it the Freshwater Sea.

Champlain[1]

HIS JOURNALS do not record what must have been his disappointment that July day in 1614 when he leaned over the gunnel of his canoe and scooped up a handful of water to taste, since if the broad waters stretching before him had been salt his fortunes and those of France would have been assured. Champlain would have found the Northwest Passage. But the water on his tongue was clear and fresh, "sweet" in the literal translation, and Champlain who described them first described them best: la Mer douce—they are not lakes, they are a sea of fresh water. He saw only a small part of the interconnected inland seas we now call the Great Lakes; their full extent would not be known for more than fifty years, and they would not be correctly charted until well into the nineteenth century. But even after the wil-

---

1. Samuel de Champlain, *The Works of Samuel de Champlain,* vol. 1, edited by H. P. Bigger (Toronto: Champlain Society, 1922–36), 1:45.

derness wars fought for them were ended and the settlers on their shores could see fleets of schooners and steamships carrying a commerce that would help build two nations, the lakes had lost none of their power to astonish. Kipling, one of many Europeans to travel the lakes in the last century, attempted to understand their effect on him; after knowing only the ocean, they seemed to him to be the stuff of a nightmare.

There is a quiet horror about the Great Lakes which grows as one revisits them. Fresh water has no right or call to dip over the horizon, pulling down and pushing up hulls of big steamers, no right to tread the slow, deep sea dance-step between wrinkled cliffs; nor to roar in on weed and sand beaches between vast headlands that run out for leagues into bays and sea fog. Lake Superior is all the same stuff towns pay taxes for (fresh water), but it engulfs and wrecks and drives ashore like a fully accredited ocean—a hideous thing to find in the heart of a continent.[2]

This Janus-faced character of the lakes that Kipling captures so well has marked their maritime culture and their literature from the earliest Indian legends to the present. Emerald and azure when spangled with the sun, silver when overspread with the Northern Lights, they have enchanted mariners with their beauty for centuries. Since they were far from the Atlantic and the passages on them took days rather than weeks, those who first sailed their limpid waters believed themselves safe from storm and danger, only to die in sudden, furious gales of roiling

---

2. Rudyard Kipling, *Letters to the Family,* in *The Collected Works of Rudyard Kipling* (New York: AMS Press, 1970), vol. 19, *Letters of Travel,* p. 157. Regarding Lake Superior, Kipling writes further: "Some people go sailing on it for pleasure, and it has produced a breed of sailors who bear the same relation to the salt-water variety as a snake-charmer to a lion-tamer."

gray water within sight of shore. Like Champlain, what these first sailors expected was not what they found, and the history and literature of the Great Lakes are a record of their attempts to accommodate themselves to a place unlike any they had experienced before: a seemingly tranquil sea they learned they could not master but only try to survive.

The wrecking and death began early in their recent recorded history, in 1679 when LaSalle's *Griffon*, the first ship to sail the upper lakes, left the Wisconsin shore against the advice of the local Indians and disappeared forever. Her pilot, an experienced sailor who had voiced his contempt for the lakes before, would listen to no one about the dangers of sailing when a storm was brewing and so, like many saltwater sailors in the next three hundred years, paid for his condescension with his life. Hennepin, the Recollect friar traveling with LaSalle, was less precipitous in his judgments and more astutely observant. Looking at the lakes, he noted that "It were easie to build on the sides of these great Lakes an infinite Number of considerable Towns which might have Communication one with another by Navigation for Five Hundred Leagues together, and by an inconceivable Commerce which would establish it self among 'em."[3] The fiction of the Great Lakes is one story of that commerce, a maritime literature inspired by the paradox of sailing a sea in the midst of a continent, where a seven-hundred-foot ship loaded with wheat from the tranquil farms nearby can be ripped apart by a gale worthy of the North Atlantic. So great is this paradox that those who have not sailed them—saltwater seamen, editors, and critics—often refuse to believe their danger and dismiss the stories about them.

Little wonder then that one of the most enduring themes of Great Lakes fiction is the humility they teach those who have

---

3. Father Louis Hennepin, *A New Discovery of a Vast Country in America*, edited by Reuben Gold Thwaites (Chicago: A. C. McClurg and Co., 1903), p. 64.

sailed only on salt water. The anonymous author of one of the first novels set on the lakes, *Scenes on Lake Huron*, had been such a person. He writes his tale, he says,

> . . . in order to place the Lake Seamen upon an equal footing, or to redeem if possible, a race of the most hardy and skillful men from the imputation, which has been often cast upon them by their Atlantic brethern, old in the profession, that they were, in fact, "no seamen at all." When in truth, after they themselves had tried the Lakes some one or two seasons, and taken lectures from our fresh water gentlemen, the more candid have universally acknowledged them to be as efficient as any other, and that they ought to be ranked among the most able on the globe.

His message seems to have fallen upon deaf ears, since James Fenimore Cooper had repeated it at length in *The Pathfinder* in 1840, and Herman Melville was still trying to convince saltwater mariners about the lakes years later in *Moby-Dick*. Melville's experience of a storm on Lake Erie left an indelible impression in his imagination, and his description of it in *Moby-Dick* has become a frequently quoted passage about the lakes:

> . . . they are swept by Borean and dismasting blasts as direful as any that lash the salted wave; they know what shipwrecks are, for out of sight of land, however inland, they have drowned full many a midnight ship with all its shrieking crew.

Perhaps if Melville had written his most famous novel about the lakes rather than the ocean, about the fur trade rather than whaling, the themes of lakes stories would have changed and the literature itself would not have been neglected. But nearly a century after *Scenes on Lake Huron*, Norman Reilly Raine wrote "The Deep Water Mate" about a saltwater sailor who scorns the lakes because their prosaic boundedness cannot compare with the romance and danger of the ocean—until he encounters a storm.

Raine, like several other writers whose work is reprinted in this volume, wrote only one story about the lakes in a career spent writing maritime fiction. He undoubtedly learned, as did they, that fiction set on the lakes would not sell to the editors in New York. Ralph Emberg, whose story "Out of the Trough" begins this book, writes in the introduction to his collection of short stories, *Phantom Caravel*, "I shall never forget the difficulty I had with editors when I first began to write stories of the Great Lakes. 'This is a good yarn and I'd buy it if it were a sea story.' was a typical editorial reaction. 'But the Great Lakes—well—we don't think our readers would be interested.'" Richard Matthews Hallet, who wrote dozens of saltwater maritime stories for the *Saturday Evening Post* early in the century, set his excellent novel, *Trial By Fire*, on the lakes, and yet it received so little attention that a few years later Eugene O'Neill could shanghai plot, characters, and theme to the ocean for *The Hairy Ape* and no one noticed.[4] Despite a rich maritime literary tradition in both the United States and Canada, the literature of the Great Lakes has often been relegated to obscure journals and small magazines specializing in adventure stories, and any maritime writer who had a living to earn by his craft soon turned to the ocean for his setting.

This determined refusal to acknowledge the experience of lakes sailing—often more demanding and dangerous than the ocean—as valid and worthy of attention is shaped by complex reasons rooted in a seldom-questioned myth that our destiny on this continent is the endless and successful conquest of the fron-

---

4. Those interested in a full discussion of O'Neill's piracy and a description of Hallet's career should read chapter 8 of *Sea-Brothers: The Tradition of American Sea fiction from Moby-Dick to the Present*, by Bert Bender (Philadelphia: University of Pennsylvania Press, 1988).

tier and the wilderness. Long ago Americans and Canadians turned their backs to the sea and embraced the land because it could be transformed and redesigned to suit our needs and conveniences.[5] For the Americans, this attitude is a heritage from the Puritans, who saw untamed wilderness as the abode of the devil, and from Thomas Jefferson, who believed the agrarian ideal of small farms and villages to be the best foundation for a free and democratic society. The Canadians faced their wilderness with the idea of turning it into an English garden, or failing that, erecting a stockade to keep it at bay. Both nations, however, made the land, not the ocean, the primary symbol for their experiences on the continent because the land could, with more or less success, be mastered. But Thoreau noted long ago that "The ocean is a wilderness reaching round the globe, wilder than a Bengal jungle, and fuller of monsters, washing the very wharves of our cities and the gardens of our seaside residences. Serpents, bears, hyenas, tigers rapidly vanish as civilization advances, but the most populous and civilized city cannot scare a shark far from its wharves."[6] And although Americans often suggest that *Moby-Dick* is their greatest novel, few would agree with Melville that "in landlessness alone resides the highest truth, shoreless, indefinite as God. . . ." For North Americans, as for all peoples in all times, the ocean, or any vast expanse of water such as the Great Lakes, is what W. H. Auden called the "primordial undifferentiated flux . . . that state of barbaric vagueness and disorder out of which civilization has emerged and into which, unless saved by the effort of gods and men, it is always liable to relapse."[7] Like the ocean, the waters of the Great Lakes remain untamed, and much of the literature written about them is devoted to tracing our inability to conquer a place. Even

---

5. J. B. Jackson, *American Space* (New York: Norton and Co., 1972), p. 36.
6. Henry David Thoreau, *Cape Cod* (New York: Bramhall House, 1951), p. 184.
7. W. H. Auden, *The Enchaféd Flood* (Charlottesville, Va.: University of Virginia, 1950), p. 6.

though they lie in the heart of a changed and plundered continent, they are a reminder that the dream of turning a wilderness into a garden does not hold for all experience.

How then are we to comprehend a literature that is nominally from the midst of one of the most agrarian and industrial places in North America and yet has little to do with it? A literature that contradicts all the surrounding landscape represents and reflects an idea of place that is not so much what we have come to regard as American, with its images of energetic confidence and successful conquest, but one where nature is seen as indifferent, if not actively hostile.[8] In other words, the untamed wilderness. This is the "hideous thing in the heart of a continent" that Kipling noticed, and it has not changed since. For all that the land around the lakes has been mined, timbered, settled, farmed, and urbanized, the maritime landscape of the lakes has changed very little from when the Indians first knew it. A few canals, breakwaters, and lighthouses are all the difference we have been able to make in three hundred years, and despite the technology that enables us to build thousand-foot ships to carry iron ore from Duluth to Detroit, ships still sink and sailors still die on the lakes, even as they did when Melville knew them. The Great Lakes give lie to the dream of conquest by settlement and technology, even as they are surrounded by it and their ships make its success possible, and their stories force us to confront far older and less comforting truths of existence we usually avoid acknowledging. Thus, we can accept stories about shipwreck and disaster on the ocean, simply because it is "out there," away from the continent, and we have a long literary tradition of ocean shipwreck and disaster; but when the ocean invades the land, bringing its age-old themes and fears in its wake, we turn away in disbelief. Water that you can drink

---

8. Margaret Atwood, *Survival* (Toronto: House of Anansi, 1972), chap. 2. Atwood's book is the best discussion of how the geography and climate of Canada has affected the art of its writers.

should not be able to kill you, particularly when you are sailing a ship longer than two football fields off a civilized shoreline.

To begin to understand Great Lakes literature in its own right and not simply as a poor imitation of saltwater themes by regional writers who could do nothing better, we must begin with the stories of the Indians. They were the first lakes mariners and had sailed in their cockleshells of birch for hundreds of years before Champlain appeared and they knew the lakes well, far better than the Europeans gave them credit for. But to the Christian Europeans who prayed to the Blessed Virgin and sang the *Te Deum* for safe passage across the lakes, the Indians' rituals of fasting and sacrifice and their offerings of tobacco sprinkled into the water were barbaric rites in service of a primitive *genius loci*, Missipeshu, the great horned lynx who raised storms and attacked canoes. But the Indian beliefs were not so different from the Europeans', since the Indians divided the cosmos into the powers of the upper world, the Thunderbirds, versus the underworld devils like Missipeshu. As Auden noted in *The Enchaféd Flood*, in all cultures "What comes from the sky is a spiritual or supernatural visitation. What lies hidden in the water is the unknown powers of nature,"[9] and, we might add, the ship sails uneasily between the two. Where the Indians did differ was in personifying these unknown powers of nature, giving them form and character and will, so that a storm was not merely a storm, but the conscious act of a vengeful or savage creature. Such beliefs were dismissed as superstition by the Europeans and Americans who took over the Indians' trade routes, sacred places, and knowledge of the water, and occasionally appropriated their myths and stories for tall tales and poetry. But Carl Jung and D. H. Lawrence felt that the spirits of a place and the spirits of men who believed in them were not so easily disavowed; both suggested that they remain to affect those cultures

---

9. Auden, p. 72.

that follow.[10] Although this is a romantic notion that too easily becomes a simplistic geographical determinism for which a landscape determines the character of its inhabitants and the literature they produce, we cannot ignore the fact that in fiction the Great Lakes are described differently from salt water.

Unlike the ocean in Melville or Conrad, the lakes are characterized not as uncaringly destructive or as a natural force with which man must reckon, but as savage and willful. This is not to say that Americans and Canadians write serious stories about water monsters in Saginaw Bay, but, submerged in the text, personification abounds in Great Lakes literature and there are several instances in this collection. One does not have sleet on Lake Superior, one has "ice devils" ("Out of the Trough"); waves are frequently described as wolves circling a ship about to sink ("The Deep Water Mate"); in the excerpt from *November Storm*, a deckhand clings to the engine room floor grating in a gale, afraid to move because it would amount to "inviting [the] storm's attention and a greater wrath. . . . to dare action, [would] deliberately infuriate the destroying force by setting puny deeds, machines in its path. . . ." In fiction that consciously appropriates Indian legends, such personification is to be expected and is often used as a cheap dramatic device; thus clouds turn into windigos and Indian drums beat along the shore each time a ship sinks. But this personification of the lakes into a presence bent on destruction occurs in all kinds of fiction, poetry, and folklore from the beginning to the present, particularly in the work of writers who have written more than once about the lakes. Whether or not one agrees with Jung and Lawrence, or whether one simply believes that any ship on any large body of water leaves behind the security of land and thereby encounters

---

10. See Carl Jung, "Mind and Earth," in *Civilization in Transition*, translated by R. F. C. Hull (Princeton: Princeton University Press, 1970), pp. 49ff., and D. H. Lawrence, *Studies in Classic American Literature* (New York: Thomas Seltzer, 1923), pp. 8–9, 44.

uncontrollable and terrifying forces of nature that prompt an atavistic urge to personify what cannot be understood, we are still left with the evidence that artists writing about the lakes describe them as something more than simply a natural threat. Caught in the crux of a baffling paradox—how is it that such seemingly calm and bounded waters, so fresh and so beautiful, can become so quickly vicious and mortal?—the writers of the lakes have, sometimes consciously and sometimes unconsciously, suggested that these waters have a nature different from the oceans, which we do not necessarily understand.

If we assume with the scholars of landscape theory that a place is neither good nor bad in itself but in the values attached to it, and that literature is one of the ways we attach value to a place,[11] we must conclude that much of the literature of the Great Lakes does not celebrate our conquest of nature, but records instead a more primitive, Northern attitude of simple survival in the face of an actively hostile environment. Technology gives only a false sense of security that leads to destruction— witness the captain of the *Blackfoot* in *November Storm*, who heads out into what he knows will be a serious gale because "They didn't come strong enough to bother these boats," and loses his ship. While the hero of lakes stories usually survives, unlike his counterpart in Canadian wilderness fiction who often does not, it is frequently a chastened survival without triumph and with a new awareness of his limitations. If his ship survives with him it is often as changed as he: battered beyond recognition, thrown up on shore, broken in two, or otherwise unsailable.[12]

The climate of the lakes and the legacy of Indian legends

---

11. Leonard Lutwack, *The Role of Place in Literature* (Syracuse: Syracuse University Press, 1984), p. 35.

12. I have referred to the heros of these stories as "he" because most stories set on the lakes are written by men about men. Heroines in lakes fiction are most often lightkeepers (as the two stories in this collection) or vessel cooks, the only maritime professions open to women until recently. Because so few stories feature women, it is difficult to generalize about their experiences on the lakes, thus the conclusions I suggest necessarily reflect a male perspective.

that permeated American and Canadian culture around them may partly explain the persistent theme of savage destruction in the literature, but they do not account for it all. Literature is inspired not only by landscape and legend but by history as well, and the shipping history of the lakes is a litany of wreck and death seldom equaled. Historians estimate that during the past two hundred years more than ten thousand ships have been torn apart by the lakes, their bones scattered on a wreck-strewn coastline as dangerous as any in the world. The life expectancy of a Great Lakes sailor in the nineteenth century was only five to seven years after first setting foot on deck; the dangers of working the lakes were greater than those of the whaling industry of the same period and more like that of English shipping a century earlier. The reasons for this carnage of ships and sailors stem from the accidents of geography and history, for the lakes were a highway into a land rich in minerals and ripe for the plow at a time when aids to navigation were few and harbors of refuge separated by hundreds of miles.

Although there were sailing ships on the lakes in the 1700s, most shipping was related to the fur trade and military garrisons until after the War of 1812. Even then lakes commerce was slow to develop until the completion of the Erie Canal in 1825 and the treaties with the Indian tribes that opened the plains for settlement. But by the 1830s more than half of the immigrants traveling west came by water, carried on steamers running between Buffalo and western lake ports. Although the rail lines began to cut into this commerce after the 1850s, passenger steamboats ran on the lakes for another hundred years, growing ever larger and more palatial and spawning travel accounts as perceptive as Kipling's, as well as a number of impossibly saccharine romantic stories and novels about one of the most popular water trips of the late nineteenth and early twentieth centuries. But side-by-side with the glittering passenger ships with their starchly uniformed crews and polished brass, the most characteristic commerce of the lakes, bulk cargo, began a stupendous growth that would endure when the steamers lay rotting at the pier. Lakes shipping had first been developed to carry bulk cargo—the canoes of the Indians and the bateaux of the French ferried bales of furs and supplies back and forth between the lakehead and the St. Lawrence for decades before passenger traffic was thought of—but with the opening of American and Canadian lands to settlement wheat soon began filling the ships that sailed down the lakes to the East. Then in the 1830s and 1840s copper and iron were discovered near the shores of Lake Superior and it quickly became apparent that shipping the raw ore to factories in the cities beginning to line the lower lakes was much cheaper than processing it in the north and shipping the finished product. With the opening of the canal at Sault Ste. Marie in 1855, the last major obstacle between the wheat fields, copper mines, and iron ranges was gone, and ships had clear passage through the lakes. In the mid-nineteenth century these ships were frequently three-masted schooners with sleek, powerful lines and towering masts, most owned by the captains who sailed them. They raced each other from Chicago to Buffalo in the spring with the first cargoes of wheat, and from the iron ranges to the cities "down below" loaded with timber or red iron ore, and around them grew up folksong and story. As one folksong chants,

> Watch her! Catch her!
> Jump up on her juberju!
> Give 'er the sheet an' let her 'er howl,
> We're the boys to drive 'er through.
> You should've of seen 'er howling,
> The wind was blowing free,
> On our passage down to Buffalo
> From Mil—wau—kee.[13]

---

13. "The Timber Drougher *Bigler*," traditional Great Lakes Song collected by Ivan H. Walton, Ivan H. Walton Papers, Michigan Historical Collections, Bentley Historical Library, Ann Arbor, Michigan.

But although this commerce was romantic and beautiful, it was also dangerous, for besides the lack of aids to navigation and harbors of refuge, the only storm warnings were what the master saw in the sky, which on the lakes is often too late. It is during this era of the mid-to-late nineteenth century that the characteristic themes of storm and death and destruction appear most frequently, and the historical reasons are not hard to find. In a *normal* year fifty to seventy ships would be total losses. In a bad year like 1880, 456 sailors died and dozens of ships never sailed again. In the one decade from 1864 to 1874, a total of 4,527 vessels were lost and 1,341 sailors were killed.[14] The ships sailed without life-saving equipment and their crews were often untrained hands who sailed only in summer and worked in the lumberwoods after freeze-up. Given these conditions, it is not hard to understand stories like "The Deep Water Mate" and "A Lake Huron Ghost Story" that attempt to make sense of the romantic yet terrifying experience of sailing the lakes before the wind.

The small bulk cargoes carried on these schooners were slowly and painfully unloaded by men and horses and later donkey engines, while the demands of the factories for raw materials and of the eastern cities for grain, coal, and timber grew unceasingly. By the 1880s the day of the schooner on the lakes was nearly over; the screw propeller had been introduced in 1840, and in 1882 the first prototype of the now characteristic class of lakes vessel, with cabins forward and engine room aft and cargo hatches between, came off the ways. Unloading machinery improved apace until what had once taken days to unload could be done in as many hours. Canal locks were repeatedly broadened and lengthened, and with each increase the ships grew longer and larger and more efficient. The old schooners were no longer profitable and no single owner could afford to build a new iron or steel vessel to compete. Shipping on the lakes became a

---

14. *Chicago Tribune*, May 7, 1874.

company concern with fleets of ships; as Morgan Robertson's story "The Survival of the Fittest" illustrates, those schooners that were still seaworthy suffered the indignity of having their masts cut down to be towed in a string like barges. The end of the nineteenth century was the end of an era of lakes shipping, and not surprisingly inspired much fiction, but while the new century saw ever longer steel ships sailed by professional seamen, the themes of the stories did not change, simply because the lakes had not. Storms still ravaged them, such as the famous 1913 blow when nineteen ships were totally destroyed and 251 sailors lost, and those who survived began to realize that improved technology could not always protect them. The losses did not stop the flow of shipping, however, and ships grew steadily larger and faster. For many years the tonnage shipped on the lakes exceeded that of the Atlantic and Pacific coast ports combined, and before the last schooner on the lakes had sunk, the parade of long ships passing through the rivers and locks was nearly continuous. The lakes had long since become international waterways, and it was no flight of poetic fancy that prompted Edgar Lee Masters to write in "The Lake Boats," "You are not Lake Leman, / Walled in by Mt. Blanc. / One sees the whole world round you / And beyond you, Lake Michigan."[15]

Although the traditional chanties had fallen silent, a new generation of singers and storytellers had grown up who knew nothing of wind-ship sailing but were sailors nevertheless. For writers like Ralph Emberg and Jay McCormick and Walter Havighurst, the sight of four- and five- and six-hundred-foot ships with their shining white upperworks fore and aft and a long, sleek stretch of cargo holds between provided romance and danger enough. There were fewer stories about storm and shipwreck as the twentieth century grew older, partly because there were

---

15. Edgar Lee Masters, "The Lake Boats," in *The New Poetry—An Anthology of Twentieth Century Verse in English*, edited by Harriet Monroe and Alice Corbin Henderson (New York: Macmillan Company, 1925), p. 329.

fewer ships, but with better equipment, and so fewer wrecks, and partly because the fashion in fiction changed from simple action and romance to a careful probing of the psyche. George Vukelich's stories, "The Sturgeon" and "The Bosun's Chair," are modern maritime fiction, but the old fears still lurk underneath: the sturgeon who kills even though it is supposed to be dead, a sailor's dread of using the bosun's chair. Yet despite the changing fashions of fiction during the last 150 years, most stories and novels written about the lakes are still set in the context of storm, their artists still seeking to understand why the lakes have not yet been tamed and why men refuse to acknowledge that. As a folksong about a recent lakes disaster puts it, "The good ship and crew was a bone to be chewed when the gales of November turned angry."[16] Ships still fall victim to the sweetwater sea, despite radar, radios, lighthouses, and nearby harbors, and artists continue to characterize the lakes as before. If the river is, in T. S. Eliot's words, "a strong, brown God," the lakes are a savage, bone-chewing one that cannot be placated or escaped no matter how much sophisticated technology man sets out to sail upon them.

If, as some suggest, the aim of stories is to make sense of experience, what then are we to think about the literature of the lakes, coming as it does from a region where the most typical way of life involves farming or urban life? That the experience represented by stories such as those collected here is an anomaly, a quirk of geography and climate, and thus only a curiosity of American and Canadian literature as a whole? Regional fiction is often denigrated for being based simply on pride, or for exploiting quaintness and eccentricity at the expense of presenting a picture of life that we recognize as true for all people, no matter where they live. Writing that celebrates a place for its own sake, without real regard for the lives lived there, becomes a travel

---

16. Gordon Lightfoot, "The Wreck of the *Edmund Fitzgerald*," *Summertime Dream*, Warner Bros. Records Inc., 1976.

narrative or a sentimental set piece, and certainly the Great Lakes have inspired a good deal of both. But the maritime fiction of the lakes seldom falls into those categories. It is, distinct from other American and Canadian fiction set in the same geographic area, a truly maritime literature and so belongs to a tradition that existed long before the first wheat ripened or the first bar of iron was forged. A ship in a gale, whether on fresh water or salt, is the same the world over, as are the sailors who struggle to keep her headed into the wind. What sets lakes literature apart is its preoccupation with the particular characteristics of sailing *this* water, characteristics that stem not only from the landscape of brooding northern seas with unpredictable weather surrounded by the lee shore, but from the history and the cultures of those who have sailed the lakes for centuries. It is in the fiction of particular places, what Wendell Berry calls "local life aware of itself," that we can see the myths we take for granted in a clearer light. "Without a complex knowledge of one's place," he continues, "the culture of a country will be superficial and decorative, functional only insofar as it may be a symbol of prestige, the affectation of an elite or ingroup."[17] Thus, to dismiss Great Lakes literature as simply regional fiction that is of scant interest to those who do not know the lakes is to cut oneself off from a potentially rich source of ideas for understanding our experience on the continent.

The stories collected in this volume represent only a small part of an intriguing body of fiction that while exploring its own landscape and experience calls into question some of the more cherished notions of American and Canadian culture, revealing them to be less universal than often thought. Even as the surrounding landscape has become a testament to our effect on the environment, the lakes in fiction have remained a symbol of the

---

17. Wendell Berry, "An Essay and a Meditation," *Southern Review* 4 (Autumn 1970): 975–76.

harsh, unchanged reality of existence itself.[18] Because lakes literature partakes of these two traditions—the ancient one of the sea that never changes, and the recent one of the attempted conquest of a continent, the literature of the Great Lakes is unique. It grew from a history of exploration and settlement without which lakes' maritime life would never have existed, and yet it hearkens back to a way of life that was old before Columbus. "Full little he thinks who has life's joy / And dwells in cities and has few disasters, / Proud and wine-flushed, how I, weary often, / Must bide my time on the brimming stream." wrote a tenth-century Anglo-Saxon poet in "The Seafarer." Another sailor, standing at the rail of a Great Lakes ship loaded with wheat and heading down to Buffalo in 1960 wrote, ". . . the time of the Sailors / men in worndown seaboots / working out the longwaters / and waiting for a season / ashore / the loneliest men in the world."[19] More than a thousand years have not changed the experience of the sea; only the shore, temporarily, has been bent to the hand of man. If nothing else, the stories of the Great Lakes serve to remind us how recent and how fragile our conquest remains.

---

18. The lakes are not the only place on the continent that symbolize another kind of existence; Leonard Lutwack, in *The Role of Place in Literature*, discusses Willa Cather's use of the rocks in the Southwest as a symbol of existence that is far different from the agrarian plains she had written about before. He suggests she uses the rocks and mountains as a symbol of what man cannot change and therefore must accommodate himself to; this is much the same way writers use the lakes.

19. George Vukelich, "Songs of the Great Inland Seas," in *Poems out of Wisconsin* (Wisconsin Fellowship of Poets, 1961), p. 70.

Editor's Note

SOME READERS may object to the widely varying quality of the stories in this collection because it contributes to a feeling of unevenness, but *Sweetwater, Storms, and Spirits* is intended to be a collection of the different sorts of stories set on the Great Lakes, not one of the finest of their kind. While such a book deserves to be done, it is appropriate, and perhaps of more interest to the professional and lay reader alike, that this first collection of Great Lakes maritime short stories be more representative of the variety of themes and types that writers of the lakes have used. If some stories seem simplistic, we must remember that their authors felt they were telling a story their readers would find interesting, if not necessarily believable. Moreover these stories have endured, sometimes in many variations for many years, and if for no other reason they deserve our thoughtful consideration as something that struck the popular fancy or was thought valuable in a time that we did not experience and can know only obliquely.

What I wished to do in this collection is to define the landscapes and to elucidate the themes of Great Lakes fiction that have persisted in several cultures over a long span of time. To do this one must look not only at serious fiction but at popular stories as well, for to consider only one and neglect the other is to ignore a large part of the cultural geography of a place. Attempting to draw fine distinctions between serious literature and popular fiction, if they can be drawn at all, would add little to the study of this subject at this time. Thus I have placed stories such as "A Lake Huron Ghost Story," which is nineteenth-century newspaper sensationalism, next to the finely crafted work of George Vukelich's "The Bosun's Chair." These may seem odd bedfellows at first, but each gains something from the other. The bosun's chair in both stories has scarcely changed, and neither have the sailors. What has changed is our attitude toward fiction, so that in this age of scientific rationality, demons and ghosts, long a staple of maritime fiction, must be internal rather than external and our sense of what constitutes poetic justice is more complex. We have in the twentieth century come to demand more realism in fiction, but many elements of maritime life have not changed: the terror of the bosun's chair and the officer who orders the sailor into it, and that sailor's dreams of revenge.

To give the reader a sense of the changing styles of fiction over the last 150 years I have left these stories as they were originally published. I have not modernized the spelling and punctuation of *Scenes on Lake Huron*, although some readers may find it difficult. Nor have I deleted passages not directly related to the plot in other nineteenth-century stories, which tend to be more discursive than we are accustomed to today. Nevertheless, since sailing ships were one of the most complex technologies of their time, with their own precise language, many of the maritime terms earlier writers took for granted are no longer known to modern readers. So despite my dislike of footnotes in the middle of a story, I have defined those sailing and cultural terms I thought most readers would not know, although for some I will have explained too much and for others not enough. When appropriate I have given the historical antecedents for a story and noted the actual location on the lakes.

"Standing Watch." (Loudon Wilson)

Masters and Men

You can take it from yours truly I don't want to be a skipper
In spite of all the salary he makes,
For I haven't got his worries an' I'm feeling pretty chipper
As an ordinary seaman on the Lakes.

"The Skipper"
Berton Brayley

Out of the Trough

Ralph Emberg

THIS STORY seems to have been inspired by the wreck of the 430-foot steel freighter *Mataafa*, which broke in two when she hit the breakwater in Duluth Harbor while trying to take refuge during the ferocious Nor'Easter of November 27, 1905. She had tried to ride out the storm on the lake, but eventually gave up and turned back to Duluth. As the townspeople watched from bonfires along the shore, the waves smashed her against first one pier and then the other, tearing off her rudder, flooding her engines, and breaking her apart. So fierce were the seas that no rescue could be attempted, even though the temperatures fell far below freezing. By morning when the first tugs could get to her, they found the men in the forepart cold but alive; nine men who had remained aft had frozen to death.

In his story Emberg has gone beyond the familiar details of the wreck to create a tale about the two greatest terrors an officer can face: an incompetent master and a fall gale on the lakes. Although the plight of Captain Shields may seem contrived, "Out of the Trough" portrays a great truth about the merchant marine: to some men the passion to command supersedes all else, even the safety of the ship and crew. The position of master is one they have spent years attaining and they seldom relinquish it lightly. It is equally difficult for a mate to decide to forcibly remove his master from command, even though he may have long suspected the captain was incompetent. Ships function by respect for one's superior and automatic obedience to orders, since in an emergency there will be no time for questioning or consensus. Thus for a crew member to refuse to obey any order is mutiny, long the most serious of crimes on water because of the danger to ship and crew it can cause. Emberg creates a graphic portrayal of a mate forced to decide between the lesser of two evils, and of his struggle to save the ship he believes is doomed to go to the bottom of Lake Superior. While the particular disability of the master in this story is uncommon, the situation is less so—the excerpt from *November Storm* that closes this collection is a different development of the same theme— for there will continue to be shipwrecks because the master would listen to no one and took his ship out in a gale he could not weather. And few are the mates who will ignore the dictates of training and risk the potential ruin of their careers to defy him.

IT WAS EARLY DUSK of a late November day. With wheat in her belly, food for America and her fighting allies, the steamer *Streakolite* with battened hatches and rigged life-lines lay under the spouts of the Northern Elevator in Duluth Harbor. A biting, snow-laden wind howled in off Lake Superior and a heavy surf pounded the Park Point Beach.

First Officer Bill Macdonald, at the head of the ladder, opened his eyes wide. Gazing at the man who had just come aboard, he seemed too astonished for words. "Just what was that, sir?" he asked.

"I'm the new captain," the old man with the thin weathered face and snow-white hair repeated. "I assume that you are the first mate?"

"Yes, sir, I'm the mate, but, well, they as good as told me that I was to take her out. We're loaded, cleared, and I've been waiting for orders. I don't understand—"

The old man gave Macdonald a letter. "I'm sorry, mister," he said sympathetically, "but here are my credentials. And the orders are Erie Elevator at Buffalo."

Macdonald read the letter. It was simply an official mem- orandum from the port-captain which said that Captain James Shields was to take command of the *Streakolite,* and that Mr. Macdonald would grant him all facilities.

"I hope we can pull together," the new captain said nervously.

Macdonald nodded dismally. "Oh, certainly, sir. Of course, I'm put out—sort of expected I'd take over—"

"I understand, mister. Went through it myself when I was a youngster. But let me tell you something. The disappointment of not getting a ship is nothing compared to having one you've commanded taken away. Believe me, I know! And now," his voice took on the snap of a shipmaster, "my luggage is on the dock. Send a man after it and get ready to single up."[1]

"Yes, sir," Macdonald gave the order to a sailor, then asked the skipper: "Shall I show you to the chartroom, sir?"

Captain Shields shook his head. "I can find the way, thanks. Come to the bridge, mister, after you've snugged down."[2]

A few minutes later the *Streakolite* backed from the dock, winded in the channel and headed toward the ship-canal. Mac- donald was depressed, irritated, as he made a last round of the deck. It wasn't fair. He was the senior mate in the line, and when Captain Ira Beldin's old heart attacks had sent him to the hospital, Macdonald had felt certain that he'd get the ship until Beldin got well. But they'd sent Shields instead . . .

The new skipper and the second mate were on the bridge. The second stood with his nose shoved into the weather-cloth,

---

1. To single up is to take in most of the lines securing a vessel to the pier so that only a few will need to be let go when she casts off.

2. To snug down is to prepare a vessel for heavy weather; here battening the hatches and securing the decks.

while the old man paced back and forth with short nervous strides.

"Snugged down, sir," Macdonald reported.

Captain Shields nodded. "You might as well turn in, mister. We're going to have a spell of weather. Get some rest while you have the chance."

Macdonald went to his cabin, shucked off his outer clothing and climbed into his bunk. It was then about eight o'clock. He would go on watch again at twelve midnight.

He couldn't sleep. The thought that line officials wouldn't trust the *Streakolite* to him cut deep. He'd had his master's ticket for the past two years. Of course it was late autumn and the very middle of the stormy season, and he supposed the brass hats felt that he was still too young to take charge of a vessel, her cargo and thirty-five lives. And they'd dug up the superannuated Shields somewhere instead of giving him a chance.

The new captain's name and face were vaguely familiar, but Macdonald couldn't remember where he'd heard of or seen the man. And from the way he had taken command it was evident that he was a competent master. For a stranger he seemed thoroughly familiar with the *Streakolite's* design, where things were, and how she handled, almost as if he'd sailed in her before.

Macdonald's thoughts wandered until in sheer exasperation with himself, the company, and the world in general, he snapped the light switch and closed his eyes.

The wind was blowing a half-gale and the ship rode into it sluggishly. Just before Macdonald turned out the light, he noticed something. Although the cabin was steam-heated, frost half an inch thick sprouted from the rivet-heads protruding through the steel walls. If it got colder they'd be chopping ice before Whitefish[3] was raised.

---

3. Whitefish Point.

An hour after the *Streakolite* had cleared Duluth Harbor the telephone in the dock office rang. A watchman answered it. It was the port-captain. He wanted to speak to acting Captain Bill Macdonald of the *Streakolite*.

"Hell," the watchman said, "she ain't here. She cleared about an hour ago."

"Cleared!" the port-captain barked, "you're crazy. She had no orders."

"Orders or no orders, she ain't here," the watchman replied. "She's gone. And if I know anything she's halfway to Two Harbors by now."

"Gawdamighty!" groaned the port-captain. "The worst gale in fifty years is sweeping west from the Soo. Ice, snow, and wind. All lake shipping's been ordered into shelter. What in hell got into that fellow—"

"I dunno," said the watchman, "he works for you."

The port-captain telephoned the Duluth Coast Guard station telling the commandant that the *Streakolite*, laden with two hundred thousand bushels of wheat had put to sea without authorization.

"What do you want us to do?" the Coast Guard man asked.

"Send a cutter after her and bring her back," the port-captain bawled. "I assume that you've had the weather reports! All hell's busted loose on Lake Superior—"

"We know it—" the commandant said tartly, "and we're not sending out any cutter in this weather. We'll radio the Soo to hold her when she gets there—"

"*If* she gets there—" the port-captain groaned.

Macdonald had his coffee in the galley and then went to the charthouse. The half-gale had increased to blizzard intensity and the air was full of sleet. Several times on the long flat deck between galley and chartroom, water swirled about his booted legs as solid green seas swept aft. And the frost glimmered in ghostly halos about the electric bulbs on the after end of the forward superstructure.

Captain Shields and the second mate were with the helmsman. So was the lookout. "It's all right, mister," the skipper explained. "I told 'em to come down. A man'd freeze to death on the bridge a night like tonight."

"Decent old fellow, after all," Macdonald thought. Some skippers insisted on the watch-officer and lookout staying on the bridge even if the hobs of hell froze up. Macdonald had always thought that a little judgment should be used.

The second mate gave him the course, the wheel and lookout were relieved, and Macdonald fell into the measured tread of a ship's watch-officer. He watched the muffled outline of Captain Shields who leaned with an elbow on the forward window.

The soft glow of the binnacle threw little light, but what did escape into the room enhanced the darkness outside. The chartroom, also steam-heated, was cold as an icebox. The old skipper shivered, drew his muffler tight about his throat and stared ahead. There was a sadness about the captain, a soft veiled sadness, without sharpness, but nevertheless with poignancy. Without knowing why, Macdonald suddenly found himself feeling sorry for the man; perhaps it was his age.

"How about some coffee, sir?" he asked.

Captain Shields shook his head.

"You look tired, sir—" the mate hesitated. "If—if you'd like to turn in for some rest, sir, I'm sure we could get along. I could call you if anything—"

The captain stiffened. "I'm staying here, mister," he said. "I'll be needed before long. Listen!" he cupped a hand to an ear. "Hear it! It's coming! I've been waiting ten years for it. Ten years is a long time, mister—"

Macdonald didn't know what the old man meant, but he did hear something. So did the wheelsman and the lookout. Above the gale, above the sandblasty rattle of sleet, above the crash of seas against the ship's bow, above the whipcrack of spindrift, above the squeak and squeal of straining rivets, was another sound. High-pitched and ominous. The groan of a million violins tuning up. Up on the bridge the weather-cloth ripped into streaming fragments.[4] Aft of the charthouse the foremast stays sang vibrantly, and within five seconds the whole ship seemed to throb in unison.

Without waiting for orders the mate jerked the telephone from the hook. "Stand by and watch your screw!" he yelled to the engine-room, "there's a hurricane or cyclone headed this way!"

Then hell was loosed in a welter of wind, snow, and water. A huge wave climbed the bow, its crest flicking to the very bridge. The pilot-house windows shattered. The four men were drenched in an icy bath.

The ship hung motionless. A second wave lifted her, passed under, and her screw out of water raced madly. Then her thousands of tons of dead weight hit the valley between the seas and a wall of water raced aft sweeping everything before it.

Captain Shields' sadness had disappeared. He seemed to exult in the storm, the smash and crash of the elements. He shook a fist at the darkness ahead. "Blow and be damned to you!" he shouted. "I'm taking her through this time!"

It was impossible to keep the vessel head on. She yawed savagely with every lift, the wheelsman spinning the wheel with every yaw.

Another great sea slammed the quarter. The ship heeled and swung over. The deck-stanchions dipped under; the men in the chartroom grabbed wildly for handholds.[5] Then just as Macdonald thought she was gone, she righted slowly, but only partly. They all knew what had happened. The cargo had shifted!

"You know what to do, mister!" the skipper barked. "All

---

4. A weather cloth is a strip of canvas lashed to the bridge railing to protect the person standing watch.

5. Deck stanchions are upright supports along the side of the deck that carry the guardrail.

hands into the hold and get that wheat trimmed!" He grabbed the engine-room telephone. "Send every man you can spare to trim cargo," he snapped into the mouthpiece. "Hurry. I'll not have it happen again."

Trimming cargo in a heavy sea is a nasty job. It's a hundred times more nasty when the cargo is bulk grain. A few electric lights encased in a wire mesh threw a dim insufficient light. The wheat came almost up to the hatch covers, and the men had to begin work on their knees. But led by Macdonald they grabbed scoops and dug in.

Attacking the shift along the side where it was up to the deck, they tore into it and tossed it back. Death flapped its wings over them. The Ice Devils of Lake Superior sneered. A roll, a twist of the vessel, and they'd be buried under a thousand tons of wheat. The dust filled their eyes, it clogged their nostrils. They tore rags from their shirts and tied them over their faces, but still the dust seeped in. They coughed, they wheezed, but they shoveled.

Macdonald shoveled too. That crew needed no supervision. It was get the vessel trimmed or die. Shadows cast by the dim lights flickered in fantastic patterns of the frost-beaded iron of the ship's inside skin. And while the crew sweated in the dusty hell below hatches, sea, wind, and snow battered the topsides.

And up in the charthouse a frightened wheelsman watched the mad antics of a white-haired captain who howled wild taunts at the sea. But he kept her head on. Seasoned sailor, he knew that once in the trough, with that list, she wouldn't stay afloat two minutes.

Down in the engine-room an apprehensive group of engineers and oilers watched the revolutions tick off. The *Streakolite*'s triple expansion reciprocating engines were turning at top speed, but every man there knew that her drift to leeward exceeded her headway.

At daybreak the ship rode without much list and the men in the hold came on deck, weary, dust-choked and red-eyed.

The cook had plenty of coffee and such food as he could cook on the crazy-pitching galley range. The sailors gulped the coffee in burning draughts and wolfed the food.

Macdonald formally reported to the captain, still in the wheelhouse, that the vessel was now in trim. The old man leaned against the smashed window frame. Frost rime was on his hair and face. He received Macdonald's report with a nod.

There was trouble to come. Macdonald hadn't been in the wheelhouse five minutes when the bosun appeared with the well-slate. He gave it to the first mate. The chalked figures were ominous. The going had been too much for the old girl. She was leaking like a sieve. And the pumps which had been coughing for the past twelve hours could not keep the water down.

Macdonald gave the slate to the captain. "If 'twas me, sir," he said, "I'd put about and run for it. We're not making a foot of headway and the strain is tearing her apart!"

Shields stared at the slate, then at Macdonald. "You think we're going down, mister? Well, we're not. And we're not putting about either. It was putting about that sent me down once before. Caught in the trough, she was, and she never righted. No, mister, we're holding our course."

"He's loony, sir," the wheelsman whispered to Macdonald. "You shoulda seen him all night, swearin', callin' names. Give me the holy creeps—"

The wheelsman's statements were confirmation of the fear that had been growing on Macdonald. The old man's actions were not those of a sane man. Should the skipper insist on holding the ship on her course, buffeting into a sea such as he'd never before witnessed, Macdonald knew that she wouldn't last another hour. The first mate made his decision. It might mean the end of his Great Lakes career—mutiny is no light thing—but he could not stand by and see a good ship and her crew go to death because of one man's stubbornness whether born of insanity or not. The commission could decide later who had been right, if the captain or owners brought charges against him.

Macdonald slipped out of the chartroom and talked to the

second mate. Together they went to the engine-room. The chief agreed that the skipper might be queer; in fact, he thought all skippers were a bit queer, but he was still the captain. If he wanted to drive the *Streakolite* through, well,—

A white-faced oiler reported water on the bunker floor-plates—he held up a pump strainer clogged with wheat. The chief changed his mind.

"When it's a choice between my ticket and my life," he said, "to hell with the ticket. Take over, Mac. And let me know when you get ready to put about."

The mates returned to the chartroom. "Captain Shields," Macdonald began. But the wild-eyed skipper would not listen.

"We're not putting about," he said grimly. "We're taking her through to the Soo. I told you it was putting about that sent the *Willowisp* to the bottom. Caught in the trough, she was, and she never righted."

"*Willowisp?*" Macdonald asked, "what do you know about the *Willowisp?*"

"I took her out on her maiden voyage," Shields cackled. "She was sister ship to the *Streakolite*. I had her seven years till she went down off Duluth in the big November blow ten years ago. I put about to go back. Caught in the trough, she was, and she foundered before you could say Jack Robinson. They said I couldn't command a ship again, ever, because I lost her. But I showed 'em!"

The picture was almost complete. Although the loss of the *Willowisp* had occurred before Macdonald came into the line, he had heard of both her and her captain, an inoffensive addled old man who now did janitor chores around the line's offices. How he had been placed in command of the *Streakolite* Macdonald could not guess, nor was there time to think of it.

Macdonald nodded to the second mate. They closed in on Shields.

"No, you don't," the old man screamed. "You're all against me just as they were that day at the hearing. I'll show all of you. I'm taking her through—right to the Soo—"

Macdonald threw his arms about the man. He picked him up bodily. The second mate held his legs.

"We're not going to hurt you, Captain," Macdonald said soothingly, "just put you out of circulation for a while." And to the second, "the paint-locker."

A minute later Shields was thrust, screaming threats and kicking like a steer, into the paint-locker in the forepeak. Macdonald closed and locked the door.

Back in the wheelhouse he telephoned the engine-room. "Stand by, Chief. We're going about and we'll need everything you have to pull her out. If we make it I'm heading for Duluth. It's our only chance."

"Okay, Mac, let her go. And if we don't make it, well, it's been nice knowing you—"

"Hard over and hold her," Macdonald gave the order to put her in the trough, the order that might mean curtains for ship and crew.

"Hard over, sir," the helmsman spoked the wheel. The telemotor steering gear clanked and the *Streakolite's* head fell off the sea. The sea was now quartering. Another yaw and the ship was in the trough. With every nerve and muscle tensed, Macdonald watched her. Now she was lengthwise in a deep valley. She lifted, rolled hard to leeward. Would the grain shift again? If it shifted now it would be the last shift. She rolled back to windward as the sea passed. Her head came a little farther around. She was answering the helm. Inch by inch, foot by foot, she fought her way out. Despite the cold the sweat stood out on the mate's forehead. The wheelsman was ashen. By the engine-room telegraph stood the second mate breathing heavily.

Macdonald was proud of the old *Streakolite* when once more her bow was at right angles to the watery ridges. The seas were all from aft now. And pooped again and again by huge seas crashing in on her fantail, she shook like a gallant old race horse and emerged from the smother. Then the new course was set and with the speed of a yacht so fierce was the press of wind on her from aft, she raced westward against time.

"God!" Macdonald breathed as he watched the mercury drop in the wheelhouse thermometer, "It'll be nip and tuck even if the ice doesn't start building up!"

Late in the afternoon the *Streakolite* was once again in hazy snow-obscured sight of the Duluth Ship Canal, a narrow strait of water, between long piers of masonry, jutting into Lake Superior from St. Louis Bay. An observer on shore would not have recognized the once smart vessel in the ice-covered, badly-listing, hard-steering freighter limping painfully toward entrance. Misfortune had dogged every mile of her voyage. Within a half-hour of Macdonald's putting about, the steel quadrant to which the rudder-post was affixed, had snapped.

It was a toss-up in that weather if a jury helm could be rigged. But it was. In water up to their waists, the crew had toiled on an ice-covered poop. With frost-bitten feet and hands they had got it working, a great iron tiller down over the rudder-post, operated with block and tackle by a half-dozen men.

But the ship didn't answer it properly in the heavy sea, and it was with forebodings that Macdonald conned her toward the harbor. He had put the ship about in the heaviest sea he had ever seen; he had beaten a bad cargo shift, removed an insane or incompetent captain, and, despite ice and a damaged rudder, brought her to within sight of safety. Was he to lose her, the lives of his crew and his own at the last moment, not to mention his ticket? He must hit that three-hundred foot entrance right on the nose, an entrance through which fifty-foot seas were surging. Only after passing through the ship canal could they find the comparative calm of a safe anchorage.

There was an alternative. He could beach her on the sands of Park Point, taking a chance that with life preservers the crew could get ashore through heavy surf before freezing to death. But that would mean loss of both vessel and cargo. No, he would take a chance at the harbor entrance, and so he told the deck and engine-room officers.

A half-mile off the entrance the *Streakolite* began to sound her siren. No tug afloat would ever dare come out into the lake, but Macdonald did think that if his signals were heard, one might venture into the harbor end of the canal and heave to where she might be reached with a hawser in an emergency. But if a tug did answer the summons he had no way of knowing, because the canal piers would hide her from observation.

Loaded down with hundreds of tons of ice, the *Streakolite*, frosty-white, lumbered sluggishly toward the entrance. She steered badly, wabbling from side to side, swept constantly by pooping seas. The men with frozen oilskins at the tiller-tackles were constantly drenched with solid water. On the spar deck of the after house, from where he could see both the fantail and the bow, Macdonald relayed his orders to the helm.

The news had spread that a vessel was in distress off the harbor, and despite the zero-cold a huge crowd gathered on lower St. Croix and Lake Avenues.

Two hundred yards from the entrance, Macdonald knew that only a miracle would take them in without mishap. Her steering was too eccentric. She might make it, but the chances were against it. A yaw one way or another would smash her head-on into the concrete.

And then before he had time to even think, an enormous wave lifted her, hurled her forward like a great battering ram, thousands of tons of ship, cargo and ice, not into the entrance but against the north pier. But as she struck, Macdonald saw that his siren-call for a tug had been heard. In a lee where the bay end of the ship canal began, a squat powerful tug rolled heavily in the swells sweeping in from the lake. Smoke poured from her funnel and steam from her blow-off valve.

The *Streakolite's* bow slid along the concrete and pointed north at right angles to the pier's nose. Again she lay in the trough, almost her entire length across the canal's mouth. Another wave smashed her. The plates aft of the bridge squealed, buckled, opened up.

Macdonald shouted orders. But they were almost unnecessary. The men forward rushed aft. The bow was breaking off and they knew it. But there was another, the man in the paint-locker. Macdonald sped forward. It was too late. The sea overwhelmed the *Streakolite*. When it had passed, careening off the pier and throwing spray a hundred feet into the air, the ship's bow had disappeared, leaving a protruding tangle of broken steel where it had been. The main section of the vessel, still afloat because the forward bulkhead held, lay free, pounded and lifted alternately by the seas.

Within a second or two, perhaps a minute, she'd be thrown against one of those concrete ramparts. Or the bulkhead would give way. Possibly, but it was very remote, she might float in a few yards before striking, but Macdonald had almost given up hope. He breathed a silent prayer.

Almost as if in answer to it, a sailor yelled, pointing toward the Bay. Emerging from the sleet was the blunt stem of the squatty tug, and on her crazy tossing bridge was the burly figure of the tug's master with a megaphone in his mittened hands.

The distance from the tug to the *Streakolite* was short, but to Macdonald and his frozen crew it seemed miles and the minutes taken to traverse it, hours. Finally, a heaving-line curled over the *Streakolite's* fantail. Frozen numbed fingers tailed onto it. A hawser followed, and as it was made fast to the after bitts the crew let out a frost-muffled cheer.

The slack in the hawser came out, ever so slowly, the ship, stern-first, eased into the harbor and alongside the nearest dock. And never before had any Great Lakes ship been berthed safely after so many disasters.

Ambulances and doctors waited. And so did beds at the Marine Hospital. Frosted ears burned, numbed fingers and toes tingled as nurses and doctors administered first aid.

Macdonald was the last to leave the battered vessel, and then only after he'd satisfied himself that with proper attention she'd remain afloat until drydocked. Then he surrendered himself to the medicoes too.

The head-nurse informed Macdonald, when he wakened the next day at noon, that the line's port-captain was waiting to see him. Which was all right with Mac. Somebody would have to do a lot of explaining. It might as well be now as later.

Macdonald told his story and asked his questions.

"It was none of our doing, Mac," the port-captain said. "And despite the magnificent job of bringing the girl in, we were set not only to fire you, but prosecute you, put you in clink if we could, instead of making you the new skipper of the *Streakolite* when she comes out of dry-dock. You see, we didn't know a thing about Shields and we couldn't understand why you had taken the vessel out. But the bow came ashore this morning and we found the old man in the paint-locker under three feet of ice. He still had those credentials, that phony letter, in his pocket. Which was our fault.

"We had no business letting him have access to our letterheads!"

Helmsmen on Lake Erie

Anonymous

DISASTROUS FIRES were common on the lakes in the mid-nineteenth century. As the railroads began to cut into the steamships' lucrative business, competition for passengers and freight grew fierce. Steamboat races became common, and while the lucky winning master filled his ship at the dock, the unlucky sometimes burned to death or drowned in the icy water of the lake, often within sight of shore. Even without the danger of racing, early steamboats were prone to explosion and fire. Built of wood, powered by high-pressure engines, and lacking the safety equipment later required by law, once they caught fire they burned like the paint-laden torches they were. One of the more dramatic losses was the burning and sinking of the steamer *Erie* in 1841; she was bound up Lake Erie from Buffalo when she caught fire at night, and of nearly three hundred passengers and crew only a few were rescued. But the heroism of her helmsman, who stayed at his post until the ship was beached, soon became legend, and the name John Maynard was known far beyond the lakes. In some versions he burned to death at the wheel, in others he survived the water only to die ashore.

In fact, he died at his post, and his name was Luther Fuller, not John Maynard. But in 1845 an unknown British traveler (some suggest Charles Dickens) heard the story and wrote it down. It appeared in a Buffalo paper that fall and was quickly reprinted by others despite the decidedly British touches in the account: the "Blue Peter" as a signal for sailing, and the renaming of the ship as the *Jersey*, an unlikely name for a lakes steamer. A few years later a poem about the wreck appeared, written by either Kate Weaver or Horatio Alger, depending on which account one believes, and the rest, as they say, is history. For fifty years school children recited:

> But where is he, that helmsman bold?
> The captain saw him reel,
> His nerveless hands released their task
> He sank beside the wheel.
> The wave received his lifeless corpse,
> Blackened with smoke and fire.
> God rest him! Never hero had
> A nobler funeral pyre!

Shrewdly aware of the dramatic and commercial possibilities of the piece, a famous temperance speaker turned it into a prose oration, even as new folklore grew that Luther Fuller had actually lived into old age and died a drunk. Others set the story to music. John Hay, Lincoln's secretary, pirated the plot and set it on the Mississippi in his poem "Jim Bludso of the *Prairie Belle*." The tale of John Maynard was the most famous story set on the Great Lakes in the nineteenth and early twentieth centuries. It is reprinted here in its 1845 version with all the Victorian sentimentality intact.

IT WAS ON A PLEASANT May morning that a steam vessel was riding at anchor, opposite the town of Buffalo, on Lake Erie. You know, I dare say, that Erie is one of those sea-lakes for which America is so famous; and as you stand on its shore, and see the green waves dashing in one after another you might well think that you were looking on the great ocean itself. The *Jer-*

sey—for that was the name of the steamer—was dressed gaily with many bright flags; the Blue Peter, the signal of her immediate sailing, was at her main-mast head; porters were hurrying along the narrow quay that juts out into the lake; boatmen quarrelling with each other for passengers; travellers hurrying backwards and forwards to look for their luggage; friends shaking hands and bidding each other farewell; idlers lounging about, with their hands in their pockets; car-drivers jangling for a larger fare; and all the various kinds of bustle and confusion that attend the departure of a packet from a watering place.

But presently the anchor was heaved, the paddles began to turn, the sails were set, and, leaving a broad track of foam behind her, the *Jersey* stood westward, and held on her course for the town of Erie. It was a bright blue day; and, as hour after hour went by, some mingled in the busy conversation of politics; some sat apart and calculated the gains of the shop or the counting-house; some were wrapped up in the book with which they were engaged, and one or two, with whom time seemed to hang heavily, composed themselves to sleep. In short, one and all were like men who thought that, let danger come to them when it might, at least it would not be that day.

It drew towards four in the afternoon, and the steamer, which had hitherto been keeping the middle of the lake, stood southward—Erie, the place to which it was bound, lying on the southern side. Old John Maynard was at the wheel—a bluff, weather-beaten sailor, tanned by many a winter tempest. He had truly learnt to be content with his situation; none could ever say that they ever heard him repine at his hard labor and scanty pay. He had, in the worst times, a cheerful word and a kind look for those with whom he was thrown—cast, often enough, into bad company, he tried, at least, and generally succeeded, to say something for its good. He was known, from one end of Lake Erie to the other, by the name of honest John Maynard; and the secret of his honesty to his neighbors was his love of God.

The land was about ten miles off, when the captain, coming up from his cabin, cried to a sailor: "Dick Fletcher, what's all that smoke I see coming out from the hold?"

"It's from the engine room, sir, I guess," said the man.

"Down with you then, and let me know."

The sailor began descending the ladder by which you go to the hold; but scarcely had he disappeared beneath the deck, when up he came again with much greater speed.

"The hold's on fire, sir," he said to the captain, who by this time was standing close to him.

The captain rushed down and found the account too true. Some sparks had fallen on a bundle of tow; no one had seen the accident; and now not only much of the luggage, but the sides of the vessel were in smouldering flame.

All hands, passengers as well as sailors, were called together; and, two lines being made, one on each side of the hold, buckets of water were passed and repassed; they were filled from the lake, they flew along a line of ready hands, were dashed hissing on the burning mass, and then passed on to the other side to be refilled. For some minutes, it seemed as if the flames were subdued.

In the meantime the women on board were clustering round John Maynard, the only man unemployed who was capable of answering their questions. "How far is it to land?" "How long shall we be in getting in?" "Is it very deep?" "Can they see us from the shore?" The helmsman answered as well as he could. There was no boat; it had been left at Buffalo to be mended; they might be seven miles from shore, they would probably be in in forty minutes; he could not tell how far the fire had reached. "But, to speak the truth," he added, "we are all in great danger, and I think if there was a little less *talking*, and a little more praying it would be the better for us, and none the worst for the boat."

"How's her head?" shouted the captain.

"West-sou'-west, sir," answered Maynard.

"Keep her south by west," cried the captain. "We must go on shore anywhere."

It happened that a draft of wind drove back the flames, which soon began to blaze up more furiously against the saloon; and the partition between it and the hold was soon on fire. Then long wreaths of smoke began to find way through the skylight, and the captain seeing this, ordered all the women forward. The engineer put on his utmost steam—the American flag was run up and reversed in token of distress; water was flung over the sails to make them hold the wind. And still John Maynard stood by the wheel, though now he was cut off, by a sheet of smoke and flames, from the ship's crew.

Great and greater grew the heat—the engineers fled from the engine room—the passengers were clustering round the vessel's bow—the sailors were sawing planks on which to lash the women—the boldest were throwing off their coats and waistcoats, and preparing for one long struggle for life. And still the coast grew plainer and plainer—the paddles as yet worked well—they could not be more than a mile from the shore, and boats were even now starting to their assistance.

"John Maynard," cried the captain.

"Aye, aye, sir!" said John.

"Can you hold on five minutes longer?"

"I'll try, sir."

And he did try; the flames came nearer and nearer, a sheet of smoke would sometimes almost suffocate him, and his hair was singed, his blood seemed on fire with the great heat. Crouching as far back as he could, he held the wheel firmly with his left hand, till the flesh shrivelled, and the muscles cracked in the flames; and then he stretched forth his right, and bore the agony without scream or a groan. It was enough for him that he heard the cheer of the sailors to the approaching boats; the cry of the captain, "The women first, and every man for himself, and God for us all." And they were the last sounds that he heard. How he perished is not known; whether dizzied by the smoke he lost his footing in endeavoring to come forward and fell overboard, or whether he was suffocated by the dense smoke, his comrades could not tell. At the moment the vessel struck the boats were at her side, passengers, sailors, and captain leaped into them, or swam for their lives; all, save he to whom they owed everything, escaped.

He had died the death of a Christian hero—I had almost said of a martyr; his spirit was commended into his Father's hands, and his body sleeps in peace by the green side of Lake Erie.

A Gold-Headed Cane

Walter Havighurst

FOR MANY DECADES it has been a Great Lakes maritime custom that the captain of the first ship into a port each spring is honored by the town. The paper may run an article, and in larger ports the television station may do a feature, but always the captain is given a present, often a cane or a top hat. "A Gold-Headed Cane" is a chapter from the novel *Signature of Time,* a chronicle about the lives of several generations of a family on one of the limestone ridged "wine" islands in eastern Lake Erie. Here, the cane figures in the intense rivalry between two brothers, one a ship's captain and the other a vintner, and it becomes a symbol of the ruthlessness that often destroys both ships and men.

But this is not just another story of a captain who wrecks his ship because of his own recalcitrance. In his carefully delineated portraits of Captain Rufus Hazard and his land-bound brother Matt, Havighurst has portrayed the classic American conflict between those who believe in progress at any price and those who prefer to live in harmony with the land. Captain Hazard is a quintessential nineteenth-century American entrepreneur: hard-driving, proud, dedicated to using the resources of nature to build the cities and locks and harbors that developed the lakes. His brother's desire to stay on the island and turn his share of it into a vineyard and a garden, much like Thoreau approached Walden Pond, seems backward if not insane, a view that would have been shared by most Americans at the time. These two brothers symbolize the great debate of American life that was beginning to be argued in the nineteenth century and has become more insistently repeated in the twentieth: What is the proper use of this land that was so pristine when we first discovered it and that has been so often destroyed in the name of progress? Is our material success worth the price we have paid, or is it better to strive for the less tangible but equally satisfying rewards that come from living in a way that does not destroy the land and the lakes? Havighurst would seem to suggest the latter, but as the novel progresses the reader discovers that there are no easy answers. The lakes will always wreak their vengeance on men who do not respect them, but even those who attempt to live a different sort of life may ultimately fail: After Matt's vines are destroyed by a fungus all he has built goes back to wilderness, and it is left to his grandsons once again to confront the questions he and Captain Hazard could not resolve.

FIFTEEN YEARS AGO, off Quarry Point, where a limestone bar ran under Lake Erie, the hulk of an old freighter marked the shoal water. Its stern was submerged, but the tilted bow rose forlorn and desperate, as though poised on a crest of sea. In winter it reared up from the pack ice, gaunt and ghostly with snow. In summer it hung above bright water with the gulls crying round it, and sometimes a city fisherman, his putt-putt idle, pulled up in its shade and tried a lure in that darkness. Across the bow ran a few corroded letters, separated by rusty spaces: J——ON—A——. That seemed name enough. Not only summer visitors, but even the island people who could remember the *Jason Hazard* loading stone under the vanished trestle dock called what was left of her "the Jonah."

For twelve-year-old Dave and Maury Hazard the hulk was a favorite and forbidden playground. They steered the dinghy, with her little kite of sail, around Province Point, and one of them said, "Let's play Jonah." Out of sight of Hazard Cove, they slacked sail and coasted into the shadow of the reared-up pilothouse. They tied their painter to the rusty chainrail and climbed aboard.

There were various ways of playing Jonah. They could leapfrog on the big iron bitts, their bare feet slapping the warped wooden decks. They could pry up the old wooden hatch covers and peer at the mounds of island limestone in the murky hold. They could peel off their shirts, dive down, and look into the sunken engine-room portholes. Sometimes fish swam through the shattered ports, and it was easy to imagine perch and pickerel nosing around the old brass driving arms and the big cylinders, or swimming down the tilted catwalk and into the shadowy fire doors where drowned clinkers buried the furnace gratings. Holding their breath, pulling themselves down the slippery stern cable, they had even explored the broken propeller blades; one of them was sheered off and the other was bent like an iris petal in that soundless dark.

Another game was sailor's swing. You stood on the pilothouse ladder and grasped the frayed rope dangling from the broken spar. You gave a push and sailed out in a slow wide circle, over the hatches, over the slanted, vanishing deck, over the rippling water. You swung back and forth in that airy arc until at last you dropped off, at the far end of the pendulum, in free water.

The best game was steering. You took your place in the tilted wheelhouse, facing the arc of windows shattered by a gale of years gone by. You grasped the big wheel with the lanyard woven around its center spoke and you looked down at the dead, corroded binnacle. You pulled the whistle lever and imagined the great voice roaring from the stack (that lay broken beneath the water). You moved the handle of the engine-room telegraph and imagined it jangling (down where the incurious fishes swam past the unresponding dials). You posted your lookout—"Take the bridge wing, watchman"—and told your mate to look sharp for the range lights. So you steered up Detroit River, between all the traffic and around the islands and past the cliff of lights that was the city, and out to the winking darkness of Lake St. Clair. You steered all night, and in the morning you were taking her up Lake Huron with blue water flashing and the bow lifting to the long lake swell. You took her through the secret passages of the St. Marys, with the Indians peering out of their tar-paper shacks on the shore. You steered through the cautious traffic of the Soo and took her into the big lock, safely. Then Whitefish Bay widened out and Lake Superior opened beyond those shattered windows. "Let me know when you pick up Stannard Rock, watchman."

"Aye, Captain Hazard. . . . Now you be watchman, Maury. It's my turn to steer."

Crippled Seth Crane had told them about the Soo and Stannard Rock Light. But they did not know they were sailing a Hazard vessel, imagining a voyage that their great-uncle had made a hundred times. They didn't know the hulk had a Hazard name—until one flashing June day when they moored the dinghy at the dock and started up the path to the house.

"The cane," Maury said. He ran back to the boat. Halfway to the house, with the cane in his hands, he stopped again. He began rubbing the tarnished metal with the tail of his T shirt.

"What's the matter?" Dave called.

"It's got writing on it."

Dave went back to his brother's side. His dark head bent over the spidery pattern on the corroded metal. "It's engraved."

"Let's shine it up," Maury said.

They took it to the carriage shed, where a can of brass polish stood on the dusty window shelf. Five minutes later they burst like a windstorm into the house where Kate Hazard, a mound of June roses in her lap, was wheeling herself toward the dining-room table.

"Gram! Look, Gram!"

The old lady swung her wheel chair round. "Hush," she said. "You'll start your mother's headache."

"Gram! There's a name on it. It says Hazard!"

The old lady held the cane across the two wheels of her chair, above the lapful of roses. She stared down at the gold head with its small flourish of engraving—*Captain Rufus Hazard, 1902.*

A change came over her face. There was a startled look, half fearful and half guilty, and then the deep-set eyes flashed sternly.

"Where did you get this?"

"On the Jonah."

Her big-knuckled hands gripped the cane. "You were on that vessel?"

"Just for a little while," Dave said.

"I found the cane under a pile of stuff in the cabin," Maury said. "There's furniture all broken and some smashed—"

"You've been told not to go there. Not to go near there."

"That was last year," Dave said, "when we only had the canoe."

Her eyes went to the empty study at the end of the long living room. "If your father was here, he'd be angry."

It was hard to think that Bart Hazard would be angry about that wreck. "Why Gram?"

"Because—you've been told."

She propelled herself away, the cane across her knees, her hands lunging at the wheels and her big shoulders rocking. They didn't see the cane again until it was brought out of her closet, with all the old things hiding there, after her death.

But before then, in the long winter while Maury was another invalid sitting beside his grandmother with his arm in a sling, the story came out. Beyond the broad window bay snow blurred the cove and raged across the empty water. Out there, unseen, it whitened the lifeless hulk and sifted in the shattered wheelhouse windows, making a smooth white mound over the warped chart table and the rusted binnacle. That winter the old lady told him, a piece at a time, how the J——ON—A——, lying wrecked off Quarry Point, was the *Jason Hazard,* broken on a wild October night thirty years ago. And Maury Hazard, staring across the wintry shore, saw that his great-uncle's vessel had been broken not so much on a limestone reef as on his grandfather's anger.

* * *

In those vanished seasons, when the smoke of the lime ovens fringed North Harbor and the dump cars rumbled on the lofty dock, Matthew Hazard's brother, Captain Rufus Hazard, brought his big freighter in to load Hazard Island stone. He carried it north to pave the spreading streets of Detroit and to build the new canal locks at Sault Sainte Marie; he carried it over Lake Erie to the new timber cribs that guarded the harbors of Ohio. On each trip, as he rounded Wolf Point where the long vineyard rows ribbed the island, he looked through the glass and found his brother patrolling the green aisles on horseback. Captain Hazard reached for the whistle cord and sent a salute roaring over the water. He listened with satisfaction while the long blasts echoed back from the island shore. He knew how that sound taunted his steadfast brother.

He brought his vessel in, around Cave Point, past Hazard Cove, and into North Harbor. Soon stone was thundering into the hold, and a white fog swirled around the dusty bins of the loading dock. Rufus took his gold-headed cane, put on his visored cap, lit his pipe and shambled down the ladder where the quarry manager waited to drive him away.

The white-dusted cart, behind the dusted chestnut horses, rattled past the yawning quarry pits and the lime furnaces seeping smoke. It skirted the green vineyard lands, with the long rows slowly turning like the spokes of a wheel. It pulled up at the rambling house, under the dark tall cedars that had sheltered

Jason Hazard's trapper's hut eighty years before. There Rufus took leave of the quarry manager and let himself in the iron gate. At the big oak door he rapped sharply with the head of his cane and went on in.

He came this way on a waning October afternoon, with a fire smoldering in the black hearth at one end of the living room. A warm light showed from the study at the far end, and through a curtain of cigarette smoke he saw a bearded face bent in the lamplight over the littered desk. Outside rang the voices of his nephews, Avery and Bart, driving cows into the milking shed. Those shrill voices always gave Rufus Hazard an unexpected stab; he had only daughters in his household in Toledo. Then, before he could interrupt his brother Julian, tracing the concentric circles of a fossil shellfish in the study, Matthew Hazard stamped in by way of the kitchen.

The brothers did not shake hands. Rufus planted his feet wide and said: "You heard my signal, likely. Kate expected me for supper."

"We heard you." Matt struck a match and turned up the wick of a reading lamp on the oval table. "Here's the Sandusky paper." He went on upstairs to change for dinner.

Julian came out of the study, his soft brown beard half hiding his thin brown face. Around him hung the smell of his medicated cigarettes, and as he sat in the wing chair by the fire his breath wheezed faintly. "Where have you been this time?" he asked his brother.

"Duluth," Rufus boomed. "Iron ore for Lorain."

"Do you ever get ashore on Lake Superior?" Julian asked softly. "There's a stegocephalian that occurs there—a fossil. I'd like to compare it—"

"I get ashore," Rufus roared, "but not to pick up rocks."

Julian gave him a lenient, twinkling smile and lighted one of his slender cigarettes. Soon Matt came down, smelling of cologne, and Kate Hazard appeared with a tray of wineglasses. She nodded with her tall dignity, "Good evening, Rufus," and served him first.

"Thank you, Kate." He scowled at the little glass in his big, weathered hand. "What is it, Dago Red?"

Matt held his glass up to the lamplight. "It's Island Cream Sherry. Grapes from the point vineyard."

Rufus raised his wind-burned face and tossed down the wine. "Rather have rum," he said.

"It won a prize," Matt declared, "at the St. Louis Fair." He looked up at the embossed decanter on the mantel.

"You've told that before," Rufus said. "How're the grapes this year—scabby?"

His brother answered without looking at him, eyeing the fire or the gathering darkness in the windows, as though he talked to a stranger whose presence he resented. When chimes sounded from the dining room, they went in to dinner.

The boys came in, faces shining and hair wet down, from the kitchen. They said, "Hello, Uncle Rufus," and slid into their places. Matt held his wife's chair and then paced around the candlelighted table. In his own place he bent his head and intoned a peremptory and meager Grace: "Feed us with the bread of life. Amen."

Then, over the soup and roast and salad, with anger leaping across the candlelight, the brothers quarreled. It would not be easy to say what they quarreled about, and it would not be hard, either. It might be some small thing like Mark Hanna's politics, or the price their grandfather, Jason Hazard, was paid for forty cords of steamer fuel wood, or the date in a long past October when their father, Joel Hazard, had driven his first sheep over the leaf-strewn roads of autumn to the stock pens at Toledo. But always it was another, deeper thing. It was the fact that Jason Hazard had run traplines from Quarry Point to Signal Cape through unbroken cedar forest, and Joel Hazard had cleared a thousand island acres, and now two brothers had put that inheritance to such different uses.

Matt Hazard's acres lay like a vast garden, aisled with vineyard and orchard from shore to shore, dotted with the white, flower-bordered houses of his Alsatian vineyardmen and turreted with the stone towers of his wineries. On these eastern acres people sang as they tended the long vineyard rows, and children played peekaboo through the green foliage and the purple clusters. Matt Hazard had built cottages of limestone dug from the spot (his only quarries were the basements of those trim dwellings), and had floored and roofed them with native cedar. Now those wide, low, solid cottages, white in the sun and gray in the rain, were spaced along the straight vineyard roads.

Rufus Hazard's acres, to the west, were a chaos of quarries, railroad tracks, lime ovens, and the big blind towers of crushing plants. The mile-long central quarry was fringed with the flimsy houses of Hungarian families who threw their kitchen refuse over the raw rock edge and let burdock and chicory grow rank around their doorsteps. Down in the excavation men blasted the stone and hauled it away, leaving ruin behind them. Already parts of the quarry were dead and desolate, and like a scar over a wound came the weedy growth of sumach and wild mustard, among which glinted tin cans and old bottles from the quarry kitchens.

"Gouge out the limestone, throw in the litter," Matt had said bitterly when his brother first brought his new ship into North Harbor. "And name your ship for a man that would set a wolf trap for you."

"He felled the trees," Rufus said easily, "we dynamite the limestone. He sold island cedar to the steamers, we sell island stone to pave the streets of Cleveland."

In Rufus Hazard was an American carelessness, restlessness, and disorder—even in the way he hacked at the roadside chicory with his gold-headed cane and wore his cap tilted on his shaggy head. He was a man always in motion, if only his big hands twisting that cane. He was at home in the chaos of loading docks, in the smoke and dust of quarries, in the raw rugged range towns of Minnesota. "You wouldn't know that place from last year," he said, his blue eyes burning. "Place called Eveleth, in the Mesabi. I bought some more shares of that iron stock."

Matthew Hazard, in his high linen collar and his derby

hat, carefully turning his cigar between puffs, was a man of order and steadfastness. He had changed the island from a pasture to a garden, and in the long, clean, undeviating vineyard rows he felt a rightness and a permanence. That ordered life expressed his pride, his conviction, and his self-righteous satisfaction. He resented all change and destruction. But at the edge of his vineyards dynamite thundered above the veins of limestone and a black snarl of smoke rose from the quarry engines. In the gray-dusted weighing shed a young city man from Toledo, with sleeve bands on his arms and a green visor over his eyes, checked the cars and tallied tonnage in the ledger. The engine whistled a taunt as it clanked away. Once Matt Hazard brought three tons of limestone from Sandusky and ostentatiously scattered it on his own deep limestone land. It was a queer wry twisted gesture, for his own comfort only—a token of his own righteousness. He was adding to the island while his brother shipped it away.

Years before, when they were still boys, the difference was there. Young Matt walked with his father through the sheep pasture and knelt beside him in the shearing pen, peeling back the mat of wool as his father worked the shears. He dug the setting holes—a boy not as tall as his spade handle—and crouched beside his father as the weblike vine roots went into the ground. He pruned the shoots of that first small vineyard, picturing in his boy's mind the long green aisles of the future.

But young Rufe could never keep at work in the fields. His eyes strayed to the white-winged schooners out in the channel, and in some mysterious way he knew the name of every freighter (the *Onaka*, the *Effingham*, the *Victory*, the *Wyandot*, the *Colonel Kentland*) that passed Border Island under its long banner of smoke. When a ship put in to North Harbor, he haunted the dock. With homesickness in his eyes, he watched it steam away in the fading windless light of evening. A package freighter coming in from Buffalo for a ton of wool or a dozen bleating sheep had for him a wonderful far-away strangeness. The raked funnel, with a film of smoke rose-colored in the sunset, the storied wheelhouse with all the windows flaming—where had it come from, and where was it going, over the water's rim?

Soon enough he found out. When he was fifteen he ran away from the island, hiding in the forepeak of a ship that carried a hundred huddled lambs from his father's pasture. He sent back a picture postcard from Chicago (a bridge jack-knifed above the river at Randolph Street). It was followed by other cards, from Marquette, Escanaba, Buffalo, Bay City, Milwaukee—each with the same message in a careless hand:

> Waved to the island last week as we went past Pelee. Had a fine voyage. Don't forget to feed my dog. RUFUS

That winter the two boys sat across the table from each other in the Hazard living room, the lamplight on their books and the air tainted with the little asthma lamp burning beside the couch where their brother Julian lay wheezing softly. The two at the table were just twenty months apart in age. Both had Joel Hazard's wide shoulders, his long straight nose, his coarse black hair, and his concentration on a job. That winter they bent in the same silence over their books, but their minds were poles apart. Rufus was studying Bowditch: *The Practical Navigator*, Asa Walker's *Navigation*, and Arkwright's *Handbook on Ship Construction*. His brother was making careful notes, in a slow square hand, on Prince's *Treatise on the Vine*, Emery's *Management of Vineyards*, and Furnival's *Insect and Fungus Enemies of the Grape*. When Joel Hazard died, fourteen years later, Rufus was steering a lumber schooner out of Saginaw Bay and Matt was supervising the pruning of vineyard rows that stretched across the island. The Hazard acres were divided between them, with the understanding that they would care for their frail brother Julian. Soon surveyors and a quarry foreman from Cleveland were pacing the western part of the island. Then began the sullen blasting thunder.

When supper was over, the brothers left the dining room, but they did not leave their differences. Over coffee and cigars in the living room, while the October wind began a thrashing in the cedars, they carried on their quarrel. Now it was about their father's sheep crossing the ice in a long-ago December.

"He drove them straight to Catawba Point," Matt said. "On hard ice all the way."

Rufus shook his head, and his big shadow wagged on the wall. "He drove them on the ice to Kelleys Island, then across the frozen South Passage to Marblehead."

"I've seen it in his records," Matt declared. "Straight to Catawba, past Mouse Island, and onto the point of land. Then over the county road to the railroad pens at Fremont."

Rufus tapped the table with his gold-headed cane. "You're wrong. Nick Newell on Kelleys Island remembers how he came with that big flock, right over the beach at North Bay, then straight up Division Street, those sheep bleating all the way. He stopped at the Newell House for a cup of coffee while the sheep pawed for grass in that little park. Then he drove them down the dock and onto the ice. He had to take a compass to keep his direction in all that snow. Nick says you couldn't see the sheep at all. You'd just see a man seesawing out there, and then the snow—"

Matt broke in. "He had dogs to keep the flock together."

On an island life has fixed boundaries. It is all confined and all concentrated. There is no spilling over, no running out and away. Go in any direction and you reach the limit. Every road is dead end, or water end. So everything is kept, and the past is closer and more accumulated because of those strict boundaries where the water pounds the shore. And so two men, with secret, unconscious envy of each other, two assertive men used to authority, could quarrel like boys over the route their father drove his sheep to market before they were born.

The windows rattled in a rush of wind. Matt called his sons

in from their chess game in the study. He told them to replenish the fire and then go up to bed. While the driftwood crackled on the irons, the argument went on—about the wolf that preyed on Joel Hazard's sheep.

Outside the wind was rising. The cedars roared around the house and the lake grew loud, smashing against the ledges. In the study, in his haze of medicated smoke, Julian Hazard bent over his drawing board. His mind was far away—in the vast ferny forest that was now Lake Erie's floor.

Matt went to the study door. "What became of the wolf that killed the sheep that winter?"

Julian turned, his cigarette feathering up into the amber lamp, his mind moving forward fifty million years to the era of wolf and sheep and Homo sapiens. "The dogs chased it into the lake, and father shot it in the water." He turned back to the trilobite on his desk, counting the flutings in its limestone shell.

Outside, the wind roared in the cedars. Kate Hazard put her embroidery hoop away. She turned the lampwick down and kissed her husband's scowling forehead. "Don't talk late, Matt. You don't have to settle anything. . . . Good night, Rufus."

He stood up, twisting the cane in his fingers. "Good night, Katherine."

A shift of wind brought another sound—not the rhythmic roar of waves, but the steady solid roar of stone pouring into a steamer's hold.

"Big stuff," Rufus said with satisfaction. "It goes to Bay Harbor, to build the breakwater."

"They drove the sheep to market," Matt said bitterly, "but they didn't haul the island away."

Rufus pressed tobacco in his pipe with a square forefinger. The match flared up, lighting his ruddy face as he sucked the flame into the blackened bowl. From the hall the man-tall clock began striking. There was the loose sound of chains and the full round beat of its bell.

Through the blue fog around him Rufus looked with a tired

tolerance at his brother. "Look, Matt." He pointed toward the clock with his cane. "Time don't stand still. If you'd get off this island, you'd know that. Take a trip with me. Come aboard tonight, it'll do you good. A couple of days in Bay City, then past the Soo to Duluth and down to Milwaukee or Chicago. You'll see things going on out there: cities growing, harbors being improved, canals walled in. And this island has a part in it. Why, there's island stone in the Indian Point Lighthouse and the canal walls at the Soo. It's in the state boundary markers of Indiana, all the way to the Ohio River. That isn't waste."

"It's ruin," Matt said.

"Forget it. Come along on a voy'ge and forget it. See what they think of Hazard Island at the Soo." He held up the cane so that the firelight danced on its gold head. "They gave me that last April for bringing the first cargo through the St. Marys ice. Come on the *Jason* with me. You've never been aboard that ship."

"I'll see it wrecked first," Matt Hazard said.

Wind buffeted the windows, and suddenly rain began a roaring on the roof. From the fireplace smoke puffed into the room. Matt poked the logs back against the chimney.

"You'll lose some grapes tonight," said Rufus comfortably.

Matt didn't even look at him. "We picked the last rows today."

Rufus's mouth twitched on his pipestem. There was a maddening rightness about his brother. He did things in time. He kept things in order. He made himself secure. Now he stood contemplating the embossed decanter on the mantel. That piece of Stiegel glass had never held wine. It was a prize, awarded by an international jury, for Erie Island claret. He sood there a solid, stubborn, tight-lipped man, with no room for risk or peril in all his ordered life. Now his grapes were heaped in baskets at the wharf shed and in boxes at the wineries. His harvest was safe from the wind. The clean-picked vines were ready for autumn's storms and winter's snow. His mile-long trellises were solidly built, with cedar posts planted like trees in the ground and wires strung through the center-drilled holes. The wrist-thick trunks held deeply to the island earth. Good vines, good for a hundred years, five hundred years, and the stone wineries standing up like fortress towers. Soon winter would ring the island shores with ice. The pruned vines would crouch under their trellises and the snow would cover them. Then Matt Hazard would drive his cutter over the white roads, relishing his possession, glad for the ice-clogged water that severed him from the violent and changing world. Under the high winter stars he would drive his family to Hazard Hall for the monthly supper and literary program. He would dignify the platform with his presence, a big man in black broadcloth, rapping with his gavel as the debaters took their chairs. *Resolved: that the tortoise is a more admirable creature than the hare.* All winter he would record temperatures and tabulate the snowfall in his neat black ledger. And in April he would ride horseback through the vineyard aisles where pale green leaves were twining round the wires. Winter and summer, the old wood and the new, and the clusters forming—it would go on in future seasons, farther than he could foresee. When he was dead, when his dust enriched the island earth, the long rows would still measure the land, the green tendrils reaching and the clusters ripening in the sun. A vineyard goes on and on. . . . If Matt Hazard had ever voyaged with his brother to the busy harbors of Lake Michigan or the long sea miles of Superior, his heart would not have pounded till he came back over the gray-green swells of Erie and breathed on the wind the fragrance of his vineyards. It takes study and planning, working and waiting, to make a vineyard. But any man with a stick of blasting powder can rend the rock apart, and any swearing steamer captain can carry off a cargo of stone. All that—all that invulnerability and contempt—were in Matt Hazard, standing in the firelight.

With a crash the terrace door blew open. A pane of glass lay scattered on the rug. Wind rushed through the room, sweeping the papers from the table. As Matt secured the door, something shattered behind him. He turned to see his brother, cane in hand, above the fragments of Stiegel glass on the stone hearth.

Matt crossed the room in four long strides. "You broke it," he said.

He seized the cane from his brother's hand and flung it at the fire. It struck the irons and rolled onto the floor. Rufus picked it up.

Through the broken pane the wet wind poured.

"Get out!" Matt ordered. "Get out of my house!"

"Your father's house," Rufus said.

"Get out!" Matt repeated. "And don't come back."

Rufus brought his stick down on the fragments of ruby glass. "So I broke it," he said, his knuckles white on the cane. "You're a fool, Matt. A blind, stupid, stubborn fool."

"Get out," Matt said in a ragged voice.

Rufus took his cap from the hall tree. The door banged behind him. In the study the lamp flame wavered, and Julian bent closer to the stone shellfish on his drawing board.

Rain drove down in sheets. Rufus stabbed the road with his cane and lunged on toward the blurred lights of the harbor. In a blind rage he climbed the ladder to his ship. He was a drenched grim figure crossing the deck where the sailors fought with floundering tarpaulins, stretching them over the hatches. His ship was loaded.

Any other time he would have waited till daylight, or till the wind slacked off. Now his voice barked in the pilothouse and he jabbed the engine-room telegraph. "Cast off the lines!" he roared down at the rain-pelted deck.

The mate said: "Bad wind, Captain Hazard. The water is piling up out there."

"I'll take her out," Rufus said.

On the dock rain swept down in a blinding curtain. It swallowed the swinging lights of the ship before they rounded the harbor point. From the reef came the roar of crashing water. Along the shore the great seas pounded in.

In the morning, under a clear October sky, across heaving water, the ship lay broken on the reef. When a boat put out, they found a dozen men huddled in the tilted foredeck cabins. But a dozen more were gone.

Two days later they found the body of Rufus Hazard washed up on Quarry Point. He was buried in the little fenced plot on the shore where the last yellow leaves were sifting down from the big cottonwood tree. . . .

In the year of Kate Hazard's death, a gale raged on the last of October, lashing the island shores all night long. In the morning the hulk off Quarry Point was gone. That winter the boys kept finding bulkhead timbers on the rocks, and once they found an old sea chest on the ledges near Cave Point. They carried it home, and Seth rubbed it down until it wore a sheen like old leather. Kate Hazard put it in the study and filled it with Julian's fossil drawings and his notes on the deep past of Hazard Island, which once lay on the bottom of a mid-continental sea.

The next spring, off Quarry Point, the lighthouse service anchored a blinker over the submerged hulk. At night it winked patiently in the lake's darkness, and the bell clanged across the water.

The Bosun's Chair

George Vukelich

THOSE WHO HAVE neither sailed on lakes freighters nor observed them closely when they dock may never have seen a bosun's chair, or a landing boom, in use. Rigged like a small swing at the end of a boom, there are usually four on each ship: portside and starboard, fore and aft. A deckhand stands or sits on the seat and is swung from the deck to the dock to handle the mooring lines as the ship ties up. Bosun's chairs are used extensively on the lakes, where often a ship will moor at an empty dock in the middle of the night. They are less common on salt water where tugs and longshoremen make them unnecessary. Using the chair, particularly in the dark in the winter, is one of the most dangerous jobs on the lakes, and many men have died doing it. Safety blocks, hundred-pound blocks of wood attached to a line, are now required on lakes ships so if the man in the chair falls in the water someone can throw over the safety block to keep him from being crushed between the ship and the dock. It was not always so. Vukelich, himself once a deckhand on the lakes, knew the terrors of the bosun's chair firsthand, and he describes one man's fear of it in the grim setting of sailing at the end of the season.

THE SEASON was November and winter was sliding into the Great Inland Seas like a spearpole. A wet, ashy snow was falling from the industrial sky when we tied up at Indiana Harbor with a load of limestone for the cement plants. The great railroad crane was up on its skinny steel legs poising like a praying mantis over our starboard side, and then the shovelmouth began filling itself at our hatches and going away and disgorging and then it came crawling forward to feed again. It was a single shovel rig and that meant we would be unloading for the next 40 hours because this was the slowest dock on the Great Lakes. In the meantime the crew would get a chance to run over to Gary and Calumet City and Mary's Place in South Chicago.

The ladder was lowered and the first offwatch men climbed down to the dock gingerly because they were dressed up for town and the handrails were wet and sooty. They turned and shouted up to the Bosun.

"Hey, you got fresh meat, Digger!"

They pointed to the little guy getting out of a taxicab and carrying a cardboard suitcase. They talked to him and hollered up to the Bosun again.

"Deck department, Digger! Fresh meat!"

The men waved and got into the muddy red, white, and blue Vet cabs and rode away. As the new man began the long climb up the ladder, Digger abruptly turned, nodded at me to follow, and headed for the galley. This was S.O.P. with Digger whenever crew replacements came aboard: Ignore them. Ignore the hell out of them.

Digger was in his thirties. A Navy veteran of World War II, he had sailed aircraft carriers in Task Force 58 against the Japanese. He was married to his high school sweetheart, had two children, and now was making a career of the Great Lakes oreboats.

"I work nine straight months," he said, "and then I curl up next to Mama for three. When I make Third Mate I'll have it knocked up."

He didn't drink too much and he didn't whore around at all and he spent most of his time studying navigation because he intended to write for his Third Mate papers during the coming off-season. This was his first season as Bosun and he knew sailing all right but he didn't know how to handle sailors and he was always calling the deckhands sonofabitch and whore and worse names that no real man would take and you had to call him on that or just get the hell off the ship. He was a rough Bosun only because he was trying so desperately to prove and reprove that he was a man, a Real Man, and that is the worst kind of Bosun a deckhand can draw.

Digger was talking as we walked into the galley for coffee and a cigarette. Digger liked to talk. If you knew anything at all about Digger, you knew that he liked to talk; and since you had heard this talk before you stopped listening.

I went over to the urn for coffee as Old Petersen came in. He had the new man with him. Petersen was always like money from home. Coming from Ashland in northern Wisconsin, he had been a lumberjack in the old days and in a way he would always be a lumberjack. He was the kind of man who was happy only with a peavy in his great hands or a doublebitted axe or a bucksaw or a marlinspike or a heavingline or anything that took a man to handle. He was six-foot-two and he walked like a young man and he knew his way around and there was life in his eyes.

Petersen got himself some coffee and sat down and he had that playful look again.

"I see your buddy's in the sack already," he said to me. "Old Buffalo."

That was the other deckhand, Billy Meyer from a little backwoods town in Minnesota. Billy was only 20 and already big as two men and Petersen called him Buffalo. Buffalo Billy. That was Petersen's sense of humor.

"He's still a growing boy," I said. "He needs his sleep."

"Well," Pete said. "You two guys won't be shorthanded anyhow. We got a new man again."

Petersen introduced me to the new man, his name was Frank, and then he showed him where the coldmeats and the bread were. Frank made himself some sandwiches and sat down. His cheeks bulged with the food and he washed it down with cold milk and kept chewing rapidly.

"I didn't get a chance to eat dinner," he said. "They wanted me to stick around the Lake Carrier's Hall."

"Sure," Petersen said, "Those bastards would let a man starve to death. It's like the army. You know, hurry up and wait." In the warmth of the galley, there was a thin stringlike whiskey smell around the new man. Petersen sniffed and looked at me and then at the new man.

"Too bad you didn't get a chance to meet the Bosun yet," Petersen said.

The new man had his mouth full. "I guess I work under him, huh?" He kept chewing and turned to Petersen. "What's his name, the Bosun?"

"Digger," Petersen said.

"That's right," the man said. "Digger. Gotta remember that. Digger."

Petersen looked around at me and then went back to cooling his coffee.

"It's an easy name," he said. "You'll remember it."

I watched Frank eating and didn't say anything.

"Well," Petersen said, "this makes how many deckhands this season for Digger? About 50?"

"About that," I said. Petersen looked at me and there was something smiling in his eyes. "But he's a good Bosun, ain't he? Gets the work out?"

"Bosun's bucking pretty goddam hard for Third Mate," Petersen explained to Frank. "That makes it rough on the deckhands. You know. They come and they go. Jesus, that's a lot of deckhands."

Petersen was still looking at me.

"Somebody's going to take him down on the dock one day. Ain't that right, kid?"

"Who?"

"Digger. One day somebody's going to take that good Bosun down on the dock."

"Is that right?" I said.

"That's right," Petersen said. "Somebody is going to take him down and clean his clock."

"I can hardly wait."

"I guess we have to," Petersen said. "Don't we?"

"Petersen," I said. "You're a nice old bastard. You are a nice troublemaking old bastard."

The new man finished his sandwiches and licked his fingers and then he asked where he could pick up his bedding.

"From the cook or one of the porters," Petersen said. He pointed through the galley and Frank said he better get his bedding now and he went to find the cook.

"Well," I said. "What kind of a guy is this one?"

"One-tripper," Petersen said. "Alky all right. Reminds me of a rabbit. You know. All twitchy and nervous. Nose like a rabbit."

"He must be hard up as hell to come decking this late."

"Alky," Petersen said. "Looking to get stakebound. He's a one-tripper all right. You know, right up Digger's alley."

We didn't say anything for a long time and Petersen was shaking his head.

"He was better off on the beach," I said.

"Said he lives in Gary and Lake Carriers sent him out," Petersen said. "He came aboard right after you guys left and I took him up forward." He paused. "Digger give him the cold shoulder at the ladder?"

"Digger's got him cased," I said. "I hope to Christ this guy's got winter clothes."

"I don't think so," Petersen said. "All he had was a little cardboard suitcase. No foulweather gear and that stuff."

"The poor bastard. He was better off."

Petersen got twinkly again.

"If you feel so sorry for him," he said, "why don't you show him your heart's in the right place and tell him he was better off on the beach?"

"Oh, screw you, Petersen."

Petersen laughed and drank his coffee.

"They all do," he said. "They always do. That's what happens when your heart is in the right place."

We got up and carried our cups to the sink drainboard and Petersen went on watch and I waited for the new man.

Frank came back with his clean padding from the Steward's department and then we went sloshing up the deck to our quarters past the gaping open cargo hatches that looked like toothless mouths and we didn't say anything until we reached the deck crane which was dogged down forward.

"I see you got an Iron Deckhand," Frank said.

"We've got four iron deckhands," I said.

"Four?"

"That crane. And Billy boy. And you. And me."

We turned at number one hatch.

"Do they put *all* the deckhands down on the dock?" Frank was pointing to the boom and the bosun's chair. The chair was like a piece of two-by-four with a rope through it strung to the boom and you rode it with a lifejacket on and were swung out over the side as the tugboats pushed inward and the ship closed with the docks because you had to get down there in a hurry and handle mooring lines.

"Yeah," I said. "You know. The more the merrier."

"That's a dangerous goddam thing," he said. "What if you fall off?"

It was a stupid question and I knew because I had asked the same question of Old Petersen when I first came aboard. The 600 feet of steel ship simply closed with the dock like a visejaw. A man in the water would be like a peanut in a nut cracker. Now I gave Frank the same answer Petersen had given me.

"Once you fall off," I said, "it stops being dangerous."

We stopped. He stared at the boom and chair, clutching his bedding tightly and shivering. We entered the ladderwell and started down.

"They serious about that sign?"

He was pointing to the big blue metal sign with the block white letters.

INTOXICATION PROHIBITED
BRINGING LIQUOR ABOARD SHIP
IS STRICTLY FORBIDDEN

"It protects the company if you get hurt," I said.

"You gotta be sober to sue them, huh?" He laughed. "You gotta be drunk to take a goddam job like this in the first place. And then you gotta be sober to sue them."

We crossed the dunnage room and entered the door stenciled, DECKHANDS.

He had taken the bunk over Billy and now he threw down the new bedding and opened up his cardboard suitcase and began pulling out balled up, dirty laundry.

"I better do some washing," he said. "We can use that machine out in the dunnage room, can't we?"

"Yes," I said. "Only they don't like us to use it when we're docked up."

He stopped pulling clothes from the suitcase.

"Why?"

"It uses up too much hot water," I said. "Christ, I don't know. Only we don't wash clothes in port."

"I really should wash this stuff," he said. "I don't have anything clean." He began pulling dirty clothes from the suitcase again.

"What the hell," he said. "It won't take me long. If anybody bitches, I can tell them nobody told me anything."

I took off my boots and worked my toes to get the chill out of them. Frank had a huge pile of clothes now and he took a good armful and went out the door. The pile left was still sizable and I knew that he wouldn't get through it in less than two or three washer loads. Then I heard Billy's soft slow voice.

"What the hell is that?"

He was looking at the sprawling pile on the flooring.

"We've got a new man," I said.

"What's he doing? Taking in washing?"

"He doesn't have anything clean."

"I can see that. What kind of a guy is this one?"

"Petersen says one-tripper."

"Boozer?"

"Smells like it."

"What did Digger say?"

"He's still thinking something up."

"Uhuh. I can see we're gonna have a real ball again. I hope this guy doesn't see snakes all night."

"I don't care about nights. I just hope this guy doesn't see anything wrong with working days."

"Oh, Digger will have him loose as a goose, buddy."

"I don't know. This guy's pretty scared. He's gonna be real rough up there. The bosun's chair scared him stiff."

"How the hell could it scare him? You mean looking at it?"

"Yeah. Looking at it."

He reached over for his cigarettes and his lighter.

"The Old Man get his orders yet?"

"I don't know," I said. "Dock boss says we've got Up Above next."

"No more stone?"

"He says not for us. A couple of self-unloaders from the Bradley fleet are taking the run right up to layup."

"Good goddam deal," he said sitting up. "We get us some overtime, Daddy."

The deck department always drew time-and-a-half when

the ship passed through the locks at Sault Ste. Marie and was lifted into the waters of Lake Superior. Coming back, the process was reversed and the ship was lowered and that was time-and-a-half too. The Company maintained a supply warehouse at the Soo Locks and a supply boat would come alongside and unload skidsful of meat and foodstores, drums of propane gas for the galley, everything and anything the ship had requisitioned in advance, and all of the stuff had to be pulled off the skids and checked and hauled and trucked away to the department that had put in the requisition.

From 100-pound bags of potatoes to 100-watt bulbs, the deckhands handled the new supplies and it was going to be a bitch at the Soo this time because we would be taking on heavy supplies for layup in addition to the usual stores and already a good cold winter was working Up Above.

"It's a goddam good deal all right," I said.

The door opened and we could hear the washing machine humming and Frank came in and stood over his pile of clothes.

"I just put one load in," he said. He saw Bill sitting on the bunk and stopped.

"Frank," I said. "This is Bill. Bill, Frank's our new man."

The door opened and there was no washing machine hum this time and there was Digger, stepping slowly inside and leaning against the bulkhead. He looked owly and was wearing slippers and now he stared slowly, tightly at the pile of laundry in front of Frank and finally his eyes came up to Frank's face.

Frank smiled uncertainly.

"I'm the new deckhand," he said. "You the Boats?"

Digger slouched with his hands in his dungarees.

"Those your clothes in the machine?"

"Yes," Frank said. "I don't have anything clean—"

"Get 'em the hell out of there."

Digger was landing on the new man with both feet. It was like watching some great bird measuring and circling and then dropping like a knifeblade into the crippled body of a small animal. Frank was not a pro and Digger was all pro and he hated the one-trippers like poison.

Frank was trembling.

"I don't have anything clean and—"

"Listen, boozer," Digger snapped. "Nobody washes clothes when this boat's in port. *Nobody.*"

Frank stood there and his lips were tight and working like he was going to cry.

"I turned off the machine," Digger said. "Now get your stuff the hell out of there." He straightened up and took his hands out of his pockets and went out the door.

Frank stood there for a long time and we didn't say anything and when he turned there were tears in his eyes. He looked at me and shook his head and bit his lips and knelt down to pick up the dirty laundry.

"Jesus Christ," he was murmuring. "Jesus Christ. Jesus Christ."

"Digger's kind of an S.O.B. Don't let him get you."

"We got a bottle," Billy said. "Do you want a shot, Frank?"

"No," he said. "No. God no."

"That's right about Digger," Billy said. "Don't let him get you."

"No more," he said. "I'm not going to drink any more. Not for the trip."

"Sure," Billy said.

The morning after we left Indiana Harbor, we ran into a heavy pus-colored sea and the thermometer on the boat deck flattened off at zero. The empty carrier was skidding high and rough like a corkfloat and the decks and hatches were coating up with ice. Digger got the deckhands out before breakfast and we rigged a lifeline back to the afterend. We had it done before Frank came on deck. He had a flapping red kerchief around his head and was wearing street shoes and his nose was running and he looked like he was going to freeze to death and blow away.

"Where the hell were you?" Digger shouted.

"I don't have any clothes," Frank said. There was that thin smell of whiskey about him again.

Digger started to say something and didn't and we finished securing the lifeline and then we went to breakfast.

"I don't have any clothes," Frank kept saying. "I was looking for some clothes to wear."

After Digger left the table we ate without talking for awhile.

"I was looking for some clothes to wear," Frank said again.

"Sure," Billy said. "That's all right, Frank."

"I wasn't trying to goof off and make it rough for you guys."

"Don't you worry about that," Billy said.

We finished eating and got into our jackets and Frank wrapped the red handkerchief around his head again. On deck we staggered and slipped our way forward along the shardhung rail. The wind was rising.

We came down the ladderwell into the dunnage room and there was Digger, dressed in his black raingear and pulling on his long rubber gloves.

"Mate says we have to hose her down, boys. Let's go."

Billy and I didn't say anything.

"Jesus Christ," Frank said. "It's freezing out there."

"We got live steam coming," Digger said. "Get your raingear and get that hose out."

"I don't have any clothes," Frank said.

Digger turned on Frank.

"That's your lookout. You boys get your foulweather gear on."

"Not me," Frank said. "I can't hose down."

"What was that, boozer?" Digger said.

"I can't hose down."

"That's mutiny," Digger said. "You refuse to work. The Coast Guard can take care of your ass."

"I don't refuse to work," Frank said. "Why can't we work

in the cargo hold or below deck somewhere? I don't refuse to work. I refuse to hose down."

Digger stared at him.

"I *don't refuse* to work," Frank said.

"Christ, you were drunk before breakfast. You can't pull that stuff out here," Digger said. "Goddammit. You signed articles on this boat and if you refuse to work, that's mutiny."

"I don't refuse to work."

Digger looked at Billy and at me.

"You guys heard him," Digger said. "He refused to work."

"No," Billy said. "He refuses to hose down."

"That's right," I said. "He only refuses to hose down."

Digger stared at me.

"Only?" he screamed. "Only!"

"It *is* pretty goddamned stormy," Billy said.

"We have work in the cargo holds," I said. "It's safer."

"That's mutiny," Digger said. "All three of you. The Coast Guard can take care of all three of you."

Billy looked at me and slowly pulled off his gloves.

"If the Coast Guard comes out in this gale, they're crazier than you are."

"He'll get 10 years," Digger said. "They can put you all in prison for 10 years."

"Why don't you just give Frank a break?" Billy said. "Let him work below?"

"Billy and I could handle it on deck. Let him work below. Right, Billy?"

"Hell, yes."

"No," Digger said. "He hoses down like everybody else."

"But we don't need him up there. He'd freeze to death out there. Like Billy says, why don't you give him a break?"

"He refuses to work. That's mutiny."

"Digger," Billy said. "You're talking foolish."

"Foolish," Digger said, "I'll show you who's talking foolish when I get the First Mate down here."

He started up the ladder and then Billy yelled at him. "Digger!"

Digger stopped and half turned.

"Yeah?"

"Digger," Billy said, "why don't you just use a gun?"

We turned and filed into our quarters and Digger went hustling up the ladderwell.

We sat on our bunks and waited and didn't say anything and the wind was running hard outside the deadlights and Billy got his fifth out and stared at it. It was half gone. He rummaged around in the drawer.

"The pint's gone," he said. "You take the pint?"

"No," I said. He was staring at Frank when the First Mate came in.

"You boys don't want to get in trouble for mutiny," he said.

"I don't refuse to work," Frank said.

"It was a misunderstanding," the Mate said. "We got a wrong weather report. The Old Man changed his mind. He wants you to work in the cargo hold." He looked at Frank for a long time.

"You don't want to get in trouble for mutiny," he said. "Do you?"

"No, sir," Frank said.

"You'll be paid off after we dock at Two Harbors. You're all done," the Mate said.

"Done?" Frank said.

"It could be worse," the Mate said. "If you were reported to the Coast Guard."

"For not hosing down in a gale," Billy said. "Crap."

"The Old Man's sore as hell at both of you, too," the Mate said. "You guys should know better. I don't think you'll sail for this company again."

Billy and I looked at each other. We had our mariners' documents and we could sail anywhere. Fresh water. Salt water.

What the hell. There were good ships and bad ships and there was a world of water to work and we looked at each other and at Frank. Frank looked stunned.

"You're breaking my heart, Mate," Billy said.

"Look, boys," the Mate said. "You know I'm not a hardnose. But I gotta be a hardnose when you don't play ball with the Bosun. You put him in a crack and I gotta back him up every time. Anyway, what the hell. Finish your drink and then get some socket wrenches and a flashlight and go check manhole covers in the cargo holds. Take all damn day but play ball with Digger now."

Billy smiled.

"Below deck, huh, Mate?"

"Hosing down was on the work sheet," the Mate said, "but we got a wrong weather report. It's not Digger's fault the gale broke."

"Like you said, Mate," Billy said. "You gotta back him up."

"Okay, kid," the Mate said. "We see eye to eye. That's why I'm paying you off in Two Harbors, Frank. Bosun can make it pretty rough on a deckhand." He paused. "Well. Don't take all damn day."

Then he was gone and we took off our heavy foulweather gear and got grease and socket wrenches and flashlights and went to check manhole covers in the cargo hold. We took our time and made the job last and we didn't see Digger at all.

"He could kill me," Frank said when we broke for a smoke. "I can see it." He grabbed Bill by the shoulder. "The Bosun *can* kill me. In that chair. That bosun's chair."

"You'll be all right," Billy said.

"Not on the chair," Frank said.

"Yes, on the chair. All you have to do is hang onto the rope."

Frank looked at him.

"And stay sober. Hang onto the rope and for Chrissake stay sober. You ride that thing drunk and you'll kill yourself."

"I can't do it," Frank said.

"Oh hell. Sure you can. Christ, it's simple."

"I can't do it."

"Jesus Christ," Billy said. "All right. You can't do it. Only what the hell did you sign on for then?"

Frank looked like he had been knifed.

"We get paid for this kind of stuff," Billy said. "What the hell did you expect, a vacation cruise?"

"I don't refuse to work," Frank said.

"Oh, crap," Billy said. "You give me that no drinking business and then you steal my booze. What the hell do you expect us to do? You want us to do your work for you too?"

Frank stared at us.

"If you want to panhandle your way, why the hell didn't you stay on the beach?"

Frank didn't say anything for a long time.

"I'm afraid of the chair," he said in almost a whisper. "You don't know how it is."

"I know all right," Billy said.

"I'm afraid," Frank said.

"You're yellow," Billy said. "You're lazy and you're a drunk and you're a thief and you're yellow to boot."

We stared at the bulkheads and listened to the wind screaming.

"Look," Billy said. "I was talking like Digger just now. I'm sorry. I didn't mean you were yellow."

"Sure," Frank said. "I know."

"Okay, Frank," Billy said.

"Only you were right," Frank said. "You hit the nail right on the head. I am yellow." He looked at us. "I'm old enough to be your father. You hit the nail right on the head." He began that whimpering little crying again.

"Jesus Christ," he said. "Jesus Christ. I'm old enough to be your father."

"Hell," Billy said. "Just hang in there. Hang tough, Frank."

Frank stopped the whimpering little crying and he reached

a pint bottle out of his jacket and it was Billy's. As he extended it, the bottle slipped from his hand. There was a crash in the black empty cargo hold far below.

"I'll pay you for the bottle," he said hoarsely. "Honest."

"That's all right," Billy said.

"And I'm not going to drink again."

"Sure," Billy said.

The night before we docked at Two Harbors, Minnesota, Old Petersen came in off watch and asked Frank how it was going. We had scrounged foulweather gear and boots for Frank. He was dressed for the deck now and he was eating three squares a day and scrounging oranges and fruit and he wasn't drinking at all and we knew he was giving himself the cold turkey treatment and we watched him trying and we didn't talk about it.

"How's it going, Frank?" Petersen asked again. "They got you looking like an old pro."

"It's going all right," Frank said. "I'm hanging tough."

"Sure," Petersen said. "A man has to stay loose. Then it's all right."

"Loose as a goose," Frank said. "Christ, I'm hanging by my thumbs."

Petersen laughed.

"That's right," he said. "Oh, it ain't so bad, you know. A man has to have clothes though. Then it ain't so bad on deck. I bet you didn't think sailing was like this, huh, Frank?"

"She's a home," he said. "She's a home. She's a feeder."

It was the time honored endorsement that sailors give to the ships that prove tolerable.

"Only that bosun's chair. I can't do that. I can't do that."

"Sure you can," Petersen said.

"No."

Petersen dug out his wallet then and opened it and took out a little card and passed it to Frank. Frank read it and read it and then he read it again.

"That's the Alky prayer," he said.

"It takes one to know one," Petersen said. "You'll be all right, Frank."

"How long you been dry?" Frank asked.

"Long time," Petersen said. "Long time, Frank. You know the score. We don't preach to anybody."

We didn't say anything about that and then the door opened and Digger came in. He was wearing slippers and a clean t-shirt and a long-billed cap.

"I made some popcorn," he said. "You guys want any popcorn?"

No one said anything.

"It gets behind my plate," Petersen said.

Digger looked around us and settled upon Frank.

No one said anything.

Digger seated himself on the flooring and crossed his legs and leaned back against the bulkhead.

"Well," he said pulling off the long-billed cap. "Won't be long now and I'll be curling up next to Mama for the winter."

He was looking past everyone and staring at the deadlight. Then he turned to Petersen.

"You know it's been a long goddam time, Pete. We fitted out March 16."

"That's a long time all right," Petersen said.

"Damn right," Digger said. He looked at us. "That's the roughest part of sailing. Fitting out. Layup's a goddam snap compared to fitting out. Chip and scrape. Hell, we got all the hull painted before the crew ever come on board. Got most of the cargo hold sprayed too."

"Yeah, that's a long time," Pete said. "I could take it when I was young. Now a couple three months is plenty. Just enough to get stakebound. You know."

Digger was squinting at Petersen.

"Let's see," he said. "I left home on March 14 and I ain't

seen the wife and kids for . . ." He broke off and was calculating. ". . . almost nine damn months. It'll be over nine when we hit the layup dock."

Frank looked up for the first time since Digger came in and now he was watching Digger closely.

"Nine months," Petersen said. "Yeah. That's a long time."

"Got a big bonus coming too," Digger said. "Company'll send that one in January sometime and I'll be cuddled up close to Mama. Hell, let her freeze tight then."

He sat there without speaking and without looking directly at any of us and we listened to the water sloshing below us in the blind tank.

"How long you been sailing oreboats?"

The question was Frank's and the voice was careful and yet clear and clean and sharp.

Digger cocked an eye at him.

"Eight years," he said.

"You been married all that time?"

"Jesus, I better be. I got a wife and two kids to prove it."

Frank shook his head.

"Eight years," he said. "That's a mistake."

Digger scowled.

"What kind of a crack is that?"

Frank leaned forward.

"You know, Boats," he said. "Most guys make a mistake when they love a woman. They tie her down with kids and then they take off. One way or another they take off. That's a mistake, Boats."

Digger was clenching and unclenching his right hand.

"What the hell are you talking about?"

"You leave a woman alone for nine months every year," Frank said. "What do you expect?"

Digger was punching his right fist into his left palm.

"Uhuh," he said. "Uhuh. You goddamn rotten drunk."

"I knew a guy once, Boats," Frank said. "Married. Left her

alone a lot. You know why he did it, Boats? Because he was afraid of her. Afraid of his own wife. I guess he was afraid of all women from way back."

Digger slid to his feet and stood spreadlegged.

"This guy wanted his wife to whore around when he was gone," Frank said. "Damn right. He wanted her to do that and then he could find out about it and he could feel better because—because he *wanted* his wife to be a whore—"

Digger cracked him then, the right fist smashing full on the bridge of Frank's nose and Frank spun into the wicked steel bunk and bounced and fell to the flooring. For a long time it looked like Digger was going to kick the life out of the thin scrubby rabbit body.

Frank raised his face slowly and his face looked like a smashed jam jar and the blood was running loosely and full from his nostrils and spattering his t-shirt.

"That guy I was talking about," he said. "That guy is me."

Digger stared at him for a full minute. Then he spun around and slammed out of the cabin.

Petersen went over to the sink and soaked a white washrag under the cold water tap and knelt down and held it over Frank's nose probing the bridge with his finger.

Petersen shook his head.

"Jesus, that's doing it the hard way," he said. He shook his head again and looked at us. "I think it's broken. Christ. That's the hard way." Frank was saying something and his words were muffled around the washrag and Petersen lifted it and went to the sink to rinse it. Frank raised himself on his elbows.

"You know," he said to Billy. "You're right about that bosun's chair. All you have to do is to hang onto the rope. How in the hell can anyone fall off if they hang onto the rope?"

"They can't," Billy said.

"That's right," Frank said. "That's right. They can't. They *can't* fall off." He was getting to his feet and peeling off his t-shirt.

"Listen," he said. "I want to go first in that bosun's chair tomorrow. I *have* to go first. Is that all right?"

Billy looked at me.

"Sure," he said. "Hell yes."

"Damn right," Frank said. "They *can't* fall off. Not if they don't want to. They plain *can't* fall off." He dropped his t-shirt on the flooring and dragged out his cardboard suitcase and dumped the contents on top of the t-shirt.

"You better get that nose looked after," Petersen said. "The Mate's got a kit."

"I'm gonna put a load in the washer first," Frank said. "Gotta have clean clothes for tomorrow." He grabbed up the dirty laundry and his nose was still bleeding and his back was small and white like the underbelly of a bird.

"I'll tell the Mate I caught my nose in the wringer," he said.

We watched him go banging out of the door and we didn't say anything until we heard the humming of the washing machine in the dunnage room.

"I'll be goddamned," Billy said. He was sitting up and reaching for his lighter. "I'll be good and double damned. Frank."

"Is his nose broken?"

"Goddamn right," Petersen said.

"Then they won't let him swing on the chair tomorrow."

"How the hell are they going to stop him now?"

"Frank." Billy repeated. "And I'll bet he'll sail through the air like a bird too." He shook his head. "Frank."

Petersen threw the dripping red washrag into the sink.

"It's an easy name," he said. "You'll remember it."

"Hanging On." (Edward Pusick; courtesy Shipwrecks Unlimited, Marquette, Michigan.)

St. Elmo's Fire

A phantom craft and a crew gone daft,
With glazed eyes staring, fore and aft,
Sails on to a nameless port.
                    "The Ghost Ship"
                              Anonymous

A Lake Huron Ghost Story

Anonymous

NINETEENTH-CENTURY NEWSPAPERS often printed short stories head-to-tail with the news, and this piece comes from the *Saginaw Courier* of 1883. Originally it had run in the *New York Sun* and is based on one of the more notorious shipwrecks of the time, the sinking of the *Chicago Board of Trade* on Lake Erie with a cargo of wheat during a gale in 1874. Although the crew was saved, rumors that the captain had deliberately scuttled his ship began to circulate, no doubt encouraged by the disastrous economic conditions of the time when owners were lucky to break even and the temptation to "sell" one's floating property to the insurance underwriters was a powerful one. Despite the captain's testimony that his ship had grounded in the Lime Kiln Crossing in the Detroit River before she sank, part of the crew told a more intriguing story—that the *Board of Trade* had begun leaking in a "mysterious manner" and that instead of heading her toward shore, the captain had steered out into the lake. With this the investigation began and the ship became a lightning rod for all the rumor, innuendo, and anxiety affecting lakes shipping, particularly the acrimonious relations between vessel owners and insurance companies.

Before the underwriters could raise her the next spring, the

Board of Trade had been spotted in several ports, then seen on Lake Michigan as a phantom ship under full sail that disappeared in an instant. The captain, meanwhile, was reported to have disappeared after the crew alleged that he was drunk. When, late the following season, the salvagers finally succeeded in raising her and towing her to Buffalo, the underwriters found suspicious holes near the water closet pipe. The owners plugged them and the ship promptly sank at the dock since all along her bottom the oakum was out and the seams were sprung, probably from where she had grounded. Both parties involved hired more experts who gave more contradictory testimony, while the *Board of Trade* sank each time they shut off the pumps to try to prove another theory. Eventually the captain surfaced in command of another vessel, the underwriters reached a compromise with the owner, and one newspaper sarcastically noted that it had cost the insurance company nearly as much to raise her and investigate as she was worth. She was repaired and sailed until 1900, but the folklore surrounding her refused to die.

In this story she is a topsail schooner renamed the *Erie Board of Trade*, and the anonymous writer focuses not on the sinking but on a previous voyage to illustrate the supposedly evil temperament of the captain. Accounts of ghostly crew members like Scotty in this story are rare on the lakes, which more often spawn water monsters and ghost ships, and stories about masters as cruel as Captain Custer seem to occur less often than in saltwater literature. A number of historical conditions account for this—voyages were shorter, pay was better, food was good, and the lakes sailors refused to tolerate the abuse saltwater men were accustomed to—but the depression of the 1870s undermined the usual relations between lake captains and their crews and encouraged the first steps toward sailor's unions. The discontent of the sailors is evident in this story, and forms a theme in a minor key underlying the writer's obvious delight in a good yarn about an unlucky ship and her tormented captain.

The Strange Yarn Spun by an Old Sailor in South Street:
The Cruise of the
Schooner Erie Board of Trade
and the Singular Mishap That
Befell Her One Starlit
Night in Saginaw Bay

DOWN IN THE LOWER part of South Street the other day, an old sailor sat on an anchor stock in front of a ship chandler's store. He was an intelligent-looking man and was fairly well-dressed for one of his calling. Other sailors were seated on a bale of oakum,[1] on a wide-mouth pump without a plunger, and on the single stone step of the store. The ship chandler and a young friend sat in chairs just inside the door. The group were talking about ghosts. One of the men had just told his experience.

"You're a sorry dog," said the ship chandler to him. "You were drunk, and the spirits you'd taken within made you see the spirits without. It's always that way."

The old sailor threw one leg over the anchor stock, faced the ship chandler, and said:

"You know I never take no grog, don't you, captain?"

The ship chandler nodded.

"Well, I saw a ghost once. I saw it as plain as ever I saw anything. The captain of the schooner I was on and the man in the waist both saw it, too. There wasn't a drop of liquor on board. It happened up on the Lakes, and I reckon you know the captain. It was the talk of the docks the whole season."

"I know a Captain Jack Custer of Milan. He's the only fresh-water captain I'm acquainted with," said the ship chandler.

"He's the man. I heard him speak of you once. It was a

---

1. Tarred hemp or manila fibers made from old and condemned ropes that have been unpicked. Oakum was used for caulking the seams of a wooden ship to make them watertight.

little over ten years ago. I was before the mast then.[2] It was at the opening of the season, and I was in Chicago. I'd been through the canal from Toronto on one of these little canallers. What with tramping through the mud with a line over my shoulder and taking turns around snubbing posts every time the schooner took a notion to run her nose into the bank, I'd got enough of canal schooners. I heard at the boarding house that some men were wanted on a three-masted schooner called the *Erie Board of Trade*. The boys gave her a pretty hard name, but they said the grub was good and that the old man paid the top wages every time, so I went down and asked him if he'd got all hands aboard. He looked at me a minute, and then asked me where my dunnage was. When I told him, he said I should get it on board right away.

"The *Board of Trade* was as handsome a craft as ever floated on the Lakes. She'd carry about 45,000 bushels of corn. Her model had as clean lines as a yacht. As I came down the dock with my bag under my arm, I had to stop and have a look at her. The old man saw me at it. He was proud of her, and I thought afterward that he rather took a fancy to me because I couldn't help showing I liked her looks.

"I was in her two round trips. The last trip up was the last on the Lakes. Not but what times were pretty good there. We were getting $2.50 a day for the first trip out and $2.00 the last. We messed with the old man, and, what with fresh meat and vegetables, and coffee with milk, it was a first-cabin passage all around. But the old man made it hot for most of us. There wasn't any watch below in the day, and we were kept painting her up on the down trip and scrubbing the paint off again on the passage up. Skippers don't handle the belaying pins[3] quite so much up there as they do down here when arguing with the

---

2. A deckhand on a sailing vessel.

3. Short lengths of wood, iron, or brass set up in convenient places in the ship and around which the running rigging can be secured or belayed. In this context the writer means that the captain used them to beat the crew.

men, because there is a lot of shysters around the docks waiting to get the men to tie the vessel up for it. A man who's handy in fisting a mainsail will generally find pretty fair cruising.

"The first trip around to Chicago every man but me got his dunnage onto the dock as soon as he was paid off. I'd seen worse times than what we'd had, and when I got my money I asked the old man if he'd want anyone to help with the lines when the schooner was towed from the coal-yard to the elevator. He said he reckoned he could keep me by if I wanted to stay, so I signed articles for the next trip there. When we were getting the wheat into her at the elevator we got the crew aboard. One of them was a red-haired Scotchman. The captain took a dislike to him from the first. It was a tough time for 'Scotty' all the way down. We were in Buffalo just twelve hours and then we cleared for Cleveland to take on soft coal for Milwaukee. The tug gave us a short pull outside the breakwater, and we had no more than got the canvas onto the schooner before the wind died out completely. Nothing would do but we must drop anchor, for the current, settling to the Niagara River, was carrying us down to Black Rock at three knots an hour.

"When we'd got things shipshape about decks, the old man called Scotty and two others aft and told them to scrape down the topmasts. Then he handed the boatswain's chairs to them. Scotty gave his chair a look and then turned around, and touching his forehead respectfully, said, 'If you please, sir, the rope's about chafed off, and I'll bend on a bit of ratlin' stuff.'[4] The captain was mighty touchy because the jug had left him so, and he just jumped up and down and swore. Scotty climbed the main rigging pretty quick. He got the halliards bent onto the chair and sung out to hoist away. I and a youngster, the captain's nephew, were standing by. We handled that rope carefully, for I'd seen how tender the chair was. When we'd got him up chock-

---

4. Ratline stuff is three-strand, loosely laid, tarred hemp. To bend on is to make a temporary, secure join between two lengths of line.

a-block, the young fellow took a turn around the pin, and I looked aloft to see what Scotty was doing. As I did so he reached for his knife with one hand and put out the other for the back-stay. Just then the chair gave way. He fell all bunched up 'til he struck the crosstrees, and then he spread out like and fell flat on the deck, just forward of the cabin on the starboard side. I was kneeling beside him in a minute, and so was the old man, too, for he'd had no idea that the man would fall. I was feeling pretty well choked up to see a shipmate killed so, and I said to the captain: 'This is pretty bad business, sir. This man's been murdered,' says I.

"When I said that Scotty opened his eyes and looked at us. Then, in a whisper, he cursed the captain and his wife and children, and the ship and her owners. It was awful. While he was still talking the blood bubbled over his lips, and his head lurched over to one side. He was dead.

"It was three days before the schooner got to Cleveland. Some of the boys were for leaving her there, but most of us stayed by, because wages were down again. Going through the rivers there were four other schooners in the tow. We were next to the tug. Just at the big end below Port Huron a squall struck us. It was too much for the tug, and some lubber cast off the towline without singing out first. We dropped our bower[5] as quick as we could, but it was not before we'd drifted astern, carrying away the head-gear of the schooner next to us and smashing in our own boat. We were a skeary lot going up Lake Huron and no boat under the stern.

"There was a fair easterly wind on the Lake, and as we had got out of the river in the morning we were standing across Saginaw Bay during the first watch that night. I had the second trick at the wheel. The stars were shining bright and clear and not a cloud was in sight. In the northwest a low, dark streak

---

5. A bow anchor attached permanently to its cable so as to be instantly ready for letting go in an emergency.

showed where the land was. Every stitch of canvas was set and drawing, though the booms sagged and creaked as the vessel rolled lazily in the varying breeze. I had just sung out to the mate to strike eight bells when the captain climbed up the companionway and out on deck. He stepped over to the starboard rail and had a look around, and then the lookout began striking the bell. The last stroke of the bell seemed to die away with a swish. A bit of spray or something struck me in the face. I wiped it away, and then I saw something rise up slowly across the mainsail from the starboard side of the deck forward of the cabin. It was white and all bunched up. I glanced at the captain, and saw he was staring at it too. When it reached the gaff near the throat halliards, it hovered over it an instant, and then struck the cross-trees.[6] There it spread out and rolled over toward us. It was Scotty. His lips were working just as they were when he cursed the captain. As he straightened out he seemed to stretch himself until he grasped the maintop mast with one hand and the mizzen with the other. Both were carried away like pipestems. The next I knew the ship was all in the wind. The squaresail yard was hanging in two pieces, the top hamper was swinging, and the booms were jibing over.[7]

"The old man fell in a dead faint on the quarter deck, and the man in the waist dived down the forecastle so fast that he knocked over the last man of the other watch. If it hadn't been for the watch coming on deck just then, she'd rolled the sticks out of her altogether. They got the headsails over,[8] and I put the wheel up without knowing what I was doing. In a minute it seemed we were laying our course again. The second mate was just beginning to curse me for going to sleep at the wheel, when the mate came along and glanced at the binnacle.

---

6. The ghost reached the section of the gaff near the mast, then struck the mast fittings just below the topmast.

7. The squaresail yard just above the gaff has broken in two and the sailing gear above it is loose.

8. Headsails are jibs and staysails raised at the forward end of the vessel.

" 'What the ——— is this?' he said. 'Laying our course and on the other tack?' "

The young man by the ship chandler had listened with intense interest. "Here," he said. "That story is true. I was there. I'm the captain's nephew you spoke about. I was reading in the cabin that night. As the bell began to strike, I felt a sudden draft through the cabin, and my paper was taken out of my hands and out of the window before I could stop it. I hurried out of the cabin after it, but as I got my head up through the companionway I heard the crash of the falling masts. When the schooner began to go off on the other tack, I saw a bit of a waterspout two miles away to the leeward, and—"

The ship chandler laughed.

"Did you find your paper?" he asked.

"No!" said the young man.

"I thought not," said the ship chandler.

"Well," said the old sailor, "the main facts in this story can be easily verified. The next voyage the schooner was sunk. The insurance company resisted payment on the grounds that she had been scuttled by her captain. During the trial of the case, the story of the death of Scotty and the loss of her topmasts under a clear sky was all told under oath. Anybody who doesn't believe it can see a copy of the printed testimony by applying to Rosberg & Barker, the ship chandlers at 1789 Central Wharf, Buffalo."

From *Scenes on Lake Huron; A Tale; Interspersed with Interesting Facts, in a Series of Letters*

A North American

Lake Mariners, Listen to This Tale

THIS SMALL, anonymously written novel is the second maritime novel set on the Great Lakes. Privately printed in 1836, it describes a month-long, wandering voyage down Lake Huron from Mackinac Island to Detroit in November and December of 1822, during which the once sturdy and well-founded vessel is reduced to a wreck by adverse winds and storms. A typical experience, the author assures us, which could happen to anyone sailing the lakes in late autumn, the better to persuade his readers that lakes sailors are among the best in the world.

Although *Scenes* is nominally about the lakes, it owes much of its technique to the voluminous voyage literature of England in the preceding centuries. Like those novels (of which *Robinson Crusoe* is one), *Scenes* purports to be an account of an actual voyage with some fictional embellishments, told in a series of diary-like letters to a friend and filled with digressions that have little to do with the actual story: *Scenes* recounts tales about impressment during the War of 1812, King Neptune's appearance on Lake Erie, and places on Mackinac Island. The writer describes his shipmates only as types—the Captain, the Mate, Three Able-Bodied Seamen, an Englishman on tour with his violin, a Pious Gentleman, a Dutchman, a Down-East Yankee, and the Cook and his dog—the better to give his tale a legendary quality as a parable of survival in a wilderness sea and to show his erudition in the earlier traditions of literature. Unlike James Fenimore Cooper, who was creating the American maritime novel at the same time *Scenes* was being written, this author is not interested in breaking new ground. His descriptions of prayers drowned out by commands is as old as Shakespeare, as is his character of the swearing Mate, a common type in Elizabethan drama. This book was obviously calculated to appeal to a popular audience addicted to travel accounts that mixed fact with fancy and promised, as this author does, that he "has endeavored to be so extravagant in his fiction, that the reader can hardly be mistaken in the perusal." A good read, in other words, with a sensational plot set in an unfamiliar place. Like many books of its type it was "not originally intended for publication, but was commenced to make a mere obituary notice of one who was very unceremoniously bereft of life," probably the "J" to whom the letters are addressed and who probably never existed except in the writer's imagination.

But as often happens in the history of literature, a work that sets out to be one thing soon becomes something quite different, and despite the author's attempt to emulate his models, his own concerns take precedence. Like many sailors before him he is quite disgusted with pious hypocrites who will not help save the ship, but *Scenes* is interesting for the author's attack on the prevailing tone of religious piety in American life and the resulting power the clergy held. Thus the author constructs his plot to pillory the Pious Gentleman at every opportunity, a situation he must have thought his readers would enjoy, if only secretly. More important, he is determined to upgrade the reputation of lakes mariners to convince his skeptical Eastern audience that while the lakes might be a wilderness in the "Western Territories," their seamen "ranked with any on the globe." To do so he has taken as his model all the sea literature he knew, complete with quotations from popular eighteenth- and nineteenth-century sea poetry, and grafted it onto a Great Lakes setting filled with gales and maritime disasters any saltwater man, or reader of sea literature, would recognize instantly. Like Captain Marryat, and presumably like many of his readers, the author of *Scenes* "had as yet never witnessed a genuine fresh water or Lake Gale; I therefore felt an anxiety to see one ushered in, in due form." Also like Captain Marryat, he soon regrets his wish.

The first letter reprinted here takes up the ship at this point, foretold by a corposant (St. Elmo's Fire) on the masts. St. Elmo's Fire is rare on the lakes and rarer still in lakes stories, but it was a staple of saltwater romances of the time and thus would have had to be included for dramatic effect. The next letters describe the ship sometime later, after a series of storms during which the cook and his dog have been swept overboard, the supplies of food and firewood are nearly exhausted, and the ship has been so damaged she is in grave danger of capsizing.

Letter III.

Dear J——

By my last letter, you learned that I was contending with adverse winds, but by no means for the first time in my life; as you must be well aware, but to proceed.

In the afternoon of the next day, we had repeated and

heavy peals of thunder to the Westward; weather thick and foggy, not any land to be seen, the thunder continuing; this was, and is always considered a perfect land mark for the "Thunder Bay Islands" (by those who navigate these waters) when the land is not visible. The place which bears this significant name consists of a group of islands, interspersed with bays, and situated on the western side of the Lake; where it seldom ceases Thundering in winter or summer, day or night: this you may perhaps think a fiction, but it is nevertheless an astonishing fact. One thing more I think worthy of note; there are no soundings to be obtained in Lake Huron; with the exception, of a rocky middle ground extending about fifteen miles in the Lake off this place, which carries six fathoms over it: with this exception, there is no soundings to be had; or should a ship master be fortunate enough to get soundings, with a cast of the lead, his good fortune would in all probability be immediately succeeded by a "mis"; and his misfortune would be; to have his jib-boom brousing among the thickets, his vessel out of her element, and hard upon the rocks.

The succeeding morning there was a slight "heave of the sea," setting from the southward and west, which increased so much during the day, that at sunset it became unpleasant. The weather was calm, with a humid, cold, and consequently unpleasant atmosphere. The Captain anxiously paced the quarter deck, but there was nothing to break in upon this monotony, except the usual exclamations of seamen at such times, of "Blow d——l," &c., and occasionally a tremulous scream from the wild fowl that were constantly hovering over, or revelling in their aquatic sports in large quantities around us.

The "heavy ground swell" as the seamen termed it; increased, and the succeeding day in the afternoon, became very heavy; the vessel rolling gunwale too at every surge, for want of wind to keep her steady, was by no means calculated to add to the comfort and convenience of the passengers, say nothing about the anxious solicitude with which our Captain's mind was agitated; for the result of the then threatening, and impending storm; and the safety of his vessel.

At three in the afternoon the fog disappeared; but the sky was still overcast with thick, dark, and low clouds, which moved rapidly to the northeast: a high promontory appeared at quite a distance off our starboard quarter, which was pronounced to be "Highland's Sauble."[1] The captain at the same time remarking, that we should have the wind out of the Bay (Saginaw Bay) before morning. "This heavy and increasing ground swell has not been upon this Lake two days for nothing." "'Tis sure to come," added the mate; "and we are sure to have enough of him, too, sir." The protracted and uncomfortable calm, with such dense fogs, together with the unpleasant and dead roll of the vessel; had become so truly irksome, that we would almost have given what our seamen were occasionally promising, provided we could have any thing like a change,—no matter what it was; or how hard it blew, if it would but blow, seemed to be the prevailing desire throughout the ship's company.

In the afternoon the flying-jib was unbent, the men were sent aloft to unrig and send down the foretop-sail; the fore-yard was also settled away, and well secured by "rolling lashings"; the Topmast struck, and in fact, the whole tophamper sent down and secured; the captain, at the same time remarking, that he "liked to have every thing snug."[2]

At nine in the evening I laid aside my book, and went upon deck; but do not recollect ever having witnessed so dark a night. The dead calm and silence still reigned, with the exception of an occasional scream from the wild fowl; and the noise made by the vessel thrashing her huge channels into the water,

---

1. Au Sable Point on the Michigan shore.

2. The flying-jib was one of up to six jibsails carried on wind ships. The foretop-sail was carried on the upper sections of the foremast. The foreyard is the lowest yard on the foremast. Here the writer describes furling the foresail around it with rolling lashings, that is, lashings that could not be blown loose. Top hamper in this context means the sailing gear aloft.

as she roll'd heavily from side to side. My eye was soon attracted by a bright light, resembling a flame, upon the cross-trees of the foremast. What is that light? I eagerly interrogated: Comprosant, replied the mate.[3] Immediately another appeared, and yet another; and in a few minutes the whole rigging was brilliantly illuminated, and apparently in a blaze, with a kind of shifting light, that was very interesting; although the superstitious forebodings of the crew were admirably well calculated to make them appear terrific. But why, how, or for what purpose these brilliant messengers should have obtruded themselves upon us, at this anxious and expecting moment, there was not any of us could presume to assign a reason.

These lights may scientifically, or perhaps philosophically, be called meteors, and are by no means an uncommon phenomenon; nor are they, strictly speaking, common, but occasionally pay a friendly visit to the "Lake Mariner," while navigating these highly interesting inland seas. I have subsequently witnessed them in dark nights, immediately preceding a thunder storm; and more frequently preceding, and during severe gales of wind. Instances I could relate, but my letter becoming already too prolix, I must forbear. Had they been an ill-omen of total destruction, as the crew prognosticated; all those who had ever witnessed them would have long since been numbered among those who have preceded us; consequently, there never could have been any persons left to report that such lights had ever made an appearance.

The captain hastily paced the quarter deck and observed, with a good deal of emphasis; we shall have wind, and plenty of it too, before morning; but adding, "we are prepared to meet whatever may come." His words were verified: for—

---

3. "Comprosant" is probably slang or the writer's mistake. The term *corposant* originally comes from the Latin, *corpo sanctus*, for holy body. It is an electrical discharge on the masts and rigging resembling a flame or a light and is commonly known as St. Elmo's Fire after St. Erasmus, the patron saint of Mediterranean sailors.

"Next morn a Storm came on at Four."[4]
"Fare thee well."

M.

Letter VIII.

Dear J——,

My last note to you did not exactly leave us as you Seamen would express it; "In the doldrums," but as usual, we were contending against adverse winds, and a prospect in the weather, that promised us not much, if any thing at all that would be favourable to the almost forlorn condition in which we were then placed.

We continued however, to Stand "Off and On," under all the "Press of Sail"[5] we could possibly make; with a hope that we should get so near in with the land as to have soundings or anchorage, before the anticipated gale set in, which we too well feared would be from the South west, the very quarter which we were deprecating against. At 3, P.M. made the land off our larboard bow, upon the British[6] coast. Our vessel (when she had any thing like an opportunity) was an excellent "sea boat," and a fine sailer: at sunset, made the land all around the southern extremity of the Lake; but so very remote, we could not discover the opening or entrance to the rivers mouth.

---

4. The author of *Scenes*, like many nineteenth-century writers, liberally sprinkles his work with quotations from poetry, a style of writing, which together with most of the poetry he quotes, has long since become unfashionable. Whenever possible I have identified the quotations, most of which come from popular poetry rather than the classics. This line comes from Falconer's "The Shipwreck," first published in 1762 and reprinted for over a hundred years.

5. They are sailing on alternate tacks under all the canvas they can carry.

6. The coast of Canada.

At half past ten at night the wind came out in a violent white squall from the Southwest, which put us in much confusion for a time. We had been extremely anxious to gain a lee under the land, or get into the mouth of the river, and leave this (what had been to us an) inhospitable Lake. Each man had therefore exerted himself to the utmost during the day, in order to accomplish this very desirable, and to us all important object. The Gale surprising us so extremely sudden, split our main sail from "Clue to earing"[7] in an instant, and with it went our beating to windward; as well as our anticipated expectations of gaining the rivers mouth that night, or even getting under a lee shore for shelter.

We were therefore driven again from the land, much to our mortification; and contrary to our wishes, and the determined and indefatigable exertions of the crew. The first thing done was to shorten sail, and secure that part of the main sail which we had remaining, and preserve the position of the vessel as near as possible; or in other words to "loose nothing," and hold on to all we had: it continuing to blow in severe gusts with the concomitants of rain, hail and a dense spray that was unusually annoying. This was truly disheartening, but we had one consolation, which is a grateful one at all times to a seaman during a gale, (and in this instance proved a very valuable one to us, for without it, we must inevitably have been wrecked) "plenty of sea room," having at least nine tenths of Lake Huron to leeward of us, "and its fathomless bottom" beneath. This was however but a pitiful compensation for our want of fire wood and provisions; say nothing of our other privations, and the extreme distress which was then pending over us, and which we too soon realized.

The morning dawned upon us with dreadful weather, blowing a perfect hurricane, and every appearance of a protracted gale; we could hardly expect any thing less at that season of the year.

---

7. The sail has torn diagonally from top to bottom.

But what had we to fear? Being yet undaunted, we had good consciences and honest hearts, we allowed no "Vultures to hover over and prey upon our minds": we were on board a vessel too, that had triumphantly carried us through one more than common "Storm," and with such perfect safety that we had every confidence in her ability too, to ride out a second or even a third; we also had an able crew;

"Whose hearts were formed in Cæsars mould;"

We had a Captain, in whom we had every confidence; inasmuch as we had most abundantly and satisfactorily tested his more than sterling worth; we had also a confidence in that (imaginary)—

"Cherub, which sat smiling aloft."

Our provisions having been quite exhausted, as a matter of coercive necessity, we were placed upon short allowance, and that not of the most pleasant kind of food; and which would have been much less desirable to us, than it then was, had we been situated in different circumstances.

This Storm lasted, and eventually wore itself out, as though exhausted by fatigue alone, at the expiration of three tedious nights, and an equal number of (to us) long days: and however severe the former one might have been, it was not a circumstance to the present; we dare not presume to show the least rag of sail, for it was totally impossible that it could have remained in the "bolt rope" a single moment; the wind exceeded every thing of the kind for severity I ever before experienced; and as the Mate hoarsely observed: "the Maker of Winds this time, is certainly doing his best; He blows hard enough to blow the vessel out of the water, or the Lake out of its bed." The sun was totally obscured, the atmosphere presented a thick, hazy reddish kind of doomsday tint, that made it appear unusually gloomy, and so dark withall; that it was absolutely necessary to keep a light constantly in the binnacle (even at mid day) in order to see the compasses. The surface of the Lake as far as we could discover, was like a tremendous sheet of boiling foam, with a dreadful heavy swell; that seemed to rise gradually, as though reluctant, and with great labor; at the same instant the wind taking and clipping off its summit, which (in the space of a breath was converted into a spray, like the drifting of snow before a gale) and came with such violence, that it wet every person exposed to the skin in a very few minutes, through the thickest clothing.

This singular darkness, together with the terrific whistlings of the wind through the rigging, the heavy toned dead, discordant and Sullen Moan of the Tempest, produced an effect upon our spirits not unlike the gloomy appearance of the atmosphere.

Yet still there was a kind of sublime grandeur in the midst of the awful and appalling howlings of this unprecedented Storm, that called the wandering mind almost involuntarily back to HIM, who was its great and grand Author with peculiar delight: and if I have ever had any thing like satisfaction, or true enjoyment with my Creator during my transitory existence, it has been in my closet, uninfluenced by Mortals; or musing alone by myself upon the relentless fury of a Tempest, or other surprising phenomena of nature.

But little could be done excepting to relieve the vessel as much as possible, and let her drift almost at the mercy of the elements. The second day was very cold, and the morning of the third, we had collected such an immense mass of ice, that the vessel which had hitherto been buoyant and lively, labored excessively; and seemed to strain upon every spike that held her together; and so severely too, that a very troublesome, and an additional leak was the consequence, which added very much to the labors of our already fatigued crew, as it took a thirty minutes spell at the pumps, out of every hour, in order to keep the vessel free from water.

The wind however lulled for a short time the third morning, and the weather lighted a little about half past eight o'clock;

but the sea which was running in tremendous mountains seemed to increase: got a view of the land under our lee, which was soon distinguished to be an Island known by the name of the "Big Manatou."[8] "Manatou" is an Indian name for evil Spirit, or Devil: hence the superstitions of the Natives are such, that they never presume to visit or land upon any of the Islands called "Manatous," there being several in the different upper Lakes bearing that Cognomen.

At half past nine A.M. "Veered Ship,"[9] and made a small part of the foresail with very great difficulty, and a determined resolution on the part of the crew; as the rigging from the extreme coldness of the weather had become so rigid, that it rendered in the blocks only with the very greatest exertions. Stood with heavy hearts and gloomy prospects to the westward, the vessel laboring and straining in a dreadful mannner. I have frequently witnessed persons laboring under great bodily pain and distress, when my sympathies have been as often extremely excited, and my mind strongly interested and engaged for their relief: Such were the condition of my feelings in this case, with regard to the distressing and arduous labors of the vessel; she seemed to make such dreadful struggles at one moment while in the trough of the sea; and at the next, so gradually, and apparently with such great labor mount the succeeding wave, triumphant. She in fact appeared; as though as sensible to her own distresses, as we were ourselves, and as though conscious of the danger, and at the same time, like a faithful animal, was exercising a desperate determination to preserve us at all hazards. All hands appeared to be equally exhausted with their fatigues, and two of them severely frostbitten; in fact, we all felt the effects of this hitherto unprecedented storm, very sensibly indeed; and as the sufferings of the crew had been much more

---

8. Manitoulin Island.

9. To veer the ship (also to wear it), they put it on the other tack by putting the stern into the wind, ran off before the wind, and sailed around to the other tack while trimming sail.

severe, owing to their exposure; and in fact were nearly
exhausted, each one of the passengers volunteered their services
(with the exception of our Pious Gentleman) to relieve their
arduous duties as much as possible, and alternately took our spell
at the pumps, and,

"Plied the Clanking Brake,"

which had become quite as tedious to us, as the prayers of "a
Hypocrite," or the monotonous sound of a hand organ.

Our pious friend continued constantly and undisturbed at
his devotions, striving hard for the Salvation of his, (and as he
said) our souls, while we labored hard for the preservation of
that boon which we considered to be a natural gift; we therefore
set the higher value upon it: as we knew not the Donor, we
therefore viewed it as truly a blessing, and its preservation of
more immediate importance than any thing that presented itself;
and, as it was more of a natural command, we looked upon it
more as a duty to attend to, and preserve it, while in our power;
besides, we could not bring our minds down to the idea that
prayer would preserve a sinking ship; nor, were we willing to
accept his services as mutual, or any thing like an equivalent
for ours; ours, was practical, his was imaginary; we therefore
"minded earthly things," while his "conversation was in
Heaven," where, I sincerely hope his soul (if he has one and
desires it) may reach and rest in peace; but for my own part, I
have not even the smallest desire to arrive at such a place of
bliss, as this ever has, and still continues to be represented; it
would in fact mar all my enjoyments, should I unfortunately fall
in with so great a Hypocrite as this Pious Gentleman subsequently proved.

Having been several days out of food, and subsisting on
cold and raw provisions, we resorted to the small spars for fuel;
and with these raised a fire in order to have a cup of warm coffee,

and such other comfortable things as we could possibly raise for a breakfast.

At half past ten we received a tremendous stroke from a sea, which gave us a violent shock; and the deep roll that it caused the vessel to take, carried every thing portable to leeward: the dishes in the pantry were in an instant displaced, and went with a general crash to the floor, and were destroyed.

Our Pious Friend had practised so much, that he had became

"Remarkably gifted in Prayer,"

remained undisturbed at his devotions, and seldom left his berth; but upon this occasion he quitted it very abruptly indeed; either by the force of gravitation, or impelled by the violent motion of the vessel, or perhaps both, and brought up against the opposite side of the cabin, amidst the overturning of tables and chairs much to his dissatisfaction and discomfiture; he recovered however, and made directly for the gangway, exclaiming at the same time Lord have mercy upon us, what shall we do, what is the matter? He was met by the Mate who deliberately replied to him, it blows like •••• ••• ••••••••; followed up with, "every man take care of himself"; at the same instant we were struck completely down by an overwhelming sea, this was truly thought I, more than we Bargained for.

Adieu,

M.

Letter IX.

"Cease, rude Boreas."[10]

---

10. This is the opening line of "The Tempest," one of the most famous maritime folksongs of the nineteenth century.

Dear J——,

The violent shock which we the first time received, retarded the motion of the vessel; and being much encumbered with ice, for the moment, lost that ability to accommodate herself to the heave of the sea, which was usual; and as she rolled heavy and sluggishly to windward, she was met by the succeeding wave, which reared itself like a tremendous mountain; broke, and boarded us just abaft the larboard fore chains; making a perfect breach over, and at the same time sweeping our decks; extended its relentless and destructive fury to our starboard and lee quarter; splitting our foresail, carrying away our fore boom, tearing our camboose from its lashings,[11] and precipitating that, with our anticipated breakfast, smoking and hissing overboard together; at the same time breaking through and carrying away our lee bulwarks in its course.

One of our best Seamen was carried off upon the combings of this surge, and made a death grasp as he was passing, and secured himself by the lee shrouds, in the "houns," and near the cross-trees of the mainmast; the topmast at the same time was pitched away.

The vessel was completely knock'd down, and lay like a log, and for a time was an unmanageable wreck upon the water. The mainmast being badly sprung by this shock, an order was given to "Cut it away immediately"; but our only axe which had been kept in the cambouse [sic] house, having passed off in the general "wreck of matter," with our anticipated coffee, of course it could not be done.

We lay in this extremely dangerous situation nearly an hour; the Captain not in the least daunted (nor did the seamen appear to be) but gave his orders as deliberate as upon any former occasion; and, as a last resort for the recovery of the vessel, went

---

11. The wave has boarded the port side between the bowsprit and the foremast and swept the deck, taking the camboose, or cookhouse, with it.

deliberately, and with much difficulty below, took a cask of whiskey from one of the state rooms, secured it with a pair of slings, "bent a hawser to the bite," and with great exertions got it overboard, veered out about fifty fathoms from our starboard and Lee Bows, this bringing the vessel's head to the wind and sea, she righted immediately.

The vessel being thus far recovered, all hands went to work at the pumps, with the usual exception: but upon this occasion He paid us another of his obtrusive visits, and urged, nay, begged of us, to "unite with him in prayer," while we were arduously engaged in freeing the vessel from water for our immediate safety; at the time too, when we were in a sinking condition. I had become disgusted with this gentlemans too apparently—hypocritical concern for our spiritual welfare, and had in fact imbibed a prejudice against this "man of God," in consequence of his having declined, and refused to participate and still persisting, to share with us in the arduous duties which our dangerous situation so much required.

I had in fact lost all charity for him, and although I had much respect, and reverence for what the happy Constitution of our Country had guaranteed to us; and which, I had ever looked upon, as truly a blessing, the enjoyment of our opinions, with regard to matters of religion, "pure and undefiled religion," as well, as for its "Pure and undefiled Professors"; this I thought the more of, as I could not but imagine that the blood, which was flowing in my veins, partook more or less of that spirit, for which millions had suffered martyrdom; and thinking of that intolerant disposition too, which has, and most likely ever will pervade community, or that part of it, who are under the thraldom of a class of people whose professions, are truly, nothing but professions; and whose deportment in life partakes too much of that of the "Proud Pharisee" to be held in estimation by the honest, ingenuous, and liberal hearted people of the community. My patience had become wearied, and in fact quite exhausted with this person's constant and useless obtrusions; He interrupted our labors and thereby the more endangered our lives; besides, I was prompted too, by those natural ties, which a numerous and young family inspired, whom I felt anxious to meet as they were dependent upon me; and I felt too, a greater regard for my own preservation on their account than I otherways should have done, fearing they might possibly be imposed upon during their juvenile years, by persons under the professions of great piety, should they lose their temporal protector. I felt constrained and therefore frankly said to him, that his obtrusions were not only useless but extremely unpleasant and injurious; that I neither could nor would put up with them any longer, and, that he must immediately cease his importunities about my "spiritual welfare," as long as he had not manifested any regard for the temporal safety of those on board the vessel; and that, if he still persisted and wished to make a Jonah of himself, and that if he did not immediately leave the deck I would head a party and throw him overboard at once, without any regard whatever of the probability of his being miraculously preserved by a Fish; and abide the consequences by myself alone; and that, if he did not immediately leave the deck, I would avail myself of the present moment. I was immediately seconded by the Mate: the gentleman left us, and crept tremblingly back to his berth, uttering a few heavy groans as he passed, and with but a single exception, did he presume to trouble us any more; this was truly a great relief.

My prejudice against this gentleman appeared to have been well founded, although perhaps premature, for on our arrival into Port, he declined, nay, refused to pay his passage, and actually cross'd the river into the British Provinces for the express purpose of defrauding and did defraud the Captain, who had been so highly instrumental in the preservation of his life. What base ingratitude.

But to return—the stroke of this sea when we received it was tremendous; every plank and timber appeared sensibly to feel its effects and the vessel trembled for the moment to her very centre, and not dissimilar to a piece of jelly when strongly agitated. At the time she righted, we were completely "water logg'd," and in a sinking condition; having shipp'd such a vast amount of water when down, that it was then ten inches deep upon the Cabin floor; this with the great weight of ice sunk the vessel so low into the water that our situation was truly deplorable:—however, by constant and very laborious exertions at the pumps, we freed her at half past three o'clock the succeeding morning; lay too, with the cask of whiskey a head during the intermediate time and would have sung,

"Cease rude Boreas;"

But our fatigues and distresses were such, that we had not the slightest disposition whatever to be musical; but endeavoured nevertheless to make ourselves as comfortable, as our cheerless and distress'd situation would admit. The sallies of Humor with which our dutch companion had been so well stored, was quite exhausted, it had ceased; the fine tones of our English friends violin sounded no longer; all, all our pleasantries were gone and the pitiful moanings of the Tempest; and the monotonous clanking of the pumps were heard in their Stead; with the frequent, cry of "Spell O!" Our Sufferings had began to be very great.

To those persons who have experienced a voyage in Stormy and frozen Seas, an attempt to give a description at this time would be superfluous. But others may imagine where immense masses of ice is continually making upon, and gradually sinking their vessel; and this too without the possibility of relief. And when every day she is still settling lower, and lower into the water, and inevitable death finally staring them in the face; and when at last their situation becomes such, that they approach the verge, and take (as we did) a fair look into the other world, they would naturally draw the conclusion, that persons placed in such a situation would have nearly pass'd the "Tempestuous ocean of life"; and that they could not but be intimidated, on approximating so important a crisis.

I had at former periods (you know well) so much, and such

frequent occasion in common with yourself to be frightened; that it had became a kind of second nature to me: my mind ever buoyant, had acquired such a degree of elasticity, as to accommodate itself to the occasion; hence I could make myself reasonably happy, under almost any circumstance or situation in which I might be placed.

....

During the night the sea run down, the Lake was calm; day light at length broke upon us, and the morning Sun arose clear, brilliant and in Splendid Majesty, from beneath a bright, smooth, transparent surface, bounded by the open Horizon of the Mighty Lake Huron.

The weather was very calm and fine, the surface of the Lake presented a silvery appearance, not unlike a vast plain or Mirror, from which objects at that time were reflected, in a very beautiful and singular manner.

We distinctly saw the Island from which we had originally taken our departure, at so remote a distance to the Westward, that it appeared nearly even with the Horizon, and not unlike the back of a "Huge turtle" upon the surface of the water.

Our cask of whiskey was hauled along side and hoisted on board, and as it had been of such vast and important service for the recovery of the vessel, we did not know but it might prove equally beneficial to ourselves, being much fatigued we ventured and took a faithful survey of its contents much to our satisfaction; our pious friend himself did not refuse upon this occasion, and worshiped at the shrine of Bacchus with more than one copious libation; he became much more sociable, even merry, and so musical that he entertained us with some fine hymns; but when he came to compliment the decanter with a reeling grasp, we reproached his insincerity, and ridiculed his hypocrisy, and set him to work at the pumps, but as the weather was calm our leak was less troublesome.

We succeeded this day in taking a fine trout, which would not have disgraced the table of a President and would have proved a delicious treat to us, had we possess'd trimmings and the means to have dress'd it, we did not murmur however as it was.

The vessel remained quite Stationary during the day; all hands were again employed in endeavouring to dislodge the great mass of Ice, which still kept her low in the water. Our salt being expended, we started the brine from the fish Barrels in the hold, and made a careful distribution of it over the ice, but having no axe we made but slow progress in this necessary, and to us important work.

The day being calm, the fatigue and long confinement very tedious, with a melancholy reflection upon the past, and an anxious solicitude for the future, I fell into a profound reverie. . . .

Adieu.

M.

Nänabushu Swallowed by the Sturgeon

Ojibwa Myth Collected by William Jones

A GREAT LAKES Indian storyteller, particularly an eloquent and inventive one whose audience waited for every word, was always welcome in the winter lodges. The best place beside the fire would be his, with a share of the best food and a gift of tobacco. In a culture that did not write its stories and put them in books, the storyteller was not only an entertainer during the long winter evenings, but also a teacher of the young and a historian, since through stories and myths the literature, history, and religion of the people were passed from generation to generation. There were two basic types of stories: those that were moral, traditional, formal, sacred stories—myths—that could be told only in the winter "when the frog and the snake were underground" so the spirits and animals talked about could not hear and be offended, and those that were the history of human events and so could be told any time of year. Because of the isolated nature of winter living, and because each storyteller added his own aesthetic elaborations, there are usually several versions for each story, but the important information remains the same. To the modern reader, however, Indian stories often seem illogical or unfinished. Accustomed to fiction that reflects an English-speaking, Western worldview, we are unfamiliar with a culture that considered much of the natural world equal to human society, and we are uncomfortable with stories where we are expected to supply information that a particular storyteller has omitted. Moreover, reading a transcription is no substitute for hearing and seeing the performance of a storyteller bringing new life to a story one has heard many times before. But despite our limitations, these are still wonderful stories, reflecting a culture that knew the lakes long before the white man came and perhaps understood them best.

The story reprinted here is a myth from the Ojibwa cycle of stories about the trickster hero Nänabushu, who was Longfellow's inspiration for *Hiawatha* and whose exploits—sometimes serious, sometimes uproariously funny—explained the creation of the world and many of the plants and animals. In "Nänabushu Swallowed by the Sturgeon" he discovers that a sturgeon killed his parents and so sets out to avenge them. He contrives to get himself swallowed by the greatest of fishes in the lakes, only to find that he must be rescued by a seagull. Stories about being swallowed by a giant fish are older than Jonah, and Trickster stories are common to all cultures in the world. But this story also explains why the seagull is white and how Nänabushu made the other kinds of fishes in the lakes, which was important cultural information for the Ojibwa.

THEREUPON TRULY was he fully prepared to go; many arrows and spears had he made. So far as the story goes, it is not told what he used when he made the great number of his arrows and spears, for he had dulled his axe; it is only told of him how that he had made himself prepared. And so it is said that Nänabushu started away. By the way, this too was what was told of him! He made a canoe; he hewed it out of a log; the measure of himself was the size he made it, so it is told of him.

Thereupon he went to assail the Great Sturgeon. And so they say that Nänabushu set out, bidding farewell to his grandmother. And then they say he was told: "Be careful, my grandson," he was told; "somewhere will you bring harm upon yourself," he was told by his grandmother.

"No, my grandmother, I shall return again to this place," he said to her. And as Nänabushu now shoved his canoe into the water, he proceeded straight out to sea; and when almost at the middle part of the sea he was come, then he cried with a loud voice, singing:

"O ye Great Sturgeons, O ye Great Sturgeons,
Come one of you and swallow me, come one of you and
    swallow me!"

And in a little while was the sea set in motion; like rapids when the current is strong, so was the flow of the waves.

Thereupon truly Nänabushu sang aloud:

"O ye Great Sturgeons, come swallow me!
Ye that have slain my parents, come swallow me too!"

As soon as he had finished speaking, then immediately he saw a great sturgeon coming to swallow him. At first round in a whirlpool spun the canoe, and then down into the water he was drawn, swallowed by the Great Sturgeon, canoe and all. All the while they say there was a hissing-sound in the ears; and when he recovered his wits, inside of a fish he was. Thereupon quietly he remained there; and they say that now he knew that the fish was carrying him away.

And so the chief of fishes returned to the home under water on the floor of the sea. And now they say that [Nänabushu] heard them holding a great smoker among themselves, and he also heard them holding forth with much talk; they were giving thanks for that he was swallowed.

Now, once they say that while he was listening, something Nänabushu saw that caught his attention. Well, on with the story. Wonder how he could see! [Nevertheless] they say that Nänabushu saw something in motion, and it happened to be the heart of the Great Sturgeon that was beating. Thereupon they say that softly he moved [and] pulled out a pointed arrow; and then he began pricking it. Whereupon they say that in a little while he heard the voice of him saying: "Oh, truly indeed but I am feeling sick at heart."[1] And then he heard him asking his wife to give him a drink of something to make him vomit. And so presently did he begin trying to vomit, but he was not able to do it. And then he heard him saying: "Impossible, for Nänabushu is making me sick at my stomach," he said.

True was it, indeed, that hard worked Nänabushu to keep from being cast out; so then crosswise he placed his arrows, and so by them he held on.

Thereupon again the Great Sturgeon spoke: "No hope. I am in distress inside on account of Nänabushu," he said. And so in a little while he was dead, him had Nänabushu slain. Even though all that were living there had come together by invitation for the purpose of bringing their chief back to life, [but it was] not [to be]; for how could any one live with his heart cut to pieces? And that was why he had died.

And as for Nänabushu, there he remained.

Thereupon truly they were doing wonderful things as they conjured for a miracle. It was no use, for already dead was the great fish. And so it is said that they were going to bury him, for really a long while had they kept him; perhaps he might come back to life, they thought. And so accordingly they say that when they were burying him, farther out upon the sea, where it was deep, they went to bury him. Ever so mightily they conjured for a miracle.

Now, Nänabushu knew everything that was happening, but yet by no one was it known that he was there and alive. They knew that he had been swallowed, but yet they did not know

---

1. This is the literal translation of the Ojibwa; the meaning is *nauseated.*

that he was alive. And so after they had finished burying [the chief of fishes], then back they came together to their home again. Exceedingly numerous they were, from every part of the sea had they come to be at the burial of their chief.

In the mean while they say that Nänabushu had been thinking out a plan how he might succeed in getting out from the inside of the fish which now was also lying buried. And so, now that Nänabushu knew what he would do, he thereupon said: "Oh, I would that there rise a mighty storm the like of which there has never been before!" Whereupon Nänabushu made a smoke offering toward the four directions where sit the manitous.

And so his prayer was answered. Thereupon truly there rose a mighty wind, everything that was on the floor of the sea came to the surface by force of the waves. And as for Nänabushu, the sand [of the mound] where he had been was washed away; and then afterwards the fish came to the surface of the water. For ten days the wind raged, and afterwards there was another great calm, whereupon to the surface [came] the Great Sturgeon.

Now once, when Nänabushu was inside of the fish, he heard something that sounded very pleasantly; and as he listened, he then heard: "[cry of gulls]." Very pleasant was the sound of the creature; it turned out to be some gulls. "Well," thus thought Nänabushu, "I will speak to them," he thought. It was true that soon again he heard the sound of them coming hitherward, whereupon again they came with the cry: "[cry of gulls]." And then he said to them: "Hark, O my younger brothers! Please peck an opening for me into the belly of this fish!"

Thereupon the gulls flew up; and as they went, they could be heard uttering a frightful cry, for such was the sound they made. Whereupon Nänabushu seized his ears [and] closed them with the hands (to keep from hearing the din). And in a little while again he listened, whereupon again he spoke to them, saying: "O my younger brothers! peck an opening for me into the belly of this fish!" he said to them.

Thereupon truly they became silent.

And so again he spoke to them, saying: "Peck an opening for me into the belly of this fish!" he said to them. "In return I will adorn you."

Thereupon the gulls spoke one with another, saying: "Nänabushu is there."

Indeed, by every creature was Nänabushu known. And so again he spoke to them, saying: "Come, my younger brothers, peck an opening for me into the belly [of this fish]. In return I shall adorn you; as beautiful as the creature of the air that surpasses [all others in beauty] is how beautiful I shall make you," he said to them.

"We surely could not [make an opening into] him," he was told.

"Yea, [you can]!" he said to them. "You can do it!"

Thereupon truly they began pecking an opening into [the fish]; and after a long while they succeeded. And then afterwards Nänabushu crawled out, and he drew out his canoe which he had hewn from a log. And then was the time that he took a careful look to see how big was the great sturgeon which had swallowed him; like an island afloat upon the water was how it looked as it lay upon the deep. Thereupon he took up one of the gulls in his hands; and then he adorned it. And then he whitened it, [white] like snow he made it. Thereupon he said to it: "You shall be called a gull from now till the end of time."

It was true that exceedingly happy was the gull when it looked upon itself and saw how beautiful it was.

"Now, then," he said to them, "now fly away!"

Now, according to the story, there was mentioned but a single gull that he took up in his hands. Yet nevertheless just as beautiful were all the rest when they all started to fly away. And then afterwards Nänabushu began cutting up the fish with a knife. And so when he had finished cutting it up, then he said, at the same time that he was flinging the pieces in every direction: "Fishes shall you be called till the end of time. And you shall be eaten by the people till the end of the world.—And you," he said to the Great Sturgeon, "never again so large shall you be as long as the world lasts, else nobody would ever live," he said to him. Therefore it truly came to pass that he created little fishes in great numbers from that Great Sturgeon.

Thereupon Nänabushu paddled home in his canoe to find his grandmother. And when he got there, he discovered his grandmother grievously sad in her thoughts. And as he peeped into the lodge, he said to her: "O my grandmother! I have now come home," he said to her.

"Oh, I should like to know why they continually say this to me, these little animal-folk!"

"Nay, my grandmother. It is really myself, Nänabushu, your grandson, who has now come home." And then into the lodge he went. Thereupon he saw that his grandmother was barely able to see, [showing] that perhaps all the while she had been weeping. And then afterwards he had made her younger.

Now Great-Lynx

Ojibwa Story Collected by William Jones

ALTHOUGH MOST Indian tribes believed in some sort of water monster, often a monstrous snake, the stories of the Great-Lynx are particular to the Ojibwa tribes living around the Great Lakes. The Lynx, in some versions called the underwater lion, was Missipeshu, a huge horned beast who raised storms by thrashing his long, spiked tail. Anyone making a trip across water, even an inland lake, was in danger of being attacked by Missipeshu unless proper prayers and sacrifices had been made before setting out and a specific route was followed. In some versions of this story the two women do not follow the correct route and therefore put themselves in danger. But one of the women has dreamed of Thunderbirds—those creatures of the air who are inimical to water monsters—and by dreaming absorbed their power. Thus she invokes their name and strikes off the beast's tail with her paddle and they escape. In other retellings, the broken part of Missipeshu's tail turns into a lump of copper when it falls into the canoe and brings riches forever to whoever owns it, since copper, to many lakes Indian tribes, was sacred and powerful. Indian rock paintings of Missipeshu that were first noted by the missionaries are still visible on the north shore of Lake Superior.

LONG AGO people often used to see something in places, especially where the current was swift. The people feared it; and that was the reason of their practice of sometimes throwing offerings to it into the water, even tobacco. Now, once yonder, at what is called Shallow-Water,[1] was where some women were once passing by in a canoe. Accordingly there happened to rise a mighty current of water, nearly were they capsized; exceedingly frightened were they. While they were paddling with all their might, they saw the tail of a Great-Lynx come up out of the water; all flung themselves up into the forward end of the canoe in their fright. Now, one of the women that was there saw that the canoe was going to sink; accordingly, when she had gone to the stern, she raised the paddle in order to strike the tail of Great-Lynx. And this she said: "While I was young, often did I fast. It was then that the Thunderers gave me their war-club." Thereupon, when she struck the tail of Great-Lynx, she then broke the tail of Great-Lynx in two. Thereupon up to the surface rose the canoe, after which they then started on their way paddling; and so they were saved.

Now, one of the women was seized by Great-Lynx. Therefore she it was who had told at home that Great-Lynx was continually harassing the people. And though the master of the Great-Lynxes would always speak to his son, saying, "Do not plague the people," yet he would never listen to his father.

Once, yonder at the Sault, together in a body were the people living. Once against a certain wigwam was leaned a child bound to a cradle-board; and then the child was missed from that place. They saw the sign of the cradle-board where it had been dragged along in the sand. Thereupon they heard the voice of the child crying beneath a rugged hill. Even though the people made offerings in the hope that Great-Lynx might set the child free, even though for a long while they besought him with prayers, yet he would not let it go. So at length the people said

---

1. The name for Ross Port. [Jones's note.]

that therefore they might as well slay Great-Lynx. Accordingly they began digging straight for the place from whence the sound of the child could be heard. And after a while they had a hole dug to the den of Great-Lynx. They saw water coming in and out (like the tide). It was true that even then they spoke kindly to Great-Lynx, yet he would not let the child go. Still yet they could hear the voice (of the child) crying. Accordingly they said: "Therefore let us dig to where he is, that we may kill him."

Truly they dug after him, following him up. By and by out came the cradle-board floating on the water, together with the child that was bound to it. And when they caught hold of the cradle-board, they observed that the child had a hole crushed into its head; Great-Lynx must have slain it. Thereupon they followed him up, digging after him; and one man that was famed for his strength said that he would kill Great-Lynx. When drawing upon him, as they dug after him, round towards them turned Great-Lynx. Thereupon him struck he who said that he would kill [Great-Lynx]. Sure enough, he slew him.

And when they pulled him out, they saw that his tail was cut off. That was the one that had been struck at Shallow-Water; by a woman with an oar had he been struck.

That was what happened. Only not long ago was seen the place where the people had once dug the hole; [it is] over toward the Big-Knife country,[2] over by the Sault.

That is all.

---

2. The United States. [Jones's note.]

The Snow Wasset

Anonymous: Collected by Ivan H. Walton

GIVEN THE DANGER involved in fishing for sturgeon, a large and extremely powerful fish, and the sudden and furious storms that lash the lakes, the foregoing Indian stories are not surprising. Modern sailors, who pride themselves on being above superstition, nevertheless talk of ships that have disappeared as having "sailed into the hole in the lake," or of ships that are unlucky because they killed someone when coming off the ways and have thirteen steps from the texas deck to the pilot house, or of the Three Sisters, waves that come in groups of three so close together that no ship can recover from them and so goes to the bottom. We all create stories to explain the inexplicable, and often we borrow from other cultures to do so. Indian stories have been collected and published for over a hundred years and long ago became part of the literature of the Great Lakes. So while the following story, "The Snow Wasset," appears to be a classic American tall tale, it is also instantly recognizable as a combination of the myths of Nänabushu being swallowed by a fish and the stories of Missipeshu. The snow wasset was originally a fearsome creature who terrorized lumber camps, but since many lakes sailors also worked in the lumberwoods during the winter when the shipping season ended, often side by side with Indians, the folklore of two cultures and two environments combined to create a hybrid monster with an American name, which explained what happened to ships that disappeared on Lake Superior. Although "The Snow Wasset" is a humorous tale and the Indian stories are not, it was probably just as useful in making young deckhands watch the water more attentively as Missipeshu was in scaring Indian children into doing what they were told in a canoe.

ABOUT THE WORST danger that sailors on Lake Superior have to face is the snow wasset, called by the Ojibwa Indians in that area the "Mish-ie-was-set-ta-gan-ie-gan-nis-sa," which in English means something like "A very big water and land monster, and you're all gone if you meet one." Sailors, however, refer to them simply as snow wassets. The animal seems to be a cross between a whale and a huge serpent. It has thick heavy scales on its under side, and tough skin over the rest of its body, and a layer of blubber just under this skin which enables it to endure the most rigorous of Canadian winters. Its head and mouth are so big that it can swallow a full-grown man in one gulp.

Like a serpent, it hibernates part of the year. But unlike a serpent, it sleeps through the summer months in great caverns on the bottom of Lake Superior where it bears its young. The young wassets rise to the surface as soon as they are born in search of their favorite food, young sailors. In autumn the adults also become active, and being very hungry, they begin their intense search for food.

The autumn is also their rutting season and a couple of adult bulls fighting can make the surface of the Lake in the area pretty rough. Wassets always try to overcome their enemies by swallowing them. It was reported as late as last season that two Indians paddled into Fort William, Ontario, in a thirty-foot wasset canoe. They had found two dead bulls locked together on the shore of Isle Royale, one half way down the gullet of the other. The Indians had stripped the hide off the outside one and stretched it over a wooden frame, and made themselves a prized canoe that would stand any amount of wave pounding on the rocky North Shore. Indians are always on the lookout for dead wassets.

These animals take to the land along in December, and a grand sight it is to see a group of them soar out of the deep water over the piled-up shore ice and coast on their scaly bellies inland over the deep snow to their feeding grounds. I forgot to tell you that during their summer sleep they grow stubby, powerful legs on which they can crawl like alligators when necessary. They shed these legs and grow heavy fins as soon as they return to the water in spring. When roaming in deep snow in the Canadian north woods in search of food, they like to burrow below trail crossings and await the approach of any large animal or any unfortunate human hunter who may come along. No animal can escape their sudden lunge.

They are most dangerous to sailors in late autumn when they have just awakened from their long sleep and are growing their shore legs. Late autumn is also, unfortunately, the season when frequent severe storms with snow and ice sweep Lake Superior, wrecking scores of vessels without leaving a trace. You have, no doubt, heard it said that the bodies of drowned sailors never rise to the surface or drift to the shore of this lake as they do on the other Great Lakes because the water is so cold that bodies are preserved and drift about forever in the depths. Well, don't believe it. I've seen hungry wassets follow vessels the length of Lake Superior, especially during bad weather, and I've seen them attack and sink a vessel while it was laboring in the big seas. Many sailors have seen the huge, dark forms circling about stricken vessels that were trying to make the lee of White Fish Point, the Keweenaw Peninsula, or one of the islands at the foot of the Lake. Sure, no drowned sailor has ever been recovered from Superior, and for a very good reason! And you'll never see no sailor go swimming in that Lake neither, and it ain't because they don't need a bath once in a while. I tell you, boy, you want to play it damn safe if you sail on Superior, especially late in the season.

An Anchor in
a Graveyard

C. H. J. Snider

ASK MOST AMERICANS what they know about the War of
1812 and they will usually respond, "Don't Give Up the Ship,"
Oliver Hazard Perry's famous battle flag during the Battle of Put-
in-Bay on September 10, 1813. Canadians often mention the
Nancy, a pert little schooner that played tag with the Americans
in upper Lake Huron. But the war on the lakes encompassed
much more than these, and this story of an American disaster
by a Canadian writer describes one such incident. "An Anchor
in a Graveyard" takes place a hundred years after the war, a
ghostly retelling of a disastrous episode in Commodore Issac
Chauncey's encounters with the British fleet near Niagara in
August, 1813. He had attacked York and returned to Niagara,
but on the morning of August 7 the British, under the command
of Sir James Yeo, appeared off the harbor. Chauncey sailed into
Lake Ontario to engage Yeo but failed, and when night fell the
two fleets were sailing in parallel lines. At two in the morning
a squall exploded with deadly force. Two of Chauncey's schooners, merchant vessels whose refitting for war had made them top-
heavy with guns and unseaworthy, sank in the storm. Fifty-three
men died, the greatest single loss of life on the lakes during the
entire war.

In 1971 a Canadian research team discovered the near-perfect remains of the *Hamilton* and the *Scourge* with their guns still standing on the decks and the shot still in the shot racks, preserved three hundred feet deep in cold waters of the Lake. Jacques Cousteau and the National Geographic Society investigated and photographed the wrecks in 1982. Emily Cain's book, *Ghost Ships Hamilton and Scourge: Historical Treasures from the War of 1812* (1983) traces the history of the two ships and reproduces many of the underwater photographs. Canadian authorities are planning to raise the ships and place them in a lakeside museum in Hamilton, Ontario. Readers who are interested in an autobiographical account by a seaman who survived the disaster should read *Ned Myers; Or, A Life Before the Mast*, edited by James Fenimore Cooper, and published by Lea and Blanchard in Philadelphia in 1843.

OUR RIDING LIGHT burned dim and blue in the fog, though 'twas a good bright lantern, hung ten feet above the top-gallant forecastle.[1] The shadows of the schooner's spars and gear made thick, whirling, spoke-like rays of darkness in the smothering white as she rolled and plunged. You couldn't see the water heaving and sobbing below us. We were bound down Lake Ontario for Kingston, from Cleveland on Lake Erie, and had anchored somewhere on the Niagara Shoal, when the wind left us and the fog set in at sundown.

It was my watch on deck from midnight till four o'clock. That is to say, the mate and his two men turned in then, and my two lads came shuffling aft from the forecastle, drowsy as opium smokers. I had been up all night before, thrashing down Lake Erie, and had been at the wheel all day, making the passage of the Welland Canal. The lads were dog-tired with the day's canalling, and I sent them below again at "one bell"—half an

---

1. A raised deck sheltering the crew's quarters forward.

hour after midnight. A sleepy lookout is worse than none, and they were so heavy-eyed they could not answer their own names. Besides, one was only a Port Hope high-school boy, working in his holidays to pay his winter's board. I myself was tired and sleepy too—"dopey," in fact—but a master *has* to keep awake.

Our ship's bell was a small affair, and clattered foolishly as she dived and rolled in the long uneasy swell. I unshipped the tongue, and slung an iron windlass-brake from the foreboom, so that with every roll it struck the capstan head, giving a deep clang that echoed back through the fog.[2] It was the best way we had of warning steamers of our presence.

Very faint and very far away the bell-buoy off the mouth of the Niagara River answered the clang of the windlass-brake with a mournful toll. The bell-ringing, the sobbing and scuffling of the uneasy water alongside, and the occasional grind of the anchor chain in the hawse-pipe, were the only sounds of the night except the clatter of the brake.

I trudged slowly forward and aft, forward and aft, staring into the blind fog until my eyes cracked, varying the dreary view with an occasional glance through the binnacle slot at the cracked, comfortable, yellow face of the cabin clock. If you look hard enough into a fog or the blackness of a dark night, or even the clean, crisp line of a sun-swept horizon, you can see almost anything; the brain throws before your eyes a false image of what you *expect* to see. I have noticed that time and again when making a landfall. I have known good lookout men to hail the deck and report headlands or lighthouses hours before they hove above the horizon—just because they were looking for them. But this that I saw and heard, after noting twenty minutes past one on the cabin clock, is not accounted for that way.

I turned suddenly from a peep through the binnacle slot,[3]

---

2. He has hung a lever used to operate the windlass from the boom so that the lever strikes the top of the windlass as the ship moves.

3. He has looked at the compass.

because I thought I heard a sound like very distant thunder. The fog smothered and blinded me like some great mass of gauze thrown over my head, but again I heard or felt the sound.

"They must be firing rockets at the mouth of the Niagara River," I thought, "to guide some fog-bound passenger steamer in."

And yet somehow the thudding reports seemed scarcely to be that. They were too irregular, sometimes clustered, as it were, sometimes single; and though very faint, they seemed to jar the thick, steaming air with concussions. They ceased abruptly, and again all I could hear was the gasping, gurgling struggle of the water alongside, the faint toll of the bell buoy, the grind of the anchor chain, and the clang of our windlass-brake.

"Those reports," thought I—"why, a long-range fleet action must have sounded like that in the old days." As the thought took words unconsciously, as thoughts will when one is alone, I sniffed something odd in the fog—a faint, pungent, smoky smell, like gunpowder.

"Here, this won't do!" I told myself. "You think of broad-sides and then smell powder smoke. Wake up!"

I walked to the scuttle butt, dipped a mug of water, and drank it to freshen my brain.

Then, distinct from the resonance of the windlass-brake or the toll of the buoy, I heard the faint tinkle as of "three bells" striking—ding-ding! ding!—half past one. *We* had no automatic striker aboard the schooner. The sound was repeated, blurred and faint, as though we were in the midst of an unseen fleet.

Looking up from my drink, I saw something which brought my heart to my mouth. Abeam of us was a vessel—a full-rigged ship, under all sail, with studding-sails out. My first impulse was to call all hands, but I choked down the cry. This was no ordinary one of the ships that pass in the night. She was square-rigged on all three masts; and the last square-rigger vanished from the lakes when I was sailing toy boats in puddles. She had "single" topsails, that is, they were each in one great square of canvas, a rig which became obsolete fifty years ago. She had a spritsail,[4] swinging from the bowsprit, a sail that has not been seen for a century, and her side was broken by a long line of open ports.

But what convinced me above all that this was some trick of my brain and not a real vessel was the way she seemed to be sailing in the sky, making good progress in a breeze so light that we had lost steerage way. As I said, the water, even alongside, was invisible; but she seemed to be floating in the air, above the horizon. Another thing which proved her unreal was the very clearness of every detail in a fog which smothered out sight of our own crosstrees. She radiated a light which illuminated her without casting a shadow. At each port a brightness—perhaps a gunner's match—was glowing. Great horn lanterns pulsed like rising moons at each corner of the taffrail[5] that ended her short high poop. Other lanterns, strung fore and aft, lighted up crowds of men, clustered around the guns, thronging the gangways, manning the yards and fighting-tops.

I could see, as plainly as in summer twilight, the colours of her Stars and Stripes, rippling in a fresh breeze, at her mizzen gaff end, and a long, twisted streamer, blowing off from her main-truck.[6] And I could see coloured signal lights, blue and white and red, rise and sink on invisible halliards.

She swept by, but a thin black, curved, line vibrated in her place, and moved in the direction she had passed, and in a moment there showed at the end of it, a squat little schooner, with an enormous cannon amidships and spars which raked till the main-truck overhung the taffrail.

I was more interested than startled by what I was seeing. I had a curious feeling of toleration for the whim of my brain which had conjured up such a vision. I continued staring. At a

---

4. A square sail set beneath the bowsprit.
5. The curved wooden rail around the stern of a man-of-war.
6. The mizzen is the third or aftermost mast; the flag flies from a short post attached to it. The main-truck is the mainmast.

short interval there loomed another old-style full-rigged ship, with deep, wide-shouldered topsails, and battle lanterns ablaze at gunports; and she had a schooner in tow like the first. And then there came a brig, and then more schooners, with raking spars, which went out of use years and years ago. They all passed within ten minutes, at a quarter-mile distance, each illumined by the strange inner light which made them plain amid the blinding fog. As each vessel drew abreast she put up her helm and wore around on to the other tack, as if in obedience to the signal lights of the flagship. The changed course brought them back across my line of vision, but further away.

I was so absorbed in the illusion that I was keeping as bad a lookout as any of my sleepy watch could have done. Pulling myself together I resolutely turned my back on the phantom fleet and stared over the opposite side. I saw the fog, of course, and more. The reason for the manœuvre was quite plain. Another line of vessels was approaching.

The leader was, I should judge, a ship of about the same size as the first one I had seen—perhaps a hundred tons smaller. She had a high sheer aft, and a light-coloured underbody. I counted twelve gunports in her side. She too had the obsolete single topsails, but, unlike the American flagship, no royals.[7] I noted particularly a large long-boat on chocks in the waist. Her figurehead was a soldier in uniform, and there was a red ensign flaming from her mizzen peak. I thought our[8] naval ensign was always white, with a red cross quartering it, and the jack in the corner; but hers was red, blood red.

Another ship, of smaller size, followed her. A lion and a unicorn, and the blue ellipse of the Order of the Garter, were emblazoned between her yawning sternports. Then there passed two brigs, and two schooners; larger, these last, than most of

---

7. Royal sails were set above the topgallants; they were the highest sails on a mast until the advent of the clipper ships.

8. "English" is to be understood here.

the Yankee fore-and-afters, and higher sided, with longer rows of grinning guns. And all flew the red flag.

I watched the spectacle fade into the fog with that twinge of regret which we experience on awakening from a curious dream. I walked quietly again to the water cask, chuckling to myself at the mildness of the beverage which had produced such an experience. Yet as I again drained the dipper I began to feel an uneasiness that I, a plain vessel captain, should be a prey to such fancies.

"It must have been a mirage," I began to tell myself.

Turning again from the scuttle butt I saw something which brought the sweat to my brow. Ahead of us was a vessel—apparently right athwart our cable. I now ran forward to call all hands, believing a collision inevitable; but when I reached the forecastle I paused, rooted to the deck. The strange vessel was then exactly the same distance away as when I had been at the opposite end of our ship, about fifty yards from me; but she was high up, as if floating in water as high as our bow-sprit end, and *that* was thirty feet above the real water level.

I had seen many mirages on the lakes, but never before one by night or in a fog. The shadow ship seemed a small two-masted schooner of a hundred tons or so. She throbbed with a dull blue glare as of continuous lightning, which made it easier to note her details than our own, in the thick fog. Her spars raked sharply, her sails were loose-footed. The foresail appeared to brail up[9] to the mast, and she had a square topsail and top-gallant-sail; a rig which had disappeared on the Great Lakes when I was a youngster. Her freeboard was low, except at the quarters, where her deck rose with a sharp break. Her bulwarks were pierced with ports from which grinned cannon, and other larger guns showed on pivots on deck.

I *knew* there was nothing there ahead of us, nothing but fog. My cheeks were hot with the shame of realizing that I was

---

9. To be tied up against the mast preparatory to stowing.

the victim of the trick of an over-wrought mind and body. But I felt a certain satisfaction in that I had not turned out the watch. I could imagine them leaning against the bulwarks, spitting into the fog overside, and muttering about the "old man" and how he was "getting them," "them" being delirium tremens.

I glanced aft into the blank fog, and then turned about for a look forward, fully assured that the phantasy of my eyes would have vanished. But the illusion schooner was exactly where I had last seen her. She seemed under weigh, but did not pass by. Her decks were covered with men—scores of them, at least—and they were all scurrying about in great confusion, pulling and hauling on the gear and lashing the guns into position. They were shortening her down for heavy weather. Her top hamper was clewed in, her foresail brailed, the tack of the mainsail triced up, when they seemed to change their minds. They began to make sail again, until every stitch was spread. Suddenly she heeled till her yardarms brushed the water, or where her waterline should have been.

It was at this moment, and had been for hours, a stark calm; but she acted exactly like a vessel hove down by a sudden overwhelming gust of wind. For a moment she hung on her beam-ends—then her hull vanished and her spars slowly straightened up, and I knew I was seeing a representation of a vessel foundering. She went down by the stern, but ere the mastheads disappeared she gave a lurch forward which threw aloft, like a tongue of blue flame, a long burgee or pennant. For an instant I watched the letters S-C-O-U-R-G-E as they disappeared one after the other. Then my ears were smitten with a thin, faint wailing, the worst sound they had ever heard—the death cries of half a hundred human beings, perishing under my very eyes.

I beat my head, I shouted to myself: "It isn't real, it *isn't* real! It's a dream, a vision, a nightmare!" but I dared not look any longer. Wheeling about I stared aft along our own solid, fog-drenched decks—and there right in front of me, was being enacted the very tragedy upon which I had just turned my back.

No further away than the end of our fore-boom I saw the steep-sloped deck of a vessel, hove down in a squall. A swarm of men were climbing and clawing up to the weather rail. Some had reached it, and were slashing at the rigging with knives and axes, to save her by letting the masts go by the board. Others slipped, grabbed wildly at the hatchcoamings, and disappeared. Four cannon on the weather side had settled back on their lashings with the ship's incline, and as my glance fell on them their tackles parted and they swept down the steep slide of the deck. Two of them disappeared, carrying a dozen men with them; the other two fetched up against a huge swivel gun, located amidships. The great heap of iron gun-barrels and lignum-vitæ carriages[10] poised for a moment, then whirled over, with a rending of deck-planks and smashing of hatchcoamings, and pitched overboard or out of sight; and at once the slanting deck in front of me began to settle and vanish, as though invisible waves were swirling through the rent made by the crashing guns.

Swiftly it disappeared utterly, leaving a tangled mass of human heads and arms, fighting rabidly for hatch-covers, deck-gratings, bits of board, even rope ends. And the voices! The awful voices! Not one separate word came through the dreadful babel; but shouts and prayers and curses and implorings were all mingled with the gasping coughs a man gives, fighting death in the water, and the smothered gurgle of the drowning victim's surrender.

The memory of the terrible distinctness of those sounds will never leave me; yet, although apparently uttered at a few yards' distance, they were all keyed down, like words over a telephone; and through all I could hear the commonplace clang of our windlass-brake, the toll of the Niagara bell-buoy, the slap and scuffle of the actual water alongside; just as, *past* the vision

---

10. Wooden gun carriages.

of the sinking deck, I could see our main and mizzen masts loom in the fog, and mark the faint halo of our lighted cabin.

I admit I was frightened, thoroughly, abjectly scared. I pounded furiously on the forescuttle, unable to speak.

"Aye, aye, sir," I heard sleepy voices rumble below, and then the tousled heads of my watch poked out.

"Hear anything, lads?" I asked sharply.

"Not me," said one.

"Seems," answered the other with a terrible yawn, "as if I—yes, it is. I can hear coween, sir. Dang them gulls, they wail at night like lost souls. Coween, that's what it is, sir. Mebbe our windlass-brake has wakened a flock of 'em, asleep on the water."

I looked sideways, forward and aft. The visions had gone. The sailors had seen nothing.

"Well, keep a good lookout, boys, and call me if you see or hear anything," I managed to say, and walked aft, limp as a wrung rag.

I tramped the quarter deck without ceasing for two hours, grateful as a starving man for food for the snatches of grumpy forecastle slang I could catch from the lads forward. *They* were human, and alive. At "eight bells" (four o'clock) I called the mate and his watch. The fog was thinning. I told him to get sail on her if it cleared, and heave short as soon as the breeze came. Then I flung myself, face downward, on my berth.

I expected a prolonged agony of trying to get to sleep would be followed by a series of terrible nightmares, but I dropped off as though drugged, and knew nothing until nearly four hours later, the mate tapped on my door and said, " 'Seven bells,' sir, and we're hove short. Wait for breakfast before breaking out?"

I sprang to my feet. The little stateroom was filled with bright sunshine. Through the port-light I saw the lake sparkling in crisp ridges of blue and green and gold. Looking along the deck I noted our lower sails were up and slatting and banging at their sheets in a cheerful westerly breeze.

"Break out first," I answered. "A fair wind's not to be wasted."

In the galley the cook's bacon and eggs sizzled joyously, and the aroma of coffee rose. Everything made a glad midsummer morning.

Like a flash came to me my visions of capsizing and foundering, but no phantasm could stand such bright sunlight, and the merry clink-clank of the windlass-pauls, while a sleep-freshened crew chantied:

> "High-ho, up she rises!
> High, high, up she rises!
> Weigh-heigh, up she rises!
> *Early* in the morning."

"Anchor's a-peak! Anchor's awash!" reported the mate. "Now lads, jib halliards, and get her going, then hook on the burton and cathead[11] our ground-tackle!"

The schooner went off smartly as soon as the headsails were sheeted home—I at the wheel, the crew busy getting the anchor aboard.

"Our hook must have fouled something," I heard one of the men say. "Picked up a plank or the like."

As the anchor flukes were lifted clear of the rail a curved board showed, locked across from one to the other, between the arms and the shank. It was weedy and black from long submersion.

"Looks like a trail-board off one o' them old-style billet-heads," said the mate, hauling it in. "We must have been anchored on a wreck. Yes, there's letters cut in it; it's an old-style name-board."

---

11. The burton was a type of tackle used to tighten shrouds or to lift heavy objects, here the anchor. A cathead was a curved timber projecting from the bow to hold an anchor.

He began scraping off the moss with one of the wedge-shaped spikes which fell from the plank.

"You'll find the first letter's S," I called to him from the wheel stand, a sudden idea possessing me.

"Wrong, sir," he hailed back. "It's N—N-O-T-L-I-M—Oh, I'm scraping it from the wrong end. It's *Hamilton*, sir. Ever hear of a vessel called the *Hamilton* being lost?"

"Not in my time," I answered. "Mightn't it be her port of hail?"

"Not likely, from the shape of the board," said he.

"Oh, sir," shouted the high-school lad, running aft, "isn't this the eighth of August, 1913?"

"Sure," I answered, rather nettled at his leaving his work, "and it'll be the ninth of next century before you get any breakfast if that anchor's not stowed on the chocks smartly."

"Why, sir," the youngster went on apologetically, "on the eighth of August, 1813, two vessels of the American Commodore Chauncey's fleet were capsized and sunk in a heavy squall while trying to escape from the British in an engagement off the Niagara river. I've read it in a history of the War of 1812, only this spring. And one of them was called the *Hamilton*!"

"What was the other one?" I asked.

"The *Scourge*," he answered. "They foundered at two o'clock in the morning, and out of a hundred men aboard only sixteen were saved. And to think of us anchoring on top of them and bringing up their old planking a century later, on the very day! Can you beat it?"

"Yes," I said, quietly. But I was very glad "eight bells" and the breakfast call saved me from telling him how.

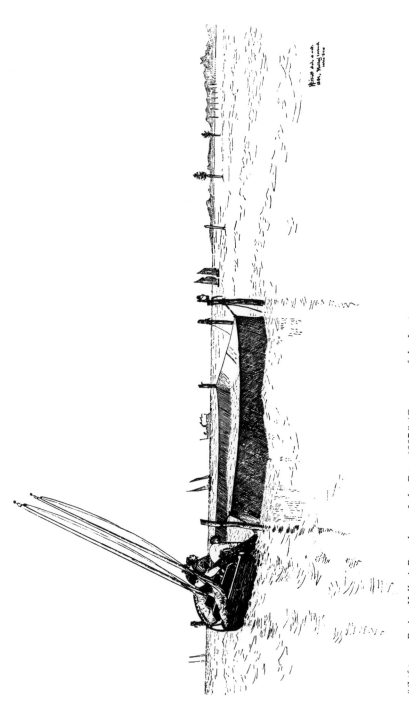

"Lifting a Pot' at Kelley's Pound-net, Lake Erie, 1887." (Courtesy of the Institute for Great Lakes Research, Bowling Green State University.)

Fishermen

His boat he calls the "Mattie," and the truth to you I'll tell,
Several times he has rebuilt her and he can sail her well.
For once when beating down the Lake he had to come about,
He heeled her in the seas so far she scooped up thirty trout.

"The Fisherman *Yankee Brown*"
Traditional Great Lakes Song

The Origin of the White Fish

Ojibwa Myth Collected by Henry Rowe Schoolcraft

HENRY ROWE SCHOOLCRAFT, who was appointed to the Indian Agency at Sault Ste. Marie in 1822, was the first person to pay serious attention to Indian stories. He had married the granddaughter of a Chippewa chief, and from her family came the tales Schoolcraft collected in *Algic Researches,* a book many have compared to the work of the brothers Grimm in Germany, and which influenced Henry Wadsworth Longfellow to compose *Hiawatha.* Later generations of ethnologists have faulted Schoolcraft for editing the tales he collected, particularly for expurgating the more ribald (and often amusing) sections, but both Schoolcraft and his wife were proper Victorians, and moreover, the science of ethnology had barely begun when he first started collecting. Whatever his faults, without his belief that Indian stories were important and deserved to be written down before they were lost, American literature would be far poorer today.

"The Origin of the Whitefish," is a serious epic of creation—an origin myth and a "rolling head" story—that was told in much the same form by many Native American tribes. This is a Chippewa version that takes place near the St. Mary's River (Pauwateeg), and the fish created is a whitefish, rather than the sturgeon of versions told by tribes farther west. Given the importance of the whitefish to the Chippewa culture of the Straits of Mackinac, this difference is easy to understand. But not only did this tale account for the origin of the whitefish, it also told how the crane clan came by their totem. This was important cultural information, since the tribes were divided into kinship groups represented by different parts of the universe, each with its own origin myth and totem, and it was necessary that the younger generation understand their heritage.

Addik Kum Maig[1]
or
The Origin of the White Fish

A LONG TIME AGO, there lived a famous hunter in a remote part of the north. He had a handsome wife and two sons, who were left in the lodge every day, while he went out in quest of the animals, upon whose flesh they subsisted. Game was very abundant in those days, and his exertions in the chase were well rewarded. The skins of animals furnished them with clothing, and their flesh with food. They lived a long distance from any other lodge, and very seldom saw any one. The two sons were still too young to follow their father to the chase, and usually diverted themselves within a short distance of the lodge. They noticed that a young man visited the lodge during their father's absence, and these visits were frequently repeated. At length the elder of the two said to his mother; "my mother, who is this tall young man that comes here so often during our father's absence?"

---

1. This term appears to be a derivative from ADDIK, the reindeer, and the plural form of the generic GUMEE water, implying deer of the waters. [Schoolcraft's note.]

"Does he wish to see him? Shall I tell him when he comes back this evening?" "Bad boy," said the mother, pettishly, "mind your bow and arrows, and do not be afraid to enter the forest in search of birds and squirrels, with your little brother. It is not manly to be ever about the lodge. Nor will you become a warrior if you tell all the little things you see and hear to your father. Say not a word to him on the subject." The boys obeyed, but as they grew older, and still saw the visits of this mysterious stranger, they resolved to speak again to their mother, and told her that they meant to inform their father of all they had observed, for they frequently saw this young man passing through the woods, and he did not walk in the path, nor did he carry anything to eat. If he had any message to deliver, they had observed that messages were always addressed to the men, and not to the women. At this, the mother flew into a rage. "I will kill you," said she, "if you speak of it." They were again intimidated to hold their peace. But observing the continuance of an improper intercourse, kept up by stealth, as it were, they resolved at last to disclose the whole matter to their father. They did so. The result was such as might have been anticipated. The father, being satisfied of the infidelity of his wife, watched a suitable occasion, when she was separated from the children, that they might not have their feelings excited, and with a single blow of his war club dispatched her. He then buried her under the ashes of his fire, took down the lodge, and removed, with his two sons, to a distant position.

But the spirit of the woman haunted the children, who were now grown up to the estate of young men. She appeared to them as they returned from hunting in the evening. They were also terrified in their dreams, which they attributed to her. She harassed their imaginations wherever they went. Life became a scene of perpetual terrors. They resolved, together with their father, to leave the country, and commenced a journey toward the south. After traveling many days along the shores of Lake Superior, they passed around a high promontory of rock where a large river issued out of the lake, and soon after came to a place called Pauwateeg.[2]

They had no sooner come in sight of these falls, than they beheld the skull of the woman rolling along the beach. They were in the utmost fear, and knew not how to elude her. At this moment one of them looked out, and saw a stately crane sitting on a rock in the middle of the rapids. They called out to the bird. "See, grandfather, we are persecuted by a spirit. Come and take us across the falls, so that we may escape her."

This crane was a bird of extraordinary size and great age. When first described by the two sons, he sat in a state of stupor, in the midst of the most violent eddies. When he heard himself addressed he stretched forth his neck with great deliberation, and lifting himself by his wings, flew across to their assistance. "Be careful," said the crane, "that you do not touch the back part of my head. It is sore, and should you press against it, I shall not be able to avoid throwing you both into the rapids." They were, however, attentive on this point, and were safely landed on the south shore of the river.

The crane then resumed his former position in the rapids. But the skull now cried out. "Come, my grandfather, and carry me over, for I have lost my children, and am sorely distressed." The aged bird flew to her assistance. He carefully repeated the injunction that she must by no means touch the back part of his head, which had been hurt, and was not yet healed. She promised to obey, but soon felt a curiosity to know where the head of her carrier had been hurt, and how so aged a bird could have received so bad a wound. She thought it strange, and before they were halfway over the rapids, could not resist the inclination she felt to touch the affected part. Instantly the crane threw her into the rapids. "There," said he, "you have been of no use during your life, you shall now be changed into something for

2. Sault Ste. Marie. [Schoolcraft's note.]

the benefit of your people, and it shall be called Addik Kum Maig." As the skull floated from rock to rock, the brains were strewed in the water, in a form resembling roes, which soon assumed the shape of a new species of fish, possessing a whiteness of color, and peculiar flavor, which have caused it, ever since, to be in great repute with the Indians.

The family of this man, in gratitude for their deliverance, adopted the crane as their totem, or mark; and this continues to be the distinguishing tribal sign of the band to this day.

The Fish Pirates

James Oliver Curwood

LONG BEFORE the lamprey eel devastated Great Lakes catches, overfishing was such a serious problem that at the turn of the century Lake Erie had become a battleground between Canadian and American fishermen fighting over declining stocks of fish. The Americans had used fine-mesh gill nets for years, a practice that had so seriously depleted the fish populations in the U.S. section of the Lake that congressional investigations were begun. When the fish did not return, the Americans headed their big steam tugs "over the line" and became pirates where the fish were still plentiful because the Canadians had used only pound nets, which do not affect the large schools of fish offshore. But the Americans were met by the Canadian cruiser *Vigilant*, armed with a four-inch cannon. The butt of the joke in Curwood's story, in reality she took no sass from the Americans and once cut a fishing tug in two. Despite its nationalism and sentimentality, "The Fish Pirates" is a realistic portrayal of commercial fishing on the lakes, an industry that continues to provoke more gunshots and lawsuits than any other commerce on fresh water.

"The Fish Pirates" occurs midway through the story cycle *Falkner of the Inland Seas*, which is about Jim Falkner, the imaginary survivor of one of the most puzzling Great Lakes shipwrecks, the disappearance of the *Bannockburn* with all hands on a calm night on Lake Superior in 1902. Curwood envisioned

Falkner's life from his rescue as a toddler on a wild shore of the Lake where his father, the captain of the *Bannockburn*, carried him before dying, through numerous adventures as a newspaperman and as a crewman on lakes. At the time of this story he has grown up, earned his Able Seaman's certificate, and graduated from college as well. He has still not decided to ship out full-time, however, and so takes a job as a cub reporter for the Detroit *Herald*: ". . . the best daily in the best city on the Great Lakes. . . ."

THE MANAGING EDITOR was studying a map when Falkner came in. He looked up, nodded and asked sharply: "Have you seen this, Jim?"

The young man picked up the afternoon edition of a rather sensational rival and noted the big head-lines running across the first three columns. The preceding night an American fishing-tug had been fired upon by a Canadian revenue cutter, and the story had been "played-up" in graphic detail.

"What do you think of that?" asked the editor, who had been told of his new cub's interest in the lakes and their people.

Jim Falkner shrugged his shoulders. He had already learned that this was a golden way of expressing himself until he had fathomed the managing editor's mind. "Interesting," he said. "Mighty interesting!"

"I'll wager a hat that it will end in something more than a little excitement, Falkner!" exclaimed the managing editor. "Our lake correspondents say that the fishermen along the Erie shore are desperate. They're not catching fish on our side, and a great many of the tug captains have turned pirates and are running their nets over the international boundary. Our Dunkirk man says the town is hot with threats against the Canadians; while in Erie, they're ready to fight, and I've got a tip that a number of captains are fitted out with guns—and there's a strong sentiment that if they're fired upon they'll use 'em. The Canadian revenue cutters are confiscating nets by the wholesale; they've captured three tugs which have been taken as prizes into Canadian ports; and two boats have been fired upon when they refused to haul to. That's the situation in a nutshell, Jim. If the Dunkirk and Erie men don't back down there's going to be a fish-pirate war; anyway, there's stacks of fun brewing, and I want you to hustle over there and take the thing in hand. Everything is up to you. Get the best special stuff you can. Our regular correspondents will attend to the routine. Here—wait a minute—I'll give you an order for transportation and funds."

Jim Falkner was instantly on his feet, ready to go. "I can make the three-twenty train," he said, glancing at his watch. "That will get me into Erie to-night."

It was already three o'clock, and the managing editor nodded in appreciation of the young man's readiness. "Then we won't waste time in getting transportation. Here's an order on the cashier. If you want more money wire for it. Get in with the pirates, if you can, and take a trip with one of them. That's what we want. Good luck to you!"

Fifteen minutes later Jim Falkner was aboard his train. He had purchased a magazine at the depot newsstand, but did not read. Lounging back comfortably in his seat, he closed his eyes and began formulating a plan of action. At the outset he realized that he would have difficulty in successfully filling his assignment. This was not the first time that the dark clouds of a fishermen's war had gathered over Erie. And it was not the first time that a newspaper man had gone down among the pirates.

He remembered that MacIlvie had almost succeeded. MacIlvie's story was a bit of cherished history in the *Herald* office. He had smuggled himself aboard a Dunkirk fish-pirate's boat, and had reached the poaching grounds before he was discovered. After that he was marooned upon a sand-bar which was not much larger than the tug which put him there. He had almost starved. Falkner chuckled as he recalled the Scotchman's adventure. Then there was Briggs, the best marine man that ever struck the *Herald* beat. Briggs came back with one arm in a sling, and so badly used-up that he was unrecognizable for a month.

Falkner himself had been among the pirates two years before, in a desultory, friendly sort of way, while writing up the fish industry during a summer vacation. He knew them for men of strong courage, toughened by storm and inured to wreck and hardship, and with a thousand fancied wrongs to right—men who talked with foxlike caution in the companionship of strangers, and who thought it no sin to seek their livelihood across a line they could neither feel nor see, and would not understand.

The young reporter admired their courage. He liked the men. He wanted to join them, and be friends, and write them up as heroes instead of outlaws. He knew that this would please the managing editor. Everybody liked the fish pirates, except the Canadians. MacIlvie and Briggs had liked them—a mental picture of MacIlvie upon his sand-bar, and Briggs in his hospital cot, flashed upon Falkner, and the humor of it tickled him.

"If that's the reward of friendship in Erie, what the deuce will they do with me?" he thought.

Unconsciously he spoke the words quite audibly. The next instant he was looking into a pair of dark, tear-filled eyes turned upon him from the seat ahead. He saw a troubled face and a mouth trembling as if upon the point of speech. Then the face was turned away.

Falkner straightened himself. He had noticed the girl when he came in, and had looked at her hair because it struck him as being exquisitely pretty. After that he had not thought of her again. But now he watched her closely, hoping that she would give him an opportunity to speak to her. But the opportunity did not come, and gradually his thoughts slipped back into their old channel.

By the time his train reached Toledo he had devised a scheme by which he hoped to make good among the pirates. He would get employment in one of the fish-houses, make the acquaintance of poachers and watch for a chance to join one of their crews. It would take time, but he believed the managing editor would stand for it.

As the train pulled into the Toledo yards, the girl ahead of him rose from her seat, and Falkner was enabled to get another view of her face. Something in it—a look of tense anxiety, almost fear—urged him to speak. "I beg your pardon," he said. "I change here—may I help you with your grip?"

A bit of color mounted into the girl's pale cheeks.

"I—I—hardly know," she faltered. The young man saw unutterable wretchedness in her eyes. "You are—going to Erie?" she asked. "I overheard you—"

"Yes, I'm going to Erie," Jim Falkner interrupted. He wanted the girl to understand that he knew she was in trouble, and there was gentle friendliness in his voice. "Won't you please tell me how I can help you?"

"You can carry my grip."

She looked up into his face, and there came a little tremble round her mouth, and her eyes were soft in the lamp-glow, as though she wanted to cry. It was a pretty face, and the young man felt his heart pounding with sympathy.

"I want to do more than that!" he said. Suddenly he reached out and caught one of her hands. "See here, little girl, something's troubling you! Won't you tell me what it is?"

The girl was crying in earnest now. The passengers had filed out of the car, but Falkner continued to hold the hand he had taken.

"Tell me!" he pleaded.

"I—I—want you to take me to a pawn-shop," sobbed the girl from behind her handkerchief.

"A pawn-shop!" cried Falkner. "What the devil—Oh, I beg your pardon."

"Yes, a pawn-shop!" repeated the girl, withdrawing her

hand and meeting his eyes squarely. "I want to go to a pawn-shop right away. I've lost my purse, and I haven't a ticket to Erie, and I'm—"

"Hungry, I'll bet a dollar!" cried the young man. "We're bound this instant for a place where they set up square meals, and do it in a hurry. We've got just thirty-five minutes. Come on!"

He caught up their grips and hurried down the aisle. There was not much beauty about Jim Falkner, but there was something unusually attractive in the boyish frankness of his face, and, as he looked back over his shoulder, his strong white teeth shining at her, the girl laughed.

"I'm a beggar!" she cried.

"The prettiest I ever met!" he flung back; and their eyes met laughingly as he reached up to help her down the car steps.

"A pawn-shop—you!" He laughed aloud.

Relief from her anxiety and the excitement of her rescue had flushed the girl's cheeks with color. Suddenly the young man halted her under a depot light. "My name is Falkner," he announced, fishing a card from his pocket. "J. Augustus Falkner, of Detroit. It's a rummy name, but I've got to keep it. I don't put on that 'J.' for style, but to make the thing passable. Altogether it's James Augustus Falkner!"

"And mine is Burton," replied the girl, smiling up into his jolly face. "Josephine Burton, of Erie."

"Jo—for short?" said Falkner.

"Ye-e-e-e-s, if you want to. You're a newspaper man?"

"Bound for Erie, to get up a few special stories about the fish pirates," he answered. He led her into the depot café and gave their orders. "Do you know any fish pirates?" he asked, after he had done so.

He noticed that she was looking at him with unusual interest.

"What are you going to say about them?" she questioned.

"You're not going to—say anything—bad?" She spoke with intense seriousness, and Falkner detected a note of alarm in her voice.

"I want to make friends with them," he assured her. "I want to turn pirate myself. And I will—if they'll let me." Then he told her about MacIlvie and Briggs. Afterward, when they were seated in their train, he described to her his plan for getting among the poachers.

"And you think that will succeed?" she asked, with a suggestive curving of her lips. "Well, it won't!"

Falkner stared at her in astonishment. "How do you know!" he retorted.

"I'd be ashamed of them if it did," continued the girl, her eyes shining with enthusiasm. "Those men whom you call pirates are old hands. They've known one another for years, and would no more think of stringing a gang over the line with a new hand aboard—" She caught herself in confusion.

"You're a pirate!" whispered Falkner. His eyes burned with admiration. "You're a pirate, Miss Jo—and so am I!"

It was late when they reached Erie. A single cab was waiting at the depot, and James Augustus Falkner led Miss Burton to it. "I am coming to see you soon," he said. "To-morrow, or the day after—may I?"

"The day after," she invited. "I shall sleep to-morrow."

The young man opened the cab door for her. After she had entered she stretched out a hand to him and said: "I will get you acquainted with a pirate, Mr. Falkner. To-morrow afternoon call at 520 Water Street, and ask for Captain Town. He will help you. Good night—and a million thanks!"

It was midnight by the time Jim Falkner had registered for a room at a hotel. But for some time after that he did not go to bed. He lighted his pipe, and went over the afternoon's adventure. Who was this Captain Town? For some reason which he did not attempt to analyze the question bothered him, and he imagined half a dozen things which might account for Miss Burton's apparent influence with him. He was quite positive that he must be a pirate, however; and a picturesque one at that, if his name stood for anything at all. Altogether, he counted himself immensely fortunate in having met the girl and in having been thus placed in line, as he was convinced, with a Lake Erie poacher.

The following morning, when the young man went down to breakfast, he stopped to chat for a few moments with the clerk, and asked him if he knew Captain Town. The clerk had never heard of him.

Until noon Falkner hung about the fish-houses. There he discovered that Captain Town was master and owner of the only "compounder" in the port.

"What's a 'compounder'?" asked the young reporter.

"A compounder," said his informant, who was a dock lounger, "is a tug wot you can only 'ear the riffles of—if y' listen 'ard!"

At a little before two o'clock, Jim Falkner walked slowly along Water Street. Before number 520 he stopped in astonishment. It was a big stone front.

"Great Scott!" he gasped; but he walked up to it and rang the door-bell.

"Rooms here, I suppose," he mentally concluded.

A moment later the door was opened by a little white-haired old lady, who stared at him with ardent curiosity. "Does Captain Town live here?" asked Falkner.

"You bet he does, my boy!" came a jovial voice from back in the hall. "Step in, will you? I suppose you're the fellow Burton's girl sent over?"

One of the oddest individuals he had ever seen confronted the young man. He was unusually tall, and unusually thin, and his long lean face shone like red tanned leather. But there was something immediately likable about him. His smile was friendly, and his grip so convincing that his visitor's hand ached for some time after he had shaken it.

"Been expecting you for some time, Falkner," he said familiarly. "Come this way, will you?"

He led him into a little room shut off from the hall, in which two men were busily engaged in smoking pipes. They were broad-built, weather-toughened men, wearing heavy seamen's jackets, and as Captain Town came in they shuffled to their feet and stood with their pipes in their hands. Falkner had previously learned that this was a custom of old lakemen when they wished to show unusual regard for a stranger.

"This is the fellow Burton's girl sent over," announced the captain. "Mr. Falkner, shake hands with the boys, will you? This is Teddy—Teddy Roosevelt, we call him, though his name is Jones; and this is Sandy—Sandy MacGunn. Both of 'em old-timers and rattling good men, as Burton's girl may have told you."

Falkner shook hands.

"We're going out to-night," continued Captain Town, relighting his pipe. "We've got our gang stretched two miles over the line, and there's a straight tip come that the *Vigilant* is going to drag there to-morrow. If she does we lose our nets—unless we get 'em out before morning. Burton's girl says you want to go, so—" He puffed hard on his pipe. "So—I guess we'll have to take you!"

For an hour Jim Falkner talked and smoked with the men. It did not take him long to see that for some reason the two fishermen, MacGunn and Jones, treated him with especial deference. Even the captain was puzzlingly attentive. At the door, as he was leaving, the master of the compounder gave him a letter.

"Burton's girl asked me to give this to you," he explained. "It's the money, I guess."

Suddenly he placed his two great hands upon the young man's shoulders and looked him squarely in the eyes. "See here, mate," he spoke in a low voice, "you did the square thing by Burton's girl. She thinks you're a brick. But if you lied to her—

if you came down here to—" he stopped. Jim Falkner thought of Briggs and the Scotchman, and understood.

"I swear that I won't betray her confidence," he replied. His voice vibrated with truth. "I'd turn back now if I thought there was a chance of it!" he finished.

"You'd be willing to die first if you knew Burton's girl as well as I do!" declared the captain. "You would, s'elp me God, you would, Falkner!" He took his hands from his visitor's shoulders and opened the door. "I don't suppose Burton's girl told you anything about herself?" he asked.

"Not a word!" cried the young man; and his eyes shone with eager interest.

"Well, mebby I'll tell you something to-night," laughed the fish pirate. "Remember, we leave at ten sharp. You're sure you can find us?"

"Perfectly!" said Jim Falkner.

He walked away as if in a dream. Twice he looked back at the handsome stone house, and more than once during the next half-hour he asked himself it it were possible that a fish pirate lived there; an outlaw, a man who staked a fortune and imperiled himself on the strength of his own cunning, and who was willing to accept the risks of the poorest fisherman for the chance of a successful haul from over the line. He had expected to meet pirates, but not of this kind. He had not associated stone fronts and pretty girls with his pictures of the poachers. He realized that, perhaps unwittingly, he was now turning traitor to his assignment.

He knew that he had already gathered material which would have created a sensation in the *Herald* office; but he had given his word not to divulge its secrets, and he had deliberately pledged himself not to use those details which his managing editor would demand. All this—he acknowledged it with a peculiar thrill of satisfaction—because he had become strangely interested in a girl!

Jim Falkner whistled as he thought, and walked without

seeking any particular direction. If he had made a fool of himself he was not in a mood to confess it. He still might follow out his original scheme, ingratiate himself into the confidence of some other pirate not associated with the girl, and write his sensation in the manner he had planned. He wondered how far Captain Town's friendship for the girl went. Perhaps they were relatives. He tried to make himself believe it.

Not until he had reached his hotel did he think to open the letter which had been given to him by the fish pirate. He was elated to find that it contained a note from Miss Burton, as well as the money which he had expended for her ticket the previous evening.

> "Dear Mr. Falkner," he read. "In this I am returning what you kindly lent me last night. I hope you liked Captain Town. Please do not forget your promise to come and see me to-morrow afternoon.   JOSEPHINE BURTON."

It was not much, but it filled the young man with pleasure. Since his interview with Captain Town he had feared that perhaps Miss Burton did not care to continue their acquaintance, and that the captain himself might not regard further attentions on his part in a friendly light.

He read the note again, and, instead of destroying it afterward, as was his custom with unimportant epistles, he placed it in his pocket. Miss Burton had become a young woman of mystery to him. He realized that she possessed unusual influence with the fish pirates,—or, at least, with Captain Town,—and each hour added to the eagerness with which he anticipated that night's adventure, in which he was confident he would learn more about her.

An hour before the appointed time he was at the slip in which the fish-pirate tug was secured. With the approach of evening a high wind had sprung up out of the northeast—although the night was clear—and from the disturbance in the

bay he knew that heavy seas were running outside. The compounder lay black and silent. Not a spark of light could he
discern aboard her, and he began to fear that the gale had driven
Captain Town and his men from their determination to leave
port. He was confident that they would at least send him word,
however, so he seated himself in the shelter of a fish-box and
waited.

A few minutes before ten two men hurried down from the
blackness of the fish-houses and jumped aboard the tug. Falkner
called to them, and found that one was MacGunn. The other
was the tug's engineer, whom he had not met before.

"Going out, MacGunn?" he asked, as he followed them
aboard.

"Sure! Didn't the cap'n say so—at ten?"

MacGunn flung open the engine-room door and a rush of
hot air poured out into the young man's face. He lighted a couple
of lanterns, and saw the puzzled look in his companion's face.
"Had steam up for half an hour," he grinned. Then he added,
with a suggestive shrug and another grin: "Hard coal!"

He flung an oil-coat over one of the lanterns and carried
it into the pilot-house, where Falkner and he sat down in
silence. A few minutes later they were joined by Captain Town
and Teddy.

When the captain spoke it was in a voice but little louder
than a whisper, and Falkner accepted the hint by maintaining
silence while the compounder was got under way. Only by the
gentle throbbing of her engine and the pitching of the boat in
the seas could he tell when she had left her mooring.

A quarter of an hour had passed when MacGunn uncovered
the lantern. He handed it to the captain. "We're off the point,"
he said. "You remember—"

Captain Town pressed his face close up to one of the port
windows. After a moment he turned and motioned Falkner to
him. "That's Presque Isle," he said. "Can you make out a light?"

The young man stared hard. A long distance away, it

seemed to him, he could see what he thought to be the glow of a lamp in a window.

"That's where Burton's girl lives," said the captain softly, "I told her that if we took you to-night we'd show a light. She must see us soon. There—look!"

Falkner's heart gave a sudden throb of pleasure. For an instant the distant light vanished, then reappeared; and in a dozen flashes of light, followed by intervals of gloom, came the signs of recognition from the watching girl. There was almost a break in the young man's voice when he spoke to Captain Town. "She's—a trump!" he breathed.

He looked again, but now the light remained steadily in the window. He watched it until the tops of the heaving seas shut it out from his vision. Never in his life had he felt the blood pulsing through his veins as it did now, and when he seated himself, facing Sandy, and the master of the compounder, he found the men eying him with keen interest.

"She is a trump!" replied MacGunn, "She's a—"

A sweeping run of the sea caught the compounder with the booming force of a ten-ton sledge-hammer, and at this first signal that she had come into the open lake, Teddy swung the tug's nose squarely out from the point, three-quarters in the teeth of the wind and on a line for the international boundary. Falkner shivered.

"She's an angel!" finished MacGunn, when the compounder had straightened herself.

Jim Falkner passed around a box of cigars. The fish pirates seemed indifferent to the roughness of the night, and the fact gave him courage. But Captain Town had discovered his nervousness.

"We've gone out in worse seas than this," he said, lighting his cigar. "It was twice as bad that night Burton went out; wasn't it, Teddy?" he asked, turning to the wheelman. "It ain't customary to go out nights—unless you've got a couple o' thousand dollars' worth of nets at stake, as we've got right now. That's

what took Burton out, in November three years ago. He had a
fifteen-hundred-dollar gang—which is a string o'gill-nets—
dropped three miles over the line in a heavy herring-run, which
ground was scheduled to be dragged the next day by the Canadian gunboat *Petrel.* It was that damned boat that settled for
Burton!" he growled.

MacGunn had pulled a piece of paper from one of his
pockets.

"Look here!" he cried, bringing a doubled fist forcefully
upon his knee. "Look here what this reads. I cut it from a fish
paper. 'Cap'n Chayter,' it says, 'of the United States revenue
cutter *Morrell,* on Lake Erie, states that all the fish this year are
on the Canadian side.' And that's right! Nine out of ten of 'em
are over there. Now, look here, Mr. Falkner," he continued, in
a voice that shook the little cabin, "fish is fish, ain't they? And
they ain't got no nationality, 'ave they? And everybody ought
to be allowed to ketch 'em, 'adn't they? But the law says not.
The law says fish is *citizens!* The fish this side of that damned
line out there it says is Americans. The fish t'other side is Canadians. If an American pike 'appens to cross that line he immediately turns Canuck—accordin' to law—and we can't ketch
'im, no matter if 'e was born 'n' bred right in Erie harbor! Think
of that! An Erie man can't go over there and bring back a
runaway Erie fish! That ain't a decent law—it's a damned out-
rage. And that's the law which killed Burton."

"You see, Burton went out in a bad night to save his nets
and was washed overboard," elucidated Captain Town. "The
lights of the cutter hove in sight, and it was in the hurry of
trying to save a part of the gang that he was lost. The tug got
away—but that was all—and it left Burton's girl and her mother
in pretty bad shape."

The wheelman spoke.

"Then she went to work as a—as a—"

"Shut up!" commanded Captain Town. "I won't have it
said, Teddy—darned if I will!"

Jim Falkner reached over and gripped the fish pirate's hand.

"I believe I understand," he said, his eyes glowing. "She was a brick, old man!"

"But it wasn't long," interrupted the other. "We rented Burton's boat to a Dunkirk man, and got her a position in one of the fish-house offices. That was just before the strike."

"Remember the big strike a couple of years ago?" asked Teddy, looking over his shoulder. "Lord—"

"Them as owned boats was all right," spoke MacGunn. "But for them that didn't it was—hell! Half of us was reduced to soup bones, sir—soup bones, by thunder!"

"And atop of that came an epidemic of diphtheria," said the captain. "It was a desperate rub for some of the poorer fellows. That was when Burton's girl showed her colors."

A deep breath came from Teddy.

"I lost my little Nell then," he said hoarsely. "I'd lost the others—three of them—and the wife, too, if it hadn't been for her. She nursed 'em through it, and fed 'em, God bless her— s'elp me, she did; she *fed* 'em!"

"There are others, Teddy," said MacGunn, a peculiar softness in his rough voice. "There was the Stimsons, the Rogerses, 'Pig' Walcott's family, and a dozen others. We didn't know what she had done for 'em until—"

He stopped, and for a time there was silence. Falkner listened to the wash of the seas, and waited. Teddy, the wheelman, was staring straight ahead into the gloom of the night. MacGunn was enveloping himself in clouds of smoke. After a while Captain Town finished what the other had begun.

'We didn't know until we found she had sold Burton's boat," he said. "The Dunkirk man had bought it at a half what it was worth, and by the time we discovered what she had done the girl had spent it all on poor devils of the fishing fleet. That's her, Falkner—that's Burton's girl!"

"We paid her back—afterward," came Terry's muffled

voice. "But she wouldn't take a cent more than she had spent, not a cent."

"And at Walcott's she took diphthery herself," rejoined MacGunn. "God, how we prayed! And in the critical days some of us didn't work, but just hung around waitin' f'r her to live."

"That was two years ago," said Falkner, after a silence. "What does she do now?"

"Nurses sick folks!" jerked MacGunn.

Teddy drew the tug a step into the wind and glanced at Captain Town. The master of the compounder thrust his head and shoulders out of the pilot-house, and, after peering for a few minutes into the darkness of the sea ahead, went forward.

Jim Falkner followed. The wind had shifted into the north, and was colder, but less violent. A mile over the starboard bow two or three steady, starlike lights were slipping swiftly up the lake.

After a little MacGunn's voice came from behind. "What is it, Cap'n?" he cried.

"It isn't her," shouted Town, over his shoulder. "Lights are too high for the *Vigilant*. We'll cut a quarter of a mile astern. Better douse the glims."[1] He made room for Falkner beside him in the bow.

"The Canucks are in port to-night," he said to him. "They're pretty sure they wouldn't catch anything in a sea like this. I'd be tied up myself if I didn't have a couple thousand dollars' worth of nets layin' out there!"

Captain Town kept a ceaseless vigil to the north. Once or twice Jim Falkner spoke to him, but received only monosyllabic replies. After a while he rejoined Teddy and MacGunn in the pilot-house.

"D'ye remember the *Laughing Lass?*" greeted Teddy. The

---

1. "Glim" once referred to the light in crew's quarters. Now it is slang for any light.

incident of the *Laughing Lass* had caused talk of war, and the young man nodded.

"Well, right here is where the *Petrel* tried to shoot hell out of her, back in 1903. She was poaching on the other side and wouldn't stop—"

Captain Town interrupted him from the pilot-house door.

"Tell the engineer to ease her down, Teddy," he called. 'We're sighting the point buoy. Sandy, give us a lift with the drag."

Falkner followed the two aft. A few days before he knew that he would have taken a keen interest in what was about to happen, but now his enthusiasm was lamentably lacking. He saw the international buoy come and go in the gloom. He heard the creaking of the net-lifter, watched Captain Town as he slowly paid out the drag-line, and was conscious of the suspense which followed.

He knew that the compounder was now in forbidden waters—that they were pirates, with certain prices upon their heads, and that at any moment a gunboat might bear down upon them. But these things did not thrill him as he had imagined they would. More than anything else they produced in his mind the picture of another night, when the father of the girl back at Presque Isle had gone to his death, perhaps very near to where he stood at this moment.

After a little he noticed that the tug was moving at a snail-like speed. She seemed to be feeling her way through the seas foot by foot.

Then came a shout from the captain, a triumphant cry from MacGunn—and the throbbing of the compounder's engine ceased. He knew that the drag had caught. For a few moments he watched the line as the creaking windlass drew it in. He saw the first of a mile of net slip over the stern,[2] and then, unob-

---

2. Curwood's command of technical matters fails here. Nets are never lifted over the stern.

served by the fish pirates, went back into the still darkness of the pilot-house.

Half an hour later Captain Town came in to get his pipe. As he lighted a match he caught sight of the young man doubled up in one of the cushioned seats. "Hello, mate!—Seasick?" he cried.

"A little uneasy," replied Falkner.

As the fish pirate turned to go, Jim Falkner jumped to his feet and caught him by the arm. "Captain, can you tell me on what date Burton was lost?" he asked.

"On the day before the season closed—November fourteenth."

"And to-morrow is the thirteenth," mused the young man as the other left the pilot-house. "Lord deliver us, Jerry, there's no time to lose!" He whistled softly and happily, in the way of a man who is far from seasick.

In the early dawn the compounder came back into Erie. There were two tons of herring in her boxes. Her nets were wet and tangled. But Captain Town did not remain to see to the unloading of his catch or to the reeling of his gang. With Jim Falkner he hurried ashore, the two almost running in their haste. A few moments later, divested of his oil-coat and sou'-wester, Teddy disappeared upon a run behind the fish-houses.

When they reached Water Street, Jim Falkner and the captain halted. "You are sure you've got time?" he asked.

"I'll have twenty boats and a hundred men by noon!" declared the fish pirate. "We'll raise hell—if you can work your end of it, Falkner!"

The *Herald* man thrust out a hand. "I'll never look Burton's girl in the face again if I don't!" he exclaimed. "Remember—I promise upon my word of honor!"

He hurried townward. A block away he glanced over his shoulder and saw Captain Town going up Water Street at a trot. It was six o'clock when he reached the Western Union telegraph office.

"I don't suppose the manager is in," he inquired of the clerk.

"He won't be in until eight."

The young man reached for a pad and began writing. Five minutes later he handed the message through the window.

"This is a matter of great importance," he explained to the clerk, "and I don't want to spare expense in getting it to the right party. I want it sent to Port Stanley, Port Burwell and Port Rowan, Ontario. If Captain Fitzgerald is not in any of these three places, have a tug sent out in search of him from each port, and I will stand the expense. He must get that message before noon at all costs."

As the clerk read he gave a low whistle of astonishment. This was the message which Falkner had written:

CAPTAIN FITZGERALD, Commander Revenue Cutter *Vigilant,*—Ontario. This afternoon a powerful fleet of tugs will leave Erie for Port Dover, where it is their intention to recapture the three American fishing-boats recently caught in Canadian waters and now held in that port. It is probable that the boats will approach from the direction of Stromness. For assurance of responsibility of writer, wire managing editor, the *Herald,* Detroit, or W. P. Samson, M. P., Windsor.   J. A. FALKNER.

Half an hour later the most sensational story of the year was being received over the *Herald* wire. It described in minute detail the daring plot of a hundred men to consummate one of the most thrilling exploits in lake history. After a column of it had gone the young man sat down and waited. Exhausted by forty-eight hours of sleepless exertion he soon fell into a slumber, from which he was aroused by the clerk an hour and a half later. The *Vigilant* had been found by a Port Rowan tug near Long Point, and the message had been delivered to Captain Fitzgerald.

After breakfast at his hotel, Falkner went to his room, but not to sleep. He had made up his mind to call upon Miss Burton as soon as possible, although he knew that she did not expect him until afternoon. He changed his clothes, shaved himself, and a little before ten o'clock appeared on Presque Isle. A small boy directed him to the Burton home. It was a comfortable-looking cottage, set well back in a group of maples. A gravel path, with flower-beds on either side, led to the big porch, and as he walked up this Falkner caught a magnificent view of the lake beyond. As he approached he heard whistling, unusually clear and musical.

"A man, by jove!" he thought. "I hope not—"

Suddenly he caught the whisk of a skirt around the edge of the cottage. He followed the path, and a moment later stopped dead still, while a flush of pleasure and embarrassment gathered in his face. Perched half-way up a ladder, a dozen feet away, was a young woman in a man's coat, a man's hat, and with a big brown shining braid of hair falling down her back. She was wielding a paint-brush upon the side of the cottage, and whistling while she worked.

As she partly turned to dip her brush into a can suspended to the ladder she saw her chance acquaintance of the other day. The whistle died on her rounded mouth. For an instant she stared in astonished confusion—and then she laughed, the merriest, sweetest laugh the young man had ever heard.

"There! I was afraid you'd go and do it!" she cried. "I told mama that just as surely as I came out to paint this morning you would show up—and you have! How do you do?" She reached down a hand, laughing, and Falkner climbed up the ladder to reach it.

"I wouldn't have missed this for anything," he said, looking up into her face. "You—you're beautiful up there! Besides, I'm here just in time to help you. I can mix paint—"

"I buy mine ready mixed," cried the girl. "See, it comes in cans." She turned to show him, and in doing so dislodged the paint receptacle which dashed its contents down the ladder, discoloring the tip of one of his shoes. She looked at him with mock dismay.

"I'm glad of it," he said, descending. "Now you must stop work!"

"I've got a dozen more cans in the kitchen," she flung down at him. "And another brush—and a ladder! If you will help me paint this side I'll let you stay to dinner."

Jim's heart fairly jumped with joy. The girl came down and surveyed her work with critical eyes. Her hat had fallen off, and Falkner stood a few steps behind to look at her unobserved.

"Isn't it fine?" she asked, turning upon him. "I'm painting it copper-brown—because—well—" Her eyes danced with fun. "That's the prevailing style in ladies' dress-goods this year, you know," she added. "I painted the fence to begin with. Mr. Tubbs, our neighbor, gave me some home-made paint for that, and it was—it was like paste. Please don't look at the fence!"

Falkner turned and looked.

"I'll do it all over for you, and paint your whole cottage, too—if you'll have an early dinner," he replied.

"Why an early dinner?" The girl pouted her red lips. "Are you hungry, or are you in a hurry to get away?"

"I came over this morning, Miss Jo, because I couldn't come this afternoon," said the young man. "I've got a very important engagement, which begins at one o'clock, and—"

"Then we won't paint," she interrupted.

"But I'll come over and help you every day for a week after to-day, if you'll let me. I'll paint it copper-brown, or red, or—no, it must be copper-brown, for that's the color of your hair—and your hair is beautiful. Will you let me come, Miss Jo?" he pleaded. "Please!"

"I'll have to ask mama about that," said the girl, laughing softly at him with her eyes. "I think—perhaps—Well, let's go in and see her. Do you mind going through the kitchen?"

When he rejoined Captain Town at one o'clock in the Water Street stone front he spoke his feelings. "I've been over to see Miss Burton," he said. "I never met a girl like her before."

"And you never will," declared the fish pirate. "Next to

Laura—that's Mrs. Town—she's the finest girl that lives!"

He led the way to the little room into which the young man was admitted the day before. "Well, I've got twenty-seven boats and a hundred and sixteen men. The tugs you want have steam up and are ready to leave at any time. You didn't let Burton's girl know?"

"Only told her part of the scheme," said Falkner. "She fairly begged me to let her go with us—said she knew Mrs. Town would go if you'd let her."

"Lord, Falkner, how Miss Jo will fight us when she discovers just why we're doing this!" laughed the captain. "If it wasn't for the mother—" He shrugged his shoulders and blew a huge cloud of smoke from his pipe.

"Have you mapped out the course, Captain?"

"This is it." The master of the compounder thumbed a much-worn map hanging on the wall. "We strike due north to the international line; follow that on the American side until we're opposite Dunkirk, then cut a point midway between Stromness and Port Dover. The Canadian boats can't help from sighting us somewhere along that course."

"And we start?"

"It's sixty-five miles. We should leave within an hour."

"That will give me just about time to run up-town and wire a few paragraphs to my paper," said Falkner. "I'll meet you at the boats."

He hurried to the telegraph office again, and found a message awaiting him. It was from W. P. Samson, member of Parliament, Windsor, and read:

> What the devil! Captain Fitzgerald, the *Vigilant*, asks who you are, and if responsible. Told him yes. Are you in trouble? SAMSON.

"Hurrah!" cried Jim Falkner.

The clerk turned a surprised face upon him from the window. "Good news?" he asked. "Money from father, perhaps?"

"Bully!" he exclaimed.

He scribbled a note of thanks to Samson, M. P., and then hurried half a column additional matter off to the *Herald.* When he came down to the docks he saw Captain Town advancing to meet him. "The *Vigilant* is taking the bait," he greeted, as the fish pirate came up. "Read this!"

He gave him Samson's telegram, and when they reached the foot of the ship Captain Town read it aloud to the little group of men assembled there. Broad grins overspread their strong faces, and each gave Jim Falkner a hearty grip of the hands.

A quarter of an hour later six of the largest and fleetest tugs in Erie trailed out of the harbor. As they passed Presque Isle, Falkner stood high up on the engine-house of the compounder, and gazed toward the Burton home. Soon he saw a figure run down to the edge of the beach, and with a joyful shout he waved his hat above his head. Then something rose in the air above the distant girl. For an instant it fluttered, only partly visible; then a gust of wind caught it, and every eye in the little fleet recognized the American flag.

From the pilot-house Captain Town shouted to his engineer, and a screeching blast from the compounder answered the salute of Burton's girl. In an instant it had been taken up by the other tugs, until a mist of steam floated out and hid the distant shore from Falkner's eyes. When he rejoined the fish-pirate captain in the pilot-house there was tense whiteness in his face which he did not know was there.

It was a strange fleet that passed along the international boundary that afternoon. According to Jim Falkner's plans, the six tugs followed one after another, in battle-ship line, and the blackest smoke that bituminous coal could be forced to make trailed over the sea behind them. Late in the afternoon a slim low craft, which was made out to be the auxiliary Canadian cruiser, was sighted in the offing. For an hour she remained parallel with them, running eastward; when darkness fell her lights showed that she was gathering great speed, and was making in the direction of Port Dover.

Opposite Dunkirk the compounder swung her course to a point between Stromness and Port Dover. At nine o'clock, with the sky faultlessly clear above them, they were in the edge of Outer Long Point Bay. In the distance the lights of Port Dover shone dimly.

Half an hour later the compounder, under low pressure, left the line and steamed silently in the direction of Stromness. Both vessels edged shoreward. It was nearly midnight when they returned to the fleet.

The compounder reported that the auxiliary cruiser was lying with steam up between Port Rowan and Normandale; the *Vigilant* had been found two miles beyond Port Dover. Both cruisers were on the watch, and ready to sweep down upon the little fleet the moment it entered the harbor.

For two hours more the tugs lay silently in the Outer Bay. Then the reconnaissance was made again. The cruisers had not changed their positions. A little after three o'clock the compounder led a course straight for Port Dover, and simultaneously with their movement the auxiliary cruiser slipped down from Port Rowan. Mile after mile, steaming slowly, the fleet of tugs approached the port in which the captured American boats were held. At dawn they had come to within half a mile of the town. Then the compounder darted eastward. In their battle-ship line they steamed boldly past the *Vigilant*, gave a simultaneous blast of their whistles, and with their crews shouting themselves hoarse with joy struck a course for the town of Dunkirk.

Meanwhile, in the unguarded Canadian fishing-grounds, forty miles away, twenty-one Erie fish-tugs were making the biggest catch of the season. When they came into port they brought fifty-two tons of Canadian herring, and that afternoon a check for six thousand dollars was handed to Captain Town by the manager of one of the big fish companies.

That evening a deputation of fish pirates, headed by Captain Town, called upon Mrs. William Burton. Jim Falkner accompanied them until he could see the lights of Josephine's home. Then he stopped. For a few moments he and the fish-pirate captain stood alone, and their hands met in a firm grip. "Falkner," said the master of the compounder, "this was your scheme. I want to tell them so. I want to let Miss Jo know that the biggest thing that ever happened in Erie came from an idea of yours. I want—"

"She would never forgive me, Captain," interrupted the young man. "I don't believe she would ever let me see her again. She will regard the whole thing as a piece of charity, and she will fight it—hard! Remember, it's for the mother. It's a six-thousand-dollar ransom taken from the Canadians for Burton's death—and it comes from the fishermen of Erie. Please leave me out!"

Captain Town returned to the waiting men and Falkner watched them until they disappeared into the cottage, but he stood in the deep shadow of a tree and waited. An almost over-mastering desire came upon him to enter the cottage and ask the girl to share her life with him. The sound of voices from a near-by shrub brought him out of his reverie. Several minutes passed before he noticed two forms coming toward him and as they approached he recognized Burton's girl.

Her companion was a tall, good-looking athletic man in his early thirties. They seemed very happy and obviously in love. When they reached a few yards from where Falkner stood the man drew the girl toward him and said in anxious tones, "I love you, Jo. Won't you give me your answer to-night? I imagine you have changed since you met this Jim Falkner and I'm afraid. Do you care for him?"

Though eavesdropping was not one of the young reporter's accomplishments, there seemed to be no place to which he might go; and after what he had already heard, disclosure of his presence in the near-by shadows was unthinkable.

The girl hesitated a moment and then said, "No, dear, I like him—but I do not love him. I'll marry you whenever you are ready!"

They moved on slowly, but Jim Falkner remained where he had hidden himself without realizing how rapidly the moments were slipping away. An hour later the cottage door reopened and the men filed out. As they came out at the gate, he joined them.

"It was a hard rub, Falkner," said Captain Town, "but we made the little widow take it!" Then glancing at the young man's face, the captain continued, "Why what—"

"I'm glad, Captain, very glad indeed. It will make it— easier for her."

The Sturgeon

George Vukelich

BIOLOGISTS DID NOT always know that the sea lamprey,
which came into the Great Lakes through the St. Lawrence
River, destroyed the lake trout. Instead, they blamed the decline
of the trout on overfishing by commercial fishermen. The lakes
states passed laws requiring that the mesh of the gill nets be
smaller and sent wardens to the docks to inspect the catches.
As Vukelich describes it:

> They dumped out the fish boxes and kicked up the cracked
> ice and the steel barrels of trout guts for the pig farmers.
> They were looking carefully for undersized fish . . . and
> the fishermen lifted their illegal nets at night even when
> the Coast Guard storm signals were out. [It was] the season
> of the state guns and the legislature against the commercial
> fishermen and the lampreys swimming down the St. Law-
> rence silently from the Atlantic Ocean.

"The Sturgeon" is an accurate portrayal of those times, of an
old Two Rivers, Wisconsin, family, and of the mightiest of Great
Lakes fishes. Although the actions of the sturgeon in this story
may seem improbable, they are not, as any commercial fisherman
will attest. Papa Le Clair's battle with the sturgeon is reminiscent
of another old man's struggle in *The Old Man and the Sea,* for

both Papa and Santiago are legendary fishermen who meet, at last, their most worthy adversaries.

THE STATE WARDENS were waiting on the high skinny docks when Germaine swung the *Ione* into the harbor mouth. The old man came back and squeezed into the tight pilot house.

"It makes a man mad to see them waiting," he said finally. Germaine sucked on his pipe and stared out through the flat dirty windows.

"They have guns," he said.

Bebe looked at the men on the pier with the herring gulls rising around them as the *Ione* closed slowly and the barb-sharp stink of river smells came in from the flat water.

"What about the sturgeon?" Bebe said to his father. "Is that why they're waiting for us?"

"I don't think they know anything about the sturgeon," the old man said. "You get up to the bow now and tell Raphael to take the stern. Tell your brothers to just unload as always. We are all right, understand? Don't even think about the sturgeon." The boy said "yes," and he went down the deck.

The state men didn't move all the while the fish-tug was mooring. None of the fishermen said anything, and after the engine cut and coughed out, the only sounds left in Bebe's ears were the silvery gull screams and the boots of his brothers slopping around the hold and getting into position to take off the fish boxes.

The wardens moved closer together and took out cigarettes and were talking low, and watching the work. They all looked like strangers to Bebe. Germaine and the old man might know them, though, and he looked to the pilot house. It was hard to see because the sun made a mirror out of the wheel-house window, and they didn't come out right away. When they did, Germaine was knocking out his pipe against the heel of his hand and coming over to the boy.

"Come on," he said, sliding the pipe stem-first into his shirt pocket. "We better give those watchdogs something to watch."

Bebe and Germaine carried the fish box from the boat onto the dock and set it down by the river wall of the gear-shack, next to the boxes already unloaded. As they walked back for another box, the state wardens moved forward and stood to one side, smoking.

The old man came up the bleached boards holding the keys to the gear-shack.

Germaine and Bebe hauled the very last fish box into shore, and the state men shifted toward the old man. The big one in the middle turned and spoke. "Le Clair?"

The old man stopped. "Yes?"

"George Le Clair," the warden said. "Is that you?"

"That's me," the old man said.

"We want to see your catch."

"It's all in the fish boxes—packed up in the ice."

The wardens looked down at the wet boxes at their feet. The one who was doing all the talking addressed the old man again. "You wouldn't have any undersized fish packed in the bottoms, would you?"

"No," the old man said. "I wouldn't have any undersized fish."

"That's what they all say," the warden said turning to the others. "It's the same every time." He turned back to the old man.

"All right," he said. "You might as well dump out the boxes."

"I am all legal," the old man said.

"You better be," the warden said. "We want to look at those boxes."

The old man seemed to sag and his sons stood watching him helplessly. "You have the guns," he said softly.

"We don't want to use them," the warden said. He pointed

to the boy. "All right; we can save the talking for some other time. Start dumping out those boxes now."

The boy looked around at the old man and at Germaine and at his brothers.

"It doesn't seem right to ask him to dump out the boxes," Germaine said, "since he spent the whole morning filling them up."

"You do it then," the warden said.

"You go to hell," Germaine said.

"What's your name?" the warden asked.

"Le Clair," Germaine said. "Germaine Le Clair. L-e-c-l-a-i-r. And I said you can go to hell."

"You gonna dump these boxes or are we?"

"We are all legal," the old man said. "We have no small laketrout."

"That's what all you bastards say. All right—we'll find out." The three wardens bent and upturned every fish box, and the deck exploded under the impact of chunked ice and skittering trout bodies. The pier looked like a slaughter-house floor. The wardens poked among the gutted fish with their toes and measured with their eyes.

Germaine got out his pipe and began to pack it.

"Notice, my friend," he said to the big warden. "The scar holes on the laketrout's bodies. The lamprey eels are killing the trout. Why don't you pass a law against the lamprey eels?"

"We just want you to stick by the law you got." They stood staring down at the fang-like scars in the trout bodies.

"You know where you can stick your law," Germaine said.

The big warden's face rippled a little, like a windshift over a sandbar. "Le Clair," he said. "Germaine Le Clair." He was going to say some more, but instead he stopped and the smile came back. "We're not looking for trouble, Le Clair. We're only doing a job. You commercial fishermen overfished the laketrout. The state of Wisconsin passed a law to protect the laketrout and you bootleg and break that law, and so the state of Wisconsin sends us here to make that law stick." The warden closed his eyes and he looked like a schoolboy reciting from memory. "If you got a grievance, take it to the Legislature. We don't make the laws, Le Clair. We just make them stick." The warden stopped and slowly opened his eyes. "That's how it stands, fisherman. You brought it on yourselves."

Germaine pulled the pipe from his mouth. "Why don't they outlaw the lamprey eels, as I said, instead of the fishermen? That's what's killing the laketrout."

The warden's voice was very low when he finally spoke. "They say there's a lot of illegal sturgeon taken in nets up here too." He stared at Germaine. "Don't make it hard for yourself, fisherman." Then he turned and led the other state men off the dock and up the rickety bleached steps to the street level.

The Le Clair brothers started to load up the loose fish in all the boxes, and everybody began talking at once.

"We could clean up on them easy," Raphael said. "We could beat the living Jesus out of them."

"That is true," Roger said. "We could show them a little steel sometime. I think they would run from a gill-knife. I think—" Roger stopped in the middle of his sentence because a trout fish caught him full in the chest. He stared at Germaine dumbly.

"When you talk like that," Germaine snapped, "you are not thinking. They could put us all on the beach. Don't you forget it. They could beach the old man."

Raphael spoke then and Bebe got a frightened feeling at the angry voice. "That big warden scared you, Germaine? Did he take the living guts right out of you?"

"All right," Germaine said, sucking out the words, "shut up now!"

"Maybe that young widow woman has taken the living guts out of him," Raphael said.

"It's not the guts she's taking," Roger said.

"All right," Germaine snapped. "Both of you at once, or

each by himself. It makes no difference. Come ahead, Goddammit," he bellowed. "Come and show me you are men."

Raphael and Roger stood like stone and looked at each other and then slowly crouched and moved on Germaine.

"Enough!" The word was like a gaff hook. It was the old man, and his great beaten face was white and looked like a trout belly. "Enough! My own flesh and blood fighting like dogfish?" The old man turned away.

Everyone stopped and the old man walked to the door of the gear-shack and stood there. No one did anything until Germaine put out his hand and shook with Raphael and with Roger.

"We can't fight them here," Germaine said. "They are the law and they could break the old man. That's what I meant—only that."

The brothers said they understood, but it was hard to keep from using their hands on somebody. They smiled slowly at each other, and then they all went back to picking up the gutted trout and repacking them in the fish boxes.

"Go by the old man," Germaine said to Bebe, slapping his buttocks. "We're all right here now."

Bebe asked what he should do there.

"Just stand by him," Germaine said, and he smiled. "Let him rub your curly little head."

Bebe always felt like a little girl when the old man did that, but he went and stood by his father.

"They take it out on each other," the old man said, "but it is my fault. They would fight the guns like that."

He stood by the old man a long time and finally thought his father didn't even know he was there any more. The old man was just looking out over the lake where there was nothing to be seen. No smoke on the horizon marking an ore boat, downbound from the lake-head. No shifting clouds of scavenger gulls marking dead fish or garbage. There was nothing that the boy could see at all.

"What are you looking at, Papa?" he asked finally. The old

man didn't answer right away, and Bebe asked him again, just to let him know that he was still there. It was a strange feeling to be watching his father and not having the old man know he was there.

"Bebe," the old man said softly, "I am looking at the greatest sturgeon in all this water. In all this world."

Bebe thought about the big armored fish in their pot-net[1] and he shivered. "Is that the greatest sturgeon fish ever?"

The old man looked down at him for the first time. "The greatest one, Bebe," and then he smiled and rubbed Bebe's head. "The greatest one ever."

Then the old man touched him on the arm as he always did when Bebe was to leave him, and Bebe went back to where his brothers were working and got down on his knees and began picking up fish. They watched the old man walk slowly into the gear-shack.

"There is not much time left for the old man," Roger said. "It's like watching the strong nets rotting."

Germaine looked up at Bebe. "What did the old man say to you?"

"He was talking about the sturgeon," Bebe said.

Germaine was silent for a time, and then nodded his head. "He knows." No one said anything, and it didn't make sense to Bebe that his brothers didn't say anything more to Germaine's words.

"He knows what?" he asked. "That this is the greatest sturgeon fish ever?"

"Even so," Germaine said. "That's what he knows."

"Have you ever seen a greater fish?" Bebe asked.

"No," Germaine said. "This is the greatest of them all."

Germaine never took Bebe along in the dory when they went out to the nets at night to lift an illegal sturgeon, and now a

---

1. A pound or pond net, used for fishing close to shore.

tingling chill moved over his back as he thought of this greatest of all sturgeon fish locked and trapped in the sunken pot-net on the fish grounds.

"Can I go when you take him out—when you go for the sturgeon?"

"It's a man's work, Bebe," Roger said.

"It is three men's work," Raphael said. "This sturgeon is no perch-fish, Bebe."

"Please, Germaine," he said. "I can help you."

"No."

"Please, Germaine. Please."

"No, Bebe. Do not beg."

"I can help you."

"No."

"Please, Germaine."

"Your turn will come."

"Please, Germaine."

"Dammit," Germaine bellowed. "No, Bebe. Now enough!"

Slowly Germaine bent to his work with the brothers, and suddenly Bebe wanted to swear at them all and hit them—and see them hurt and bleeding. He picked up a laketrout and flung it like a rock into Germaine's face. It slopped loosely in his slickered lap.

"Goddamn you," he screamed. "Goddamn you! I'm not a baby!" And then he shook and cried and closed his eyes as tightly as he could. He wanted Germaine to hit him as hard as he could, and then he would be hurt and bleeding, and then before he died he would forgive Germaine everything and feel Germaine's beard against his face. When Bebe opened his eyes Germaine was not even looking at him.

"He goes," Germaine said. "Bebe goes."

"In place of who?" Roger asked.

"In place of no one," Germaine said. "The three of us and Bebe. We make room for him."

Bebe crouched like a puppy and felt the tears on his face.

"What of the old man?" Raphael asked.

"He is not to know," Germaine said. "Until perhaps later. Bebe," he continued, looking at the boy directly for the first time, "you will come with us after the sturgeon, but you will not tell a word to the old man at all. Do you understand? Not a word to Mamma either!"

Bebe nodded slowly. The chill began on his back again, and though he tried to control it his whole body shook a little bit, even though the sun was like hot water on his back.

"Now," Germaine said, "don't think about that any more."

Bebe almost shouted out the words as he asked his brothers the most important question of all. "Are we going after the sturgeon *tonight?*"

"Tonight," Germaine said, and then from his lap he picked up the trout thrown at him and gently lobbed it into the fish box. "Now think of something else, Bebe. And say for the old man's great fish a few Hail Marys."

"They never say that in school . . . to pray for a fish," he said. "A fish is not like people."

"Why not?" Roger said. "People are like fish."

Bebe didn't understand but Roger didn't laugh, and so he prayed to the Blessed Virgin for the great sturgeon.

"And what shall I pray for," Bebe said in a moment. "I mean, should I pray for something special for this fish?"

"Just pray that he has a happy death," Germaine said. "That's all a great fish can want."

Bebe still did not understand completely, but his brothers all fell silent, and so he was silent too, although his lips moved as they always did in school when he said his prayers to himself—half whispering and seeing the Blessed Virgin Mary wearing her blue robe and smiling like his mother in the pictures of her when she was young.

Germaine watched Bebe carefully and slowly wipe the fish-wet of the laketrout from his face.

At the supper table, the talk was all of the big sturgeon in the pot-net nearly a mile out in the lake. The brothers spoke carefully of getting the fish out, and Bebe nearly burst with the excitement of listening and knowing he would be helping them, yet not being able to talk about it in front of the old man. The booming of the surf outside sharpened his senses like barbed hooks, and he could see the great six-foot body of the sturgeon rolling like some animal fenced in by the cable-like nets. He went to the kitchen window and stared out over the darkening lake. The old man rubbed his head as he went by to the living room for the pipe and tobacco.

Then Bebe was aware of his mother and the laundry starch smell of her as she held him by the shoulders. He just stood there waiting for her to let him go.

"This is not a life for an honest man, Bebe." She was speaking as if to herself. "To sneak like a thief for the illegal sturgeon fish and always the deep waters waiting. You must not bring a woman into this life, Bebe." Then she released him quickly and he followed her back to the table.

"There is a heavy swell running," his mother said loudly. "It is going to storm. I do not think that you can lift tonight."

"We can lift tonight, all right," Roger said, moving his cup for more coffee. "Or any night of the blessed week for that matter."

"Can you not wait for a quiet night?"

"What's to wait, Mamma?" Raphael said. "The state wardens are like mosquitoes on quiet nights. A little wind and a little sea running will hold them to the beach like flies."

"Yes? And what of this excitement for your father? You all know what the doctor said."

Bebe did not know anything about a doctor at all.

"What did the doctor say, Mamma?" he asked.

"Mamma," Germaine said quickly, "you are making the excitement. We must get the fish out of there tonight or he tears up the nets and the whole rig comes out for repair."

His mother started to interrupt.

"Now, enough," Germaine said, raising his hand. "That fish is in our pot-net and he comes out tonight."

"What about the doctor?" Bebe repeated loudly, and no one answered because at the moment the old man came into the kitchen, lighting his pipe. He walked slowly to the head of the table and seated himself. After he got the pipe going strong and there were blue clouds of smoke around his head, he leaned back and folded his arms.

"Now then, Bebe," he said. "What about what doctor?"

Bebe said that he didn't know anything about a doctor at all.

"That is a true statement of fact," the old man said. "You do not know about the doctor because no one here thinks that you are a man. If they thought you were a man, then you would know about the doctor." He pulled the pipe from his mouth and stared at the bowl. "Are you a man, Bebe?"

He did not know what the old man was talking about but it made his mother mad. "What foolishness are you filling the boy with?" she snapped. "What good will it do for him to know?"

"Every good in the world. Even a minnow learns from the big fish, Mamma. This will do him every good in the world." At his words she turned her head sharply to one side and that was a sure sign that she was very angry.

"Bebe," the old man began, "I believe you are a man, or perhaps I say this only to be the first to say it. A man must see things always as they are, and not be pretending things are not that way."

Bebe didn't know what to say and then the old man started talking again. "Everything in this world, Bebe. Everything that is living, must one day die. That is the way things are."

Bebe got a very cold feeling inside, and he remembered when his class at school had to go to the little girl's funeral who had fallen into the river and drowned by the bridge.

"No one knows when he is going to die, Bebe. I cannot tell you and you cannot tell me. Some people do not like to think about dying at all, but that is pretending. Anyway, no one can tell for sure when you will die. Except perhaps a person like a doctor, Bebe."

"Did the doctor say when you were going to die, Papa?"

"Yes, Bebe. That is what the doctor said."

Bebe did not know what to say. "When?" he asked loudly.

The old man looked at him and smiled.

"My very own word," he said. "My very first word. Tell me, Bebe, do you feel a little bigger now? Do you feel like a man at all?"

Bebe was so confused he did not know what to say. His brothers were smoking their cigarettes and staring down at their coffee cups. The old man seemed to be the only happy person there. He beckoned to Bebe with his pipe and Bebe went to stand by his side.

"It is the heart," the old man said, fixing the young fingers on his pulse. "Feel it now for a moment."

No one moved, and the beat of his father's heart pounded up Bebe's arm like a man hammering on a bent nail and stopping and hammering again.

"The doctor says that very soon, this—this hammering—will stop. Then I will be dead. It is very much like the old engine in the fish-tug before we got this one. It simply runs down and breaks, Bebe. That is all. That is living—or rather—that is dying."

No one said anything until the mother spoke.

"What of the sturgeon now? The wardens will be watching."

"We will get him out tonight," the old man said. "He is money in the bank."

Raphael agreed. "We can peddle him in Milwaukee like nothing."

"Tail and all," Roger said.

"*You* will get him out," the mother said angrily, glancing at her husband. "What do you mean *you?*"

"The boys and I will go for him tonight."

"The boys and you!" She turned angry again. "Are you gone crazy in your old age? I will not let you leave this house. You will kill yourself with that fish. And what of the wardens? My God!"

"I will not die in jail," the old man said. "Not an old gull like me. They would have every fisherman an outlaw. What the hell. Is it against the law for a man to feed his family?"

No one said anything.

"A black, rough night," the old man said. "They won't be able to see their noses."

The brothers looked like they wanted to do something for the old man.

"I think it will be all right tonight, Pa," Germaine said. "I don't think this fish will give us any trouble."

The old man started to argue with Germaine. "This last one time," he said. "I wanted to go for one last great fish." He looked at his sons. "It is something a man understands, I think."

Germaine nodded his head in agreement. "We would like you to come, Pa, except that we will be crowded in the boat tonight."

"There would be just the four of us," the old man said.

"The five of us," Germaine corrected him. "Since this morning we have agreed that our brother Bebe is to help us tonight."

"Bebe?" The old man's hand came crashing down on the table and everything rattled. "Bebe! I forbid it. A boy to go after that sturgeon? Germaine, you do not act wisely with your talk. Is this your doing?"

"This is Bebe's doing," Germaine said. "This morning he declared to us that he was a man. We believe him, and we count him one of us now."

The old man relaxed his hold on the table and turned slowly to look at the boy. "This is so, Bebe?"

"Yes, sir."

"And you are a man now? A man?"

Before Bebe could answer, Germaine was speaking. "You yourself said so, Pa. When you told him about the doctor."

The old man stared at his sons without speaking, and then he pulled Bebe to him and asked that he feel the pulse again. As the erratic hammering came up the boy's arm, the old man smiled and then slapped him on the buttocks.

"So then, your first great fish! For the old man this one, yes?" Bebe told him yes. "So Bebe will no more be Bebe? We are all men here now."

The brothers began to smile, and Bebe thought the old man was going to stroke his head again but he didn't.

"What did he say?" the old man asked. "How did you know this manhood was upon him?"

Germaine rubbed his nose. "He threw a trout into my face. A very large splendid fish."

The old man shook his head and punched Bebe's arm. "You did not want to miss him at all, it seems."

The old man called for whisky glasses then and said that he wanted to drink once with his menfolk all together. The mother didn't exactly smile, but she did what he asked.

"And bring a glass for Bebe also," the old man said. "This day he has a little something with his ginger ale."

He pulled the boy close again, and Bebe could hear his brothers laughing and the pounding of the old man's heart and, over all, the Lake Michigan surf boiling onto the beachlands beyond the dunes.

Bebe did not know if it was the excitement of actually starting for the pot-nets or the rolling water that dipped under the dory, but when they were a half-mile out from shore his mouth filled up with supper and the taste of whisky and he hung over the gunwales and was sick. The wind was blowing in straight off the lake. It carried cold spray into the back of his neck, and he wanted to huddle under a thwart and fall asleep. It was completely dark without stars or moon, and the wind and the waves moving sounded like a thousand waterfalls. Only the long, swinging yellowbeam of Point Beach light seemed secure and not floating. They were jammed into the little dory, like survivors on a raft, and Bebe was afraid because they were thrown about so much and he couldn't see anything around them.

He reached his hand down over the gunwale, and as they dipped the water swallowed up his hand and part of his jacket sleeve. He wiped his mouth and face clean. Then he heard Germaine yelling in his ear. "How do you feel now?"

He told Germaine he felt all right. "I was feeding the fish a little bit," he said.

Germaine slapped him on the leg. "She is rough tonight, man." He was still speaking, but the wind was blowing away his words.

"What did you say?" Bebe yelled.

"I said we are almost there now."

"The hell you say," Roger shouted. He and Raphael were working the oars, and they hadn't said anything at all until now. Roger was still talking but the boy couldn't hear, and he yelled at Roger. Roger's voice came back slicing the wind like a knife.

"You were feeding the fishes, hey?" There was laughter on the wind.

Bebe still felt sick and was breathing in every time the dory went up and breathing out when it went down in the wave troughs. He was glad Germaine was not asking him anything so he would have to talk.

They just kept rising and falling and sliding, and he tried hard not to think about anything that would bring back the sickness. He watched the Point Beach light swinging around, and he counted one-hundred thirty-nine revolutions and then stopped counting. He watched the light so long it seemed to be getting closer, and he had the feeling they were sliding stern first back onto the old man's beach.

Then Germaine was shading a flashlight in his hands, and

snapping it on and off and swinging it quickly. In the bending beam of the little light Bebe could see the forest of spiletops that poked out of the rolling waters like fence posts and the webby stiff glistening nets that strung out in great sprawling perimeters. They were in the fish-grounds.

Instinctively, his brothers had their position fixed and the light snapped out, and they pulled for the lead side of the pot-net—the side that could be loosened and lifted, the side to which they would moor while they brought up the net and the great sturgeon. They made fast to two towering spiles with bow and stern lines, and the water rolled through the nets and lifted and banged them into the spile sticks with a grinding, crushing sound.

"Keep your arms and hands inside," Germaine shouted. "She plays for keeps tonight."

The lead lines of the pot-net were loosened from the spiles, and they began the work of lifting the net by hand. As the sturgeon was free to swim around in the pot-net, the plan was to raise the net under him, forcing him to the surface where he could be shot and hauled into the boat.

The net was tarred stiff like iron cable and it seemed to weigh tons. Germaine and Bebe were in the stern, Roger and Raphael up front. Bebe knew he was not much help to Germaine because Roger was calling constantly about the net coming up evenly.

"Your end," Roger would shout. "Your end, Germaine!"

"My end," Germaine would mutter. "My Royal Canadian end. All right, pull, Bebe. Put your back into it. Now, *pull!*" They pulled and pulled, and together they rested and held their purchase and felt the current working against them below, and then they pulled again. It seemed like hours were going by every time the Point Beach light swung past, and then the nets were swinging too, and the spiles and their dory, and the boy was convinced that the light was stationary and not moving, and that he was swinging past the light like a stone on a string.

"Germaine," Roger yelled. "The light! I think we have him up."

Bebe's pulse nearly pounded out of his temples.

Germaine played the flashlight out over the pot-net. "There he is, Bebe! Look at the size of him."

The sturgeon rolled on the surface like some heavy log and sank out of sight. He was longer than a man. Germaine snapped out the light. "Another ten feet," he yelled.

"Ten, all right," Roger answered.

"Another ten feet, Bebe. Then our net will be under his belly. He has no place to go but up. Pull, Bebe, *pull!*"

The ten feet of net came up slowly like scrap iron. "I can't pull any more," Bebe said. "My hands are raw."

"Pull, Bebe! Just hold tight like for your life. Pull for the old man's sturgeon fish, Bebe. Pull!"

They got the ten feet. The boy didn't know how. He was crying. The net was taut, like a floor under the fish. The sturgeon had only a few feet of water and then the iron-cabled net.

"Now, Bebe," Germaine said. He worked the net around the spiles somehow so that it hung, and then he switched on the flash and handed it to Bebe and loaded the rifle. "Keep the light on his head, Bebe. On his head. On his head!"

The boy watched the glistening armored body as it twisted and rolled in the wash of water. He grabbed hold of a spile to steady the light, and then Germaine fired and Bebe bolted upright from the thwart. The fish was thrashing against the net like an animal against a cage. Tears were blinding the boy.

"Bebe, get down!" Roger was screaming. "Get down!"

The the dory lifted as the water slid into them with a sickening slow rush, and the boy toppled into the water. *The flashlight,* he thought. *The flashlight will get wet. The flashlight is not waterproof.* That is what the boy was thinking and then the flashlight and everything else went out, and there was warm water filling up his nose.

The next thing he knew, the flashlight was swinging

around and around his head like a stone on a string. He tried
to grab for it before it went to the bottom.

"How do you feel, Bebe?" Germaine's face was in front of him,
but upside down. Then the boy knew he was lying down between
Germaine's knees, and Germaine was behind him and bending
over him.

"I fell in," he said.

"You were going to feed the fish again, eh?" Germaine
pulled something around the boy's neck and he knew that it was
Germaine's jacket.

"Hey," Germaine called. "Bebe's okay. He sends his love."

Roger and Raphael began talking at once.

"I feel very religious tonight," Germaine said. "First we
baptize him and then we wet-nurse him."

"That describes Germaine like I never heard," Roger said.

"I'm sorry I fell in," Bebe said.

"She was rough tonight," Germaine said. "It could happen
to anyone."

"That fish knew you meant business," Roger said. "When
he saw you come into the pot-net I thought he'd have died of
fright."

"Where is the fish?" Bebe asked.

"We are all sitting on top of him, the big bastard!"

"If he was any bigger he could have this boat all to
himself."

"Close your eyes now, Bebe. We will be on the beach in
a little while now."

The boy watched the slickered wide backs of Roger and
Raphael swing toward him and then away and then back again.
He felt with his legs under the thwarts, and he could feel the
sturgeon fish. He remembered what the old man said about this
great fish . . . *The oldest thing in these fresh waters. Before there
was this world, and even before that, there was this fish in these
waters swimming . . . The skin like rocks all wrapped in steel . . .*

Feeding, it must have fed on the bottoms where the beaches are now . . . Always swimming. It must have moved along and against the currents for a million years without touching shores . . . Without touching shores. Without touching shores.

They pulled for shore and the boy straddled the terrible stone body with his legs. *For a million years, where the beaches are now.*

He remembered what Germaine had told him that morning and he prayed that the great fish had a happy death. He was very sleepy and warm, and the boat was rocking less now, and the wind was far away.

"Is Papa going to die?" he said out loud, although he did not mean to ask it. There was no answer and he began to think he had only put the question to himself after all.

"We are all going to die, Bebe," the answer came back.

And because of being sleepy, and the rocking and the far-away wind, he could not tell who it was that finally answered. He tried very hard to know who it was, but then he could not tell at all.

They carried the sturgeon up the beach in the dark and the boy held the door open as his brothers struggled the fish into the house and down into the fruit cellar. The old man came to watch in his slippers, with his pipe dead in his mouth. They watched him without talking because they knew he was thinking and going to say something, and they did not want to spoil it by speaking first.

"It is a great one, this fish," the old man said. "There will be no other like this one."

He turned and Germaine closed the fruit cellar door, and they followed the old man upstairs and into the kitchen.

Germaine got out the bottle of brandy, poured the shots, and handed the glasses around. The water from their slickers and the boots puddled on the floor, and the boy felt the excitement of being a real part of this for the first time. This was a ritual on the Fisherman's Beach: to drink a toast to the great illegal fish that were fought out of the nets the hard way—at night with a big sea running, and the pot-nets lifted by hand and everything against the law.

Germaine smiled and gave Bebe mostly ginger ale and not much whisky, but that did not change the boy's feeling at all. He felt the slime on his hands, and saw it on the sides of the glass, and thought of the great stone body in the basement. *The oldest thing in the fresh waters.*

"So then," the old man said. "How did it go, Bebe, your first great fish?"

The boy thought about being sick in the boat and falling into the pot-net, and the fear he had of the sturgeon.

"Good," he said. "It went good, Papa."

"That is the way," the old man said. "With me tonight it went hard. We waited, Mamma and me, like two old women. She was wanting you back here with her, and I was wanting to be out there with you." The old man sighed. "That is the way."

"Yes, sir," the boy said because he did not know what else to say.

"It is not so easy at night," the old man said. "It takes a good man at night in the small dory."

Germaine cleared his throat and motioned with his glass to the old man. "Pa. You toast, Pa. This is your fish."

"No," the old man said. "No. This is not my fish, but I toast this last time." He looked at the boy. "Bebe, for you! For your fish!" He held up the heavy green glass. "You will see many great things from this water and on the beach." He stopped and looked squarely at the boy. "Do not be afraid of them. To Bebe!" He held out the glass.

"To Bebe!" the brothers answered. The glasses clinked and the brothers looked into the boy's eyes, while the boy sipped from the drink and Germaine refilled the glasses with his bottle and told the old man how it was on the water, leaving out only about the boy falling into the net.

"I have been thinking tonight," the old man said, "about these wardens."

"Those bastards!" Roger said.

"That makes nothing," the old man said. "I have been thinking about how to change the law for the nets."

The brothers looked at each other and back at the old man. The boy knew the look in their eyes to be pity.

"I am not crazy," the old man said. "I will go to Madison."

"Pa," Roger said patiently. "You can't lobby against those bastards."

"I do not go to lobby," the old man said. "I will go to make the law of this land."

"You mean politics?"

"Even so. I will go as a State Senator," the old man smiled. "The warden told you how many friends I have with the lake-trout fishermen. Good. They will elect me and I will go. I will tell our story to the whole state—about these sea lampreys."

Germaine finished pouring the brandy, and the brothers looked at each other and shifted on their feet and no one said anything.

"You're damned right," Germaine said finally. "It's a good idea, Pa. We need you down there."

The boy saw how the old man was full of color again and talking and using his hands like he did when the *Ione* was over the fish grounds and the work was fast and hard and plentiful and there was almost no time to think.

"Bebe steps into my shoes," the old man said. "It is not so bad to be on the beach then."

"You are a tough old gull, Pa."

Then the thrashing noises came like crashing glass from the basement. The old man, because he was standing in front of the cellar door, was the first through it. Bebe did not know if it was a dream or he had fainted or was in shock, or dead. When he followed them down, the old man had it all done. The white fruit cellar was horrible with broken glass and berry juice. The old man was straddling the sturgeon with his back to his sons and the hatchet for kindling raised over his head, flashing and falling, flashing and falling like the breakers on the beach until the sturgeon stopped its swimming motion on the concrete floor and shivered like a man in the cold.

Bebe closed his eyes, and squeezed them tightly, and prayed, and when he opened his eyes again the old man was standing, leaning in the doorway, with his mouth closed, breathing deeply through his nose. His bathrobe was flung with blood and smashed-down berries and juice, and he looked past his older sons, watching Bebe closely. The slime from the hatchet dripped onto the concrete and then the hatchet dropped from his hand and the old man slumped and fell forward to the floor.

The boy screamed and Germaine leaped to the old man and bent over, and the boy closed his eyes. It was all a dream—a dream. A dream. Dear God. Sweet God.

Bebe opened his eyes and Roger and Raphael were slowly rising from around the old man and looking at each other. The boy was afraid to ask the question because of what the answer would be.

Germaine ran his hand over the old man's face and wiped the blood away and closed the old man's eyes and smoothed his hair.

"The fish was dead!" Roger said. "My God, the fish was dead!"

Germaine looked up and his face was painful to watch. "I did not shoot him cleanly," Germaine said. "It is my fault. I should have shot him again."

They stared down at the old man and their faces were wet with slime and water, and still the boy knew they were crying. The fish, the sturgeon, had killed the old man. The boy ran to the black fish body and kicked it until it slid heavily. The boy kicked it again and again. "God damn you," he cried. "God damn you! God damn you!"

Then he felt his arms pinned and his feet lifted from the

floor, and he was staring into Germaine's wet bearded face. "No, Bebe," Germaine was saying gently yet rapidly. "No, Bebe, no, no!"

Germaine held him tightly, off the floor, and then the boy began to sob and Germaine led him to the basement steps and they sat down together. Germaine took out cigarettes and the brothers stood there smoking and looking at the glistening floor of the fruit cellar.

The boy blinked and blinked and blinked his eyes, and finally there were no more tears to come and he stared at the two bodies on the basement floor and he huddled against Germaine.

"They were two great hearts," Germaine said, gently rubbing the boy's head. "There is no reason to feel bad for anybody."

The boy stared and then the tears began again and he closed his eyes tightly and bit his lips and he plunged his head into Germaine's lap and cried, for the last time, like a baby.

"Bois Blanche Island Light." (Courtesy Leo V. Kuschel.)

Lighthouses and Lockkeepers

"Ah come with me" you cry,
"Each day you tend this lock, you're one day older,
While your blood grows colder."

But that anchor chain's a fetter,
And with it you are tethered to the foam,
And I wouldn't trade your life for one hour of home.
"The Lock-Keeper"
Stan Rogers

Ballast Island

Constance Fenimore Woolson

WOOLSON WAS a literary pioneer in many ways. She was the first woman to write fiction about the Great Lakes, one of the first northerners to write of the Reconstruction South, and one of the first serious artists of the post–Civil War period. A witty realist who despised the sentimental romantic fiction of her day, she became one of the first American women writers to create strong, independent women characters who renounce love and survive by determination and effort. But Woolson supported herself and her mother by writing, and since her marketplace demanded that any story involving romance must end in marriage, she often tempered her instincts to give readers what they expected. That compromise is evident in this story, one of her earliest, in which the fate of the lightkeeper, Miss Jonah, rings like a buoy amid the shining waters of romance, a warning to the credulous young female reader that not all love ends happily.

Her marketplace was also hungry for what is now called local color fiction—stories of curious characters who live in remote areas—which had caught the fancy of the public as the United States was discovering itself after the Civil War. The hallmark of this style of writing was the presupposition that one's readers were of a different class than one's characters, that they were better educated (thus Woolson's many classical allusions), and had more money and more leisure. The form is inherently condescending to the people written about, but Woolson manages to rise above its limitations by creating characters like Miss Jonah, who is very different from the frozen, withered, insane creatures that populate much other fiction of this kind. She stands on her island like a figure in a Winslow Homer painting, looking out to sea from a great height and radiating a feeling of security and power.

Miss Jonah's island is one of the Lake Erie Islands that had been Woolson's summer playground since childhood and figured several times in her work. She sets several stories and a travel article at summer resorts frequented by vacationers, many of whom were, like herself, from Cleveland. But despite her familiarity with the area, "Ballast Island" departs from reality in a number of ways, as any sailor who knows the Islands will recognize. Woolson's Ballast is probably Green Island, not only from the descriptions she gives, but also because there was no light on the real Ballast when Woolson knew it. While the inspiration for Miss Jonah may have been one of the several unmarried woman lightkeepers on the lakes in the mid-nineteenth century, her character came naturally to Woolson, a singular, lonely artist who never married and whose later life in Europe bore an uncanny resemblance to the lightkeeper's she had created twenty years before.

THE LAKE was blue, deep blue, and fairy wavelets broke on the island-beaches, each with its miniature foam-crest and gentle wash. The sun had vanished, but all the banners of his royal army flamed in the sky, a mighty host of colors marching down to the west, rank by rank, leaving vacant behind them the pale-golden field of the evening, where already an advance-guard of the night had appeared—the star Hesperus in his silver armor. The islands near and far were veiled in the shadows of twilight; familiar cliffs showed strange profiles, as if rock-deities had come to the surface to gaze over the water for a while; an unseen, whispering presence lurked in the groves; the caverns into which the wavelets ran put on an air of mystery, as if they might be fathomless; and Elizabeth forgot that only that very morning she had pushed her skiff within, and gathered the little shells from their utmost beach. Dusky vineyards, stretching from shore to shore, looked like enchanted labyrinths, in which a man might wander forever in a twilight that never changed; and the out-lying islands seemed hundreds of miles away, so vague and purple were their outlines in the golden haze. Only Lake Erie and its group of wine-islands—a Western archipelago, without poetry or fame, but beautiful as the charmed waters of the Old World! Fame, after all, is often but a question of time. If the Pacific held in store another undiscovered continent, we in our turn might hope to become classical: Grant might live again as a species of Hercules, Emerson as a Socrates, Theodore Thomas as an Orpheus, Bret Harte as a Horace, and dear, delightful Sothern as a Thespis; school-boys, several thousand years hence, might be translating "Dundreary," and pedants might be writing learned notes upon the Geological Society of the Stanislow. The wine-islands of Lake Erie, also, might then have their Sappho.[1]

But the Pacific holds no continent, and future generations will tread the same ground we are treading. No romantic pilgrims will sigh among the ruins of New York. We cannot hope to become classic. It takes a continent to discover a continent, and an age to discover an age, which, being interpreted, signifies that a prophet is not without honor, save in his own country.

Elizabeth Pyne was floating in a skiff alone on the blue water. Behind, on the island, stood the long, white hotel, with

---

1. Woolson is comparing famous Americans of her time to actual and leg-endary Greek figures. Theodore Thomas (1835–1905) was a violinist and conductor; Orpheus was a mythical poet so powerful he could move inanimate objects with his music; Edward A. Sothern (1826–1881) was an actor whose most famous role was Lord Dundreary in *Our American Cousin,* the play Lincoln was watching when he was assassinated; Thespis was the father of Greek tragedy. Sappho (ca. 620–565 B.C.) was a poetess and Woolson is making a sly comparison to herself here.

its rows of green blinds and piazzas, its oak-grove, and its little dock.[2] Here, during the summer months, came languid people from the Southwestern rivers—the Mississippi, the Tennessee, the Ohio—and from the Blue-Grass region; and here, in the early autumn, when the vineyards were purple, came the wiser people of the lake-cities, culling the best of the grapes and the weather, and bringing back full game-bags from their shooting-expeditions into the marshy wilderness of Sandusky Bay. The Southerners had gone back to their rivers, and the lake-city people were in possession. Already September had passed its meridian, but the golden weather held them in its spell. "Only one day more," they said to each other every evening; but still they remained, like the singers whose last appearances are long drawn out, dependent upon the lingering golden sunshine of popular favor.

But all the loveliness of air, earth, sky, and water, could not charm away from Elizabeth's mind the certainty that she was angry; her cheeks were flushed, her eyes shone, and by fits and starts she rowed with quick dashes, very different from the long, sweeping strokes natural to her skilled wrists and the peaceful evening. Needless to hesitate over the cause of this mood! Given a girl of beauty, a fair Juliet in anger, and instantly there arises, on the opposite side of the picture, a dark Romeo, who is the cause of all. In this case Romeo was Frederick Harper, and a clergyman, but a Romeo still, for he loved. He was a clergyman, but vigorous, energetic, and up even with the march of knowledge scientific, philosophic, and political; a man whom it did your heart good to see in the ranks; a man with brain, heart, and muscle enough for success in any of the worldly occupations, where fortunes are offered as prizes; a man who, capable of any thing, had chosen this. The thoughtless said: "What a pity!" But the earnest answered: "This is as it should be. Would that the greatest profession could always have the greatest! Whereas we all know how—" and a sigh closed the sentence.

---

2. Middle Bass Island.

Miss Pyne and Mr. Harper were in that lovely shadow-land of expectation through the vista of which there shines from beyond a golden light; the path leads toward it, but the vague aisles are full of enchantment, and the travellers linger to gather flowers, or step aside to follow the course of a brook, sure, however, to come back again to the beaten path, each time nearer and still nearer to the open sunshine beyond. In this case the plain words "Wilt thou?" had not been spoken; but, as the church-gossips said, "they understood each other." O busy tongues, ye spoke better than ye knew! To understand each other—what can express more? We all long to be understood; but only a rare, true love can penetrate to the sanctuary where each soul waits for its interpreter, as the beautiful sleeper in the wood waited for the prince. The mother thinks that she understands her child, but there are chambers in that daughter's heart which she can never enter. Sisters, brothers, friends, and, alas! even husbands and wives, live through life waiting, waiting, but the prince comes not. When we meet him, at last, face to face, that will be heaven enough for some of us.

Yes; Frederick and Elizabeth understood each other. They read the same books, and compared their opinions; they kept for each other treasure-troves of fugitive verses; they loved the same music—Mendelssohn, Wagner, and German folk-songs, with some of the plaintive negro melodies of the Southern rivers, for they did not belong to the musicians of one idea; the one-idea people become wearisome after a time. (Mont Blanc is grand, and we like to ascend to its summit; but must we therefore choose it as a residence? Great is classical music! And, having thus saluted it, we are quietly thankful that there are still cakes and ale.) They enjoyed the long personal conversations possible only to lovers, in which the hidden feelings come to the surface, and take delight in communion face to face. To each the other's mere presence made every-day life glorious. With Elizabeth, the whether or not to go always resolved itself into the question, "Shall I see him?" To Frederick, with whom the going was seldom a matter of choice, the possibility of enjoyment meant,

"Will she be there?" Generally she was. Clergymen are fortunate. Or is it unfortunate? They have a weekly round which they must tread; nor can they flit to the right or the left, as fancy might suggest. But Mohammed comes to the mountain. It is remarkable how that weekly round is brightened by the fair faces that smile upon its borders.

Elizabeth and Frederick understood each other—to a certain extent; but the woman was nervous from inaction, the man lethargic from fatigue. Elizabeth did so little that she was constantly longing for excitement; Frederick so much that he was constantly longing for rest. Spending an autumn vacation among the vineyards of the vine-islands, the young man gave way to a full enjoyment of that delicious brain-idleness which only a brain-worker can know; the cares and interests of a large city parish, with its dependent missions, were for the moment gone, and the pastor rested as he worked, fully. But Elizabeth needed no rest. She was charged with an overplus of vitality, energy unemployed made her restless, and urged her to numerous daring freaks. She proposed joining the hunting expeditions to Sandusky Bay; she was seized with a desire to visit the uninhabited Sister Islands, dimly visible on the horizon; she was sure that the grapes on Rattlesnake were sweeter than those in the vineyards near the hotel; why not try a midnight sail, or a sunrise fishing-party? To all of which Mr. Harper returned a lethargic "*Cui bono?*" and remained lying at ease upon the rocks, listening to the wash of the wavelets, and gazing dreamily off over the blue lake.

That evening Elizabeth had remarked, "I hate a humdrum life."

"Only humdrum people have humdrum lives," answered Frederick, sketching a little profile on a smooth lake-pebble.

"I hate humdrum people, then," pursued Elizabeth.

"So do I; that is, I am not fond of them."

"Every thing here is humdrum."

"What! This lovely view?"

"Yes, and every thing at Lakeport also," continued the young lady, aggressively.[3]

"Sad for Lakeport," answered the young clergyman, shading the countenance of his pebble portrait.

"There is no chivalry left in the world."

"But plenty of self-sacrifice."

"There is no romance."

"But plenty of love."

"I do not believe it," said Elizabeth, shortly. Now, Frederick might have gone on a mission then and there, and converted this unbeliever, but he was indolent, and so only smiled.

"I see nothing of it," continued Miss Pyne, advancing a step farther in search of excitement, going, indeed, to the extreme limit of her domain. No sooner had she thus spoken, than she became painfully aware of the significance of her words; but confusion changed rapidly into anger, when she perceived that no advantage was taken of them. An advance unnoticed, a retreat unpursued, are both mortifying. She waited a full minute, while Frederick Harper tranquilly darkened the eyelashes of his little stone face; then she rose and walked down the beach, angry with the world, with herself, but most of all with the tall, dark young man she left behind her. Frederick said to himself, "I will follow her in a moment," and went on with his sketch; to do him justice, he had no idea she was angry, for he had not taken in the full meaning of her words. Busy, practical men require some strong excitement to tone them up to all the infinite and delicate variations of a woman's feelings and moods; but there was no excitement in the hazy evening air, and, besides, the brain-worker was enjoying his annual rest. So he tarried. And when he followed, she was gone.

Around the rock-corner, out of sight, Elizabeth rowed her skiff, and the water showed no trace. She had never ventured out alone so late in the day, and therefore the masculine mind

---

3. Cleveland.

thought not of such a possibility; but what is precedent to a woman of the quicksilver type! "I will row over to the Rattlesnake," she said to herself, "it is but a short distance;" and the daring idea chimed in with her angry mood. She settled to her oars, and was soon far out in the lake. The Snake was four miles away, lying in the water with his two rattles behind; the sunset glow faded, the twilight grew dusky, clouds rolled up from the west, and still the girl rowed on. She was lost in reverie, and rowed mechanically. Gradually, however, she became aware that it took more force to pull back the oars, and that the strain on her hands was heavier. She glanced around; it was night on shore, but on the water the light lingers late, a bank of black clouds was rising slowly in the west, and a swell setting in from the outside showed that beyond the islands there was a sea running. The Snake was nearer now than the Hotel-island, and Elizabeth, no longer in a reverie, bent to her oars, and often turned her head, steering the skiff so as not to lose an inch on her way. She was not alarmed, for she was a skillful oarswoman, but she had no wish to be driven out to sea, and rescued by some prosaic old lumber-barge. If it were a yacht, now, or a privateer! But Lake Erie has no such romantic craft.

Heavier grew the swell, and darker the sky, crests of foam appeared here and there, and at last the wind got into the island-corner, and wound in and out through the archipelago, bringing the waves in its track. The Snake was not far distant, but its head hissed angrily as the wind struck it and raised the seething foam. The landing was on the outer side, and Elizabeth hesitated an instant; but the angry daring which had taken her out, took her on, and she ventured. Another moment, and the skiff was swept out to sea. She kept the boat's head in the wind and counted the chances; there were, however, but three: to outride the storm; to turn and row back to the Hotel-island; or to land on Ballast, whose range-light shone out ahead. Ballast Islet was the outpost of the group; beyond was the open lake. She decided for Ballast.

Half an hour passed, and a pale girl sat in a skiff driving before the wind, which was fast growing into a gale; the sea was high, and the skiff plunged and rocked, but she kept it on its course and sat with her head turned, intently watching. Ballast was near, but too far to the left. The wind would not take her, as she had hoped, far up on its sandy beach—she must turn and row sideways across the current of the wind and water. Could she do it? It was all Lake Erie against one pair of rounded arms. Elizabeth was alarmed now. She recognized the storm. It was the so-called equinoctial—the September gale which surely rides over the lake sooner or later, and cannot be mistaken when it comes. Yearly, Erie is strewed with the wrecks of this storm, whose approach is masked in soft, purple haze, and whose departure is followed by brilliant sunshine, as if in mockery of the victims. There is a fatality about the equinoctial on the Lower Lakes; no one ever expects it. "Not to-day," say the sailors; "not to-day," say the pleasure-travellers; and that very night their souls are required of them.

Elizabeth, a child of the lake-country, had realized during this last half-hour that the year had come; her face was pale and pinched, her round hat had gone, and her hair floated unheeded around her shoulders; only her eyes and her arms seemed alive as she watched and rowed. Rocks lay jagged around Ballast; there was but one landing, a short strip of sloping beach, and on either side rocky needles and hooks to tear the boat in pieces, and deep water to drown its one passenger. The chances now were but one, and that a slender one. To outride the three days' gale, to go back to the Hotel-island, were both impossible; there remained only the dangerous alternative of a landing on the narrow beach. Nearer and nearer swept the skiff, the moment was almost there. Elizabeth thought of—her sins? Of her guardian-angel? No; she thought of Frederick Harper, who took the place of both. "He will mourn for me if I am drowned," she thought, pathetically. And with that she seized the oars tightly, and, bracing her feet, turned the skiff short to the left, bending double with her effort to force the boat broadside to the wind, across the current. It was a mighty effort for a girl, but she did not covet the being mourned for, if it could be prevented. The tense muscles on her arms, and blisters on her hands, showed that. A short and desperate contest. But the well-developed physique, the superabundant vitality and electricity that tormented her in the idleness of peace, gained the victory in this war with the elements, and, panting for breath, with singing noises in her head and blood-spots dancing before her eyes, Elizabeth Pyne beached the skiff with a last tremendous stroke, and, gaining the higher ground behind, sank exhausted on the grass. Vertigo swam in her brain for some moments, then followed a lethargic faintness, and gradually a chill crept through her frame, and she felt the pain of strained muscles and blistered palms. Rising wearily she started for the lighthouse. But the light was an old-man-of-the-mountain—visible only from a distance; though she had guided her course by its twinkle for the last half-hour, once upon the island, it vanished. It was dark, and the wind sounded among the trees with a wild cry; tired, cold, and disheartened, the girl wandered on at random, looking for the light, and thinking of Frederick Harper. She derived some comfort in the thought that he was probably "perfectly distracted." In reality, however, Mr. Harper was comfortably seated on the sheltered piazza watching the on-coming storm; he supposed that Elizabeth had followed one of her freaks and immured herself in her own room for the evening. He missed her, of course, and he allowed himself to hope that after their marriage there would be fewer of these freaks. This settled, he had an evening cigar of peace.

In the mean time, poor Elizabeth wandered on, her little kid boots torn and wet, her summer dress a trailing, tattered train, holding her hair with one hand to keep herself from Absalom's fate,[4] and with the other guarding her face from the trees

4. 2 Samuel 18:9.

and bushes unseen in the darkness. She was exhausted and mis-erable, and on the verge of hysterics; but of course she could not have hysterics all alone, no one ever did. At last, when she had been dragging herself about for more than an hour, her tired eyes caught a low-down gleam. "The keeper's house," she thought, and a glow surprised her cold veins; she was still alive. But it was like chasing a will-o'-the-wisp; again and again she lost the light, and again and again it gleamed out in an unex-pected quarter, for in the darkness she made many circles. At last the cabin came into view, or rather its window, and without trying to find the door, Elizabeth tapped on the curtained pane. Another minute, and she was under a roof, and face to face with a fire. Then she had her hysterics.

Through it all she was dimly conscious that a woman was tending her; the wet boots were taken off, her hair smoothed, and her bruised hands bound up in soft balm. Then the warmth of the fire began to soothe, and a fragrant aroma to arouse her, and finally she dried her tears, and drank the hot coffee with eagerness. A state of beatitude followed, and she fell asleep.

Late in the evening, when the storm was fierce, Elizabeth's aunt appeared on the piazza. "Bessie! Bessie!" she cried. "Come in, child. You will take cold."

"Elizabeth is not here, Miss Sage," answered Frederick Har-per, rising; "she has been in her room all the evening."

"Indeed," replied Aunt Anne, retreating out of the wind; then to herself, "I wonder if they have quarrelled?" For Aunt Anne, like most maiden aunts, fancied clergymen, and looked forward to the position of oracle in the parish, and the head directorship of sewing-societies. A few moments later she came running down the hall, with her cap-strings floating behind her. "She is not there, Mr. Harper," she cried; "the door is locked, and the key under the mat, as usual. She has not been there since afternoon."

Then came confusion and anxiety, many tongues and many suggestions. "Could she have strayed—?" "Could she have fallen—?" "Could she have ventured—?" but no one ended his question, for the cliffs were abrupt, and the rocks below cruel. At last a boy was found, who said, "She went out in a skiff at sunset; I saw her pass the point."

This was worse than all. "Elizabeth, Elizabeth!" cried Aunt Anne. "Elizabeth is drowned!"

"No," answered Frederick Harper, in a voice that startled the chattering crowd; "she is not dead." And he ran out into the darkness, taking the path that led down to the dock.

The crowd gazed after him, and then, with that impulse that leads a crowd to follow a master-spirit, out they streamed into the wild night, these summer visitors from the city, and ran down to the shore.

Some fishermen sat in the boat-house, mending their nets by the light of a coal-oil lamp. They heard the story, and shook their heads. "It is the equinox, and it'll last three days," they said. "Nothing can go out of harbor to-night." Money was offered; but "Life is more than money," replied old Commodore Perry, an aged fisherman, whose name, happening to be the same as that of the hero of Lake Erie, the summer visitors had adorned with the gallant officer's title, and amused themselves gravely questioning the old man as to the battle and its incidents, until he almost believed he had taken part.

"I believe it was at one o'clock precisely, commodore, that you wrote your famous dispatch, 'We have met the enemy, and we are theirs,' " said one.

"No, no," interrupted another; "at one, the commodore crossed in a small boat, amid the terrific broadsides of the iron-clads, bearing in his hand a pennon containing these words, "If any man attempts to shoot up the American flag, haul him on the spot!' "

"You're both wrong," remarked a third. "At one, the commodore was lashed to the main-mast, and proposed 'To fight it out in those lines, if it took all summer.' "

"Nothing of the kind," added a fourth. "The commodore

was about to leave, his trunks were all packed, when Pontiac and Tecumseh came off in a small boat, and cried, with tears, 'Don't give up the ship!' So he didn't."

"Jess so, gentlemen," the old fisherman would reply, "jess so." But, now that there was an end of chaffing, and real danger abroad, the commodore, unlike his prototype, drew back; "Life is more than money, gentlemen," he said. "Ef one of the steamers was in, we might venture; but we can't tempt the equinox in a sail-boat."

"What are you doing, Harper?" said one.

"I am going out in the Pickerel," answered a voice from the end of the dock.

Then arose a chorus of remonstrance, wonder, and alarm; each person had something to say against the idea; only Aunt Anne held her peace. "He is mad." "He can never find her; they will both be lost." "A boat cannot live in such a gale." "He must not be allowed to go."

Through this shower of words Frederick worked on. Then, without answer, he pushed off and set sail. The wind whistled over the island, and the lake was black; they could only see the boat a short distance, then it vanished into the darkness. "He is lost." "He will never return." "Such a strong young life!" "So earnest and so eloquent!"

Thus the requiem was chanted. But Aunt Anne went quietly back through the grove. "I shall see them both again," she said to herself; and, in the strength of this faith, she slept quietly through the long, wild night.

Frederick Harper was a good sailor on both salt- and freshwater; let it be understood, also, that being the one does not by any means imply the other. He knew the position of the islands, and could make his way among them without the aid of daylight; such knowledge, however, was but slight help in a storm like this. "How can he tell which way she went?" said Junior-warden Graham, as he turned back toward the house. "Such an expedition is beyond all reason." And it was. But love is not always reasonable, fortunately for the poetry of life. Frederick Harper literally could not stay in safety on shore when Elizabeth Pyne was in danger on the water; that was the whole truth.

Out he sailed over the bay, and passing the "Parsons' Snug-harbor," dimly seen through the darkness (not forgetting, even then, to dislike it as a Low-Church institution), he turned into the broad water beyond, running before the wind under a jib.[5] His plan was to approach each island by turn; something would tell him if he came near her. Is this superstitious? Is it not rather a kind of desperate faith? He never once admitted the idea that Elizabeth might never have reached the land at all. . . .

After a short but profound sleep Elizabeth awoke and gazed around the little room. A drift-wood fire crackled on the hearth, and a candle burned in the window; wooden chairs and tables, a clock, the settle on which she lay, and a few cooking-utensils, completed the furniture; but the whole was in blossom. Flowers were everywhere—in boxes, pots, and baskets, on shelves, on the floor, hanging from the ceiling, and climbing over the plastered walls—all kinds, the rare and the common, the hot-house princess, and the way-side peasant, the rose, the fuchsia, and the orange-blossom, side by side with the flower-de-luce, the daisy, and even the red clover. All blossoms, with as little green as possible; the leaves seemed to have been pruned away to make room for the flower. "That poor rose—all its leaves are gone," said Elizabeth, dreamily.

"Oh, you're awake, are ye? I'm glad, for I want to know which side to set the watch-fire on," said a voice. It was a woman who spoke, and Elizabeth turned and looked at her. She was a tall, slender person, with hair, eyes, and skin, of a pale yellow; only her clearly-cut profile kept her face from fading into nonentity. Small, rough hands peeped from the long, close sleeves, but the limp gown hung about her form in shapeless folds, and, altogether, she looked like a faded sunflower. Eliza-

---

5. Snug Harbor is a rest home for retired seamen, this one obviously run by a denomination other than High-Church Episcopalian.

beth took in all these details at a glance, after the manner of woman; and then she answered, "What for?"

"Why, you come from somewhere, I suppose, and your folks will be anxious after you, won't they? If you'll tell me which way you come from, I'll set a fire on that side, and they can see it."

"I came from Bass Island," said Elizabeth.

"Bass Island? I thought so. You're one of the city folks, I reckon. I'll set the fire on that side." The hostess left the room, and a few minutes later Elizabeth saw through the window a gleam, a shooting flame, and then a steady red glare. "It's set," said the woman, reentering.

"Are you the light-house keeper's wife?" asked Miss Pyne, after a sleepy pause; both her ideas and words seemed to come slowly.

"*I'm* the keeper; there ain't no other that I know of."

"You live here?"

"Yes."

"Alone?"

"Yes."

"Why?"

"Because I want to."

"Oh!" said Miss Pyne, gazing at this singular person, who wanted to live alone upon a Lake-Erie island. She was dimly conscious throughout this dialogue that she was not speaking with her usual courtesy, but she could command only the shortest phrases. She was not herself—she was somebody else; she felt that her questions had belonged to country-bred curiosity. After a pause, she solved the puzzle: "You put something in my coffee," she said, slowly.

"Yes; yarbs to make you sleep."

"Oh!" said Elizabeth again, too hazy to push the investigation further. "What is your name?" she continued, after a pause, returning to the laconic curiosity produced apparently by the "yarbs."

"Jonah—Miss Jonah!"

"That is a man's name; no woman ever had it."

"I have it."

"I don't believe it is your name at all," pursued Elizabeth, after pondering a while.

"Well, then, don't. It's no consequence."

"Where did you get all those flowers?" said the visitor, abandoning the subject of the name.

"Growed 'em."

"Why do you keep them in the house in summer?"

"'Cause I want to."

"I wish my head would stop whirling," said Elizabeth, abandoning the flowers also, and turning wearily upon the settle.

"Eat a bit, and then you'll doze and sleep it all off," said the light-keeper, rising. She busied herself among the dishes and over the fire, and Elizabeth dreamily wondered over her yellow hue and extreme length; she seemed half a mile long to the dazed visitor. At length came a bowl of broth, a piece of pilot-bread, and a cup of coffee. "No yarbs this time," said the yellow woman, smiling, and, after eating, the tired girl fell asleep. She was awakened suddenly by a vigorous shake. "Some one's off the island," said the light-keeper. "I heard him hollering on the wind. Is there anybody such a fool as to sail out after you in such a storm?"

"Yes," answered Elizabeth, springing up; "but you need not call him a fool."

"Pretty near it, I reckon. You want to go, too, do you? There's a shawl and some shoes."

The two women went out into the night. The beacon-fire blazed brightly and flared in the wind, dazzling Elizabeth's eyes so that she saw nothing but flame-spots in every direction; but the yellow woman's eyes were like the eyes of a cat. "There, there," she cried, "a little sloop! If they don't run upon this beach they're gone, sure. Come along, girl." And snatching a brand from the fire, she ran down to the sand. Elizabeth followed her example, and the two took their stations, one at each end of the little harbor, like two pier-lights, to show the way. By this time the sleep, the excitement, and the cold air, had overcome the narcotic, and Elizabeth began to realize her love and her mortal fear. Frederick Harper was in the boat, and death was very near him. She never doubted that it was he. "Two minutes more," said the yellow woman, "and either we or the lake will have them, poor fellows!"

As it is in drowning, all her past life seemed to glide before Elizabeth's eyes during those two minutes, and she saw her own faults standing out in glaring colors against the earnest, active good wrought by her lover. "Spare him," she prayed silently, and gazed with anguish out into the darkness before her.

"Halloa!" shouted the yellow woman.—"Shout, girl; now, both together!" And as the sloop came into the glare of the fire, the two shouted with all their might. The unseen sailor heard, for the little boat turned—a dangerous turn—and leaped forward, head-on toward the beach. Another half-moment, and the yellow woman had plunged into the water, waist-deep, and, clutching the bow with the strength of a man, dragged it ashore, while Frederick Harper, all unmindful of her help, sprang out and clasped Elizabeth in his arms.

The woman hauled up the Pickerel, and made it fast to the rocks; then, "Well, folks," she said, "when you get through, we'll go back to the house. I'm a little damp myself." The "getting through" consisted of broken exclamations, half-uttered questions, and answers all astray. The yellow woman listened a while, and then she said, half to herself, "But they'll never get through. I might have known it. I'll go and get things ready for them." So off she started in her dripping clothes, holding a brand for a lantern, and the lovers unconsciously followed, entering the little house and sitting down upon the settle in the same trance—a pale girl, in a tattered dress and clumsy overshoes, and a young man, in wet clothes, with dripping hair, and worn, white face. Thus the light-keeper found them when she came from the inner room clad in a dry gown. "Chills and fever, sure," she said. "Goodness, children, you don't even know you're wet, I suppose!—Young man, if you'll step into the outer room, you'll find old Kit's best clothes laid out on a chair."

"Madam," said Frederick Harper, coming out of his trance, "we owe our lives to you; Elizabeth and I—"

"Let that debt wait," interrupted the yellow woman, "and get dry things on you, do. I ain't a madam, either; Jonah's my name, Miss Jonah. There's the door."

The young man obeyed the pointing finger, and Miss Jonah rattled among her cooking-utensils. "You'd better help; it will warm you up," she said to Elizabeth. "What can you cook?"

Miss Pyne hesitated, and mentally ran over the list of her culinary accomplishments.

"Thought so," said Miss Jonah, severely. "What's the good of your hands?"

This remark opened a door of escape to the visitor. "My hands are blistered; I cannot use them over the fire," she said.

"Don't believe you can cook, all the same," answered the hostess, bending over the coals.

"Yes, I can."

"What?"

"Oh—oh—cream-pies," said Elizabeth, bringing out her one dish in triumph.

"Cream-pies!" echoed Miss Jonah, contemptuously. "Will *they* save the nation?"

"Does the nation need saving?" asked the visitor, amused with the oddities of the light-keeper.

"It did a short time ago, child.—At least, can you set a table?"

"Yes; but my dress hangs about my feet, and I cannot walk in these great shoes."

"Well, you *do* look like the 'draggle-tail Gypsies, O!' I haven't any Sunday clothes, as old Kit has, but you can help yourself to whatever there is in the press. Take the candle. I can cook by the firelight."

When Miss Pyne came back, she was transformed into a Würtemberg peasant-girl. One of the light-keeper's straight blue gowns hung about her; she wore a white kerchief over her shoulders and an apron tied close up under her arms; her hair was braided in the German style, and a handkerchief tied quaintly around her head, and in her blooming beauty she looked sixteen, and a princess in masquerade.

"Well, you-'ns *do* know more than we-'ns," said Miss Jonah, setting down her basin to gaze.

"If I only had buckled shoes," said Elizabeth, holding out a little stockinged foot.

"You've managed to make a fancy dress out of my old duds; what won't vanity do? But I don't blame you, child; and as for shoes, I can fix that." And, stepping to a chest, Miss Jonah brought out a pair of black-satin slippers, of the style of 1800, somewhat worn, but dainty still.

"Oh, the beauties!" cried Elizabeth, slipping them on, and looking at her feet with admiration.

"My grandmother's," said Miss Jonah. "*Now,* can you set the table!"

"Certainly; motion becomes a pleasure in such fairy godmother slippers," answered Miss Pyne, gayly.

When, after some delay, Frederick Harper returned, he found a midnight meal ready on the table, decked with a central mound of blossoms. Fish, potatoes, hoe-cake, bacon, smoking hominy, pilot-bread, and honey. All these, and a Würtemberg peasant-girl in satin slippers as waitress.

"How charming!" exclaimed Frederick.

"How funny!" exclaimed Elizabeth.

For the young man had not the skill to transform himself into any thing but a bulky athlete, uncomfortably attired in clothes much too small for him, with a length of ankle, throat, and wrist, escaping from the well-worn garments.

"How tall you are!" said Elizabeth.

"None too tall," said Miss Jonah. "Little men are always a

mistake; all you can do is, make the best of 'em.—Help yourself,
Fred."

"The Reverend Frederick Harper," said Elizabeth, quickly.

"And allow me, Miss Jonah, to introduce to you Miss Elizabeth Pyne," said the young clergyman.

"Yes, yes, I know. And now, Fred and Betsy, do eat something; it will be daylight before long."

The two guests glanced at each other in amusement. "Let
me give you some fish, Betsy," said Frederick, smiling.

"The blooms don't look so bad on the table," remarked
Miss Jonah, looking at the impromptu *épergne*. "I never thought
of mixing flowers with victuals myself, though."

"You are fond of flowers," said Frederick.

"Yes; they're sisters and brothers to me, and more.—Well,
you're through, are ye? Then just get to sleep as quick as you
can. You'll find Kit's cot in the outer room, Fred. Good-night;
I'll call you when breakfast is ready." And, holding open the
door, she sent out her guest in spite of his half-laughing
objections.

"Now, Betsy, trot into the inner room and curl yourself up
in the bed. I never like to see a girl get peaked for want of
sleep."

"And you?" said Elizabeth.

"Oh, I am an owl," answered Miss Jonah. "Half the time
I don't sleep nights at all;" and in the firelight, with her yellow
eyes and pointed nose, she looked not unlike the nightbird.
Elizabeth's watch showed one o'clock, and she fell asleep with
a hazy cloud of owl-faces hovering around her.

The next morning the storm was at its wildest; all the winds
were abroad, and the lake was white with flattened foam, the
clouds flew across the sky with lurid gleams between. But, in
spite of the gloom, the peasant-girl and the awkward athlete
made good cheer within the little house, and found it impossible
to feel depressed. "We ought to, you know," said Elizabeth at

the breakfast-table. "No doubt they are sadly anxious at the hotel, and—and, we may have to stay here days."

"Dreadful," said Frederick, bringing the coffee-pot from the trevet on the hearth. "Ours is indeed a melancholy lot. Have some more coffee?"

In truth the friends at the hotel were sadly anxious; they clustered around the fire and said to each other: "How young they were!" "How well loved!" The past tense gave significance to their eulogies. Only Aunt Anne hoped on. The next evening after the long, sad day of storm, Commodore Perry covered himself with glory by bringing the tidings that a fisherman who lived around the point reported a beacon-light on Ballast. "The range is there as usual," he said to the listening group in the parlor, "but this here's a watch-fire on the beach, and it stands to reason it means something. Miss Jonah, she don't make bonfires for fun in weather like this."

"Miss Jonah?"

"Yes; the light-keeper's a woman, a lone, lorn female, that stays over on Ballast all the year round. She's queer, she is! Old Kit brings her victuals, and the like."

"One or both of them must be there," said Junior-warden Graham, hopefully.

"Both," said Aunt Anne.

The curious asked many questions about this recluse of Ballast, but the commodore had no more to say. "She lives there; that's all I know," he answered. He saw nothing surprising in the fact; he took the world as he found it, and was surprised at nothing, that wise old man!

All through the day the two on the island were happy, laughing, and enjoying the adventure like school-children. All through the day the yellow woman sat grimly by, and looked on. She allowed them to prepare dinner, and she ate their burned and dried-up concoctions with equanimity; she relieved them from the prosaic after-piece of dish-washing; she suffered a rearrangement of all her plants, and various improvements in the position of her furniture. She was amused, poor, lonely soul.

Toward night she rose, half reluctantly. "Well, I must go out, milk the cow, light the range, and set the watch-fire," she said, taking down a pail.

"I will go too," said Elizabeth. "I want to feel the storm."

"Not in my grandmother's slippers, Betsy."

"The slippers shall not be injured," said the athlete, and he lifted the peasant-girl in his arms. "Now, then, for the storm."

"Well, you *are* strong," said Miss Jonah, approvingly. "I never did like puny people. Sit still, Betsy, and don't make a fuss. Can't you take a bit of fun, child?"

So the procession started in high glee, the storm was felt, the cow milked, the range lighted, the beacon-fire started, and, through it all, the grandmother's slippers never once touched the ground.

Then came supper and a merry evening; Frederick was even betrayed into a college-song.

"I can sing," said Miss Jonah.

"Pray favor us," urged the two guests; and she favored them: "Barbara Allen" and the ballad of the "Draggle-tail Gypsies, O!"

"You two are lovers, of course," she said, as late in the evening they still sat around the fire, listening to the wild wind outside. This sudden question brought the red to Elizabeth's face, but Frederick answered calmly:

"Of course."

"When are you going to be married?"

"In November."

"What day?"

"The 24th."

Now, be it known, that the word marriage had never yet been spoken by either of these two young persons. Elizabeth, with scarlet face, interposed a "No."

"Don't you make any objections, Betsy," said Miss Jonah, "for you know you like him."

"Of course she does," said the audacious Frederick.

"It is very late," said Elizabeth, hastily, rising and taking a candle. "Good-night." And so she escaped.

The opening of the next day was gloomy with gusts of heavy rain; the gay mood had passed, and Elizabeth sat silently at the little window, gazing out over the dark, stormy water. She had slept little, and her mind was divided between two feelings—pleasure that would not down, and anger that would not up, at least to the desired point. She loved Frederick Harper, and she knew that she loved him; but her proud spirit chafed against this easy conquest. Should it be for him to win without difficulty? Was she his without even an asking? And all the time she knew she was, and had hard work to keep herself up to the proper indignation; which last was the most humiliating of all.

But Frederick, who had risked his life for this girl and counted it as nothing, thought not of moods and fancies; he rested content with his great thankfulness for life and love.

The day wore on, and the three were quiet, Elizabeth moody; the yellow woman quietly watchful, and Frederick lapsing back into that lethargy of complete rest, which had been so rudely broken.

"To-morrow you can go home," said Miss Jonah, toward evening. "The wind will go down some time to-night, and Kit will be coming across from Middle Bass as soon as the sea goes down; he can take you back."

"Don't you think I am a good sailor, Miss Jonah?" said Frederick, smiling.

"Yes; but you'll have to look after her; she's out of sorts," with a gesture toward Elizabeth, who stood in the inner room, looking out at the rain.

"Is she ill," asked Frederick, rising quickly.

"Young man," said Miss Jonah, in a low voice, "I can't abear to see trouble growing out of nothing. She feels bad, and, of course, you're the cause, somehow. Now, you just go right in there and make up." And Frederick went.

"Well, children, supper's ready, and can't wait," called a voice through the half-open door, an hour afterward.

Forth came the lovers at their hostess's summons, and Elizabeth was radiant, with the traces of tears still on her cheeks. For Frederick had then and there been on a mission, and converted this unbeliever. There was no uncertainty about the asking now. O Miss Jonah, you did bravely as a Cupid!

The yellow woman busied herself about the table, and seemed not to see this new radiance; but all the same she sighed when they were not observing her, and pressed her hand to her head.

"This is our last evening," she said, as, the work over and fresh drift-wood heaped on the fire, she sat down in her splint rocking-chair with her knitting.

Outside the wind was still rushing through the sky, and the watch-fire burned on the beach; inside the two were together on the settle, making quarrels with their words and love with their eyes, after the manner of young persons who "understand each other." The hostess sat opposite, and listened, and looked.

"Miss Jonah," said Frederick, remembering at last that there was a third, "you do not, of course, remain here during the winter?"

"Yes, I do, Fred."

"But is it not dreary and lonely?"

"Dreary and lonely, dreary and lonely," repeated the woman; "God knows it is!" And two tears rolled slowly down her yellow cheeks.

"Dear Miss Jonah," said Elizabeth, taking her hand, "do not stay here. Come with us to Lakeport."

"No, no, child. I must keep my place."

"I can easily find a better place for you in Lakeport," said Frederick. "Come back with us. Let us help you to make a home in the city near ours, where we can often see you."

"Do," pleaded Elizabeth, bending down her happy, winsome face—"do, my dear." And she kissed the faded cheek.

Miss Jonah burst into tears, and rocked herself to and fro.

"It is so long since any one has kissed me, so long since any one has called me 'dear!' " she said, with sobs. "It isn't easy to be dead before you've died. If I was really dead, I shouldn't be hungering after what can't be. At least, I hope not. Else, what's the use of death? Children, you've opened my heart tonight, and I'll tell you my story. Then, perhaps, you'll help me to end every thing right." She wiped her eyes, and motioned them back to the settle. "Sit there like you was before," she said. "'Twas seeing you so happy that first set me off. I don't begrudge you, my dears; but even the poorest human creature has its feelings.

"I was born in Northern Georgia, near the mountain called Yonah. We were poor, but not exactly poor white trash, for we came from a good stock, and grandmother was a real lady. I went to school some, and didn't have to work hard. My name was Rose; I look like it, don't I? Well, at eighteen I was engaged to Joe; and, seven years after, I was still only engaged, for he was too poor to marry. Mattie, my sister, was seventeen, and I loved her dearly. She was a pretty blossom of a child, like that carnation-pink in the window. I had taken care of her always, for we had no mother, and father had died when she was still young. Well, all at once a far-away cousin died, and left her farm up in the hills to me—a queer old body like I am now, I suppose. Joe had not been in that evening, and I sat working in the keeping-room, burning to tell him the good news. Still, he didn't come. At last, I got nervous, and thought I'd feel better out in the garden, where I could hear the gate creak. I went out; I didn't hear the gate creak, but I heard something else— Joe and Mattie, he talking, she crying, and both of 'em loving each other with all their hearts. Yes; I couldn't mistake. He spoke to her as he never spoke to me; his very voice was tenderer. And Mattie, too—the child was breaking her heart.

Through it all they both stood firm. He had no thoughts of giving me up; she had no thoughts of getting him away. It was only that they had happened to meet, and misery will out. If either of 'em had been false—but no. I couldn't even have the comfort of anger. It stood just this way: Joe had given me a boy's fancy, but Mattie he loved; she loved him with all her heart; and I—well, I was only in the way. I won't take the time to tell you all I thought, but this is what I did: I got a little bundle of things that I set store by—things that wouldn't be missed; those slippers is one, for I was vain of my foot, and had planned to be married in 'em—and then I went to the river, and threw my shawl over so it would lodge on the reeds. I wasn't an hour doing it all; and, while they were still in the garden, I was coming North. I've never been back, and I never mean to go. After a time, I got on this island, and here I'm going to stay. I like it. It's lonely, but I'm best alone. In the war I helped the prisoners over there a bit—the boys on Johnson's Island down in the bay, the Johnny Rebs, you know. I was something of a nurse, and I used to take care of the sick ones. 'Twas all for the sake of old Georgia. But peace came; the boys are home again; and the barracks are gone from Johnson's. Since then I've taken to flow-ers. We're pining creatures, after all; we must have something to fuss over. Well, I don't even know if my two are married, but I did the best I could. I'm drowned, you see, and the farm is Mattie's. All I care for now is to have the end all right. I have a fancy I shall not live long, and I want to be buried here on Ballast. There mustn't be any stone or even a mound, for I want to be clean forgotten; and this is what I ask you two to do for me."

"O Miss Jonah," said Elizabeth, earnestly, "give up these gloomy ideas, and come with us!"

"Eh, child, you're kind, but I couldn't be happy nowheres; I can't make myself over."

"But we will write—we will send to your old home—"

"No, no. I can stand being away from Joe, but I couldn't

stand being near him. I love him the same as ever. You look at me with your pretty eyes wide open, but it's so. I suppose I seem an old woman to you. I'm forty-two; but if I was seventy it would be just the same."

"But, Miss Jonah, at least you can know—"

"I don't want to know, child. All I have to do is just keep still. If I have done wrong, it can't be mended now; if I have done right, it mustn't be spoiled."

"But, dear Miss Jonah—"

"Stay, Elizabeth," interposed Frederick Harper, "this is a question we cannot answer. Miss Jonah must judge for herself."

"Yes, young man. The heart knoweth its own bitterness. Good-night."

And, passing through the outer door, Miss Jonah left them, nor did they see her again that evening. She did not enter the room where Elizabeth slept, and, although the clergyman watched late before the fire, she did not appear. In the morning, however, there she was, not the broken-voiced, sad woman who had told her story as if she longed for sympathy, but pale, grim Miss Jonah, the light-keeper of Ballast Island.

"We have been dreaming," said Elizabeth, in a low tone. "Those hard, yellow eyes never shed tears."

"It is that very stony endurance that I pity most," answered Frederick. "It is her armor against suffering, and shows how long and hard has been the battle."

Old Kit, the fisherman, came across from Middle Bass early in the afternoon. The sky was drifted with ragged clouds, the lake rough, and the air cold; but the storm was over. Frederick and Elizabeth were now attired in their own shrunken clothes, but the kid boots were hopelessly torn. "Keep the slippers," said Miss Jonah; "I like to see 'em on you."

The yellow woman had held herself aloof from her guests during the day; she seemed in a sombre mood, and averse to any conversation. "I do not like to go away without a word as to what she told us last night," said Elizabeth, as old Kit made ready the Pickerel for the voyage to the Hotel-island. "Poor soul!—see how lonely she looks!"

"We have tried several times this morning, and she has refused to speak; we must not force ourselves upon her," answered Frederick. "She knows we are going; if she wishes to say any thing, she will come. Telling her story was a relief at the time; but she has been in a dumb agony ever since. Last night she was out in the wind wandering up and down on the beach like a wild creature; she did not come in until dawn."

"Let me go and comfort her," said the warm-hearted Elizabeth, looking with tearful eyes toward the solitary figure on the rocks.

"No, dear. No one can comfort her. But I think she will come to us when the boat is ready to sail." And she did.

"Good-by, children," she said, quietly. "I have trusted you with my all, but I know you will not betray me. I should like to ask you, if word comes, to help me in the end; but—it might be troublesome."

"Dear friend," said Frederick, taking the cold hand in both his own, "life is uncertain; you may outlive us both."

"And, may not."

"In that case, freely do I give my promise."

"God bless you," said Miss Jonah, solemnly. They pressed each other's hands in farewell, and then Elizabeth threw her arms around the yellow woman's neck and kissed her.

"Oh, my little blossom," cried Miss Jonah, with tears, "may you be happy, ever so happy, my sweet one!" She turned away, and Frederick lifted Elizabeth over the wet sand and placed her in the boat, already rising and falling on the surf, as if impatient to be off.

"All ready," said old Kit.

Miss Jonah did not turn, and Frederick, seeing her purpose, gave the sign, and the boat glided away from the little log dock out into the broad lake. When a wide space of water lay between them, Miss Jonah climbed upon a rock and stood gazing after the sloop, her tall form outlined against the gloomy sky. As a change in the course hid her from view, the two watchers in the boat saw her hand waving a last farewell. . . .

No need to tell of the joy at the Hotel-island. "I knew they would return," said Aunt Anne, triumphantly.

Early the next morning the little island steamer, weather-bound at Sandusky, ventured out, and carried back on her return voyage to the main-land every summer visitor. The islands were left to themselves until another summer; but their grapes and their wine kept their memory warm through the long, cold winter.

Early in the spring, when ice was still floating in the lake, the Rev. Frederick Harper received a letter:

> DEAR CHILDREN: I feel that death is not far off. When I am gone Kit will mail this, and then wait. Keep your promise. Goodby, both of you.
>
> "MISS JONAH."

"Will you go with me?" he said, giving the letter to his wife.

"Yes," answered Elizabeth.

Reaching Sandusky, they took a little sloop and sailed out over the cold lake toward Ballast Island. Old Kit was waiting for them, and in the house was a closed box.

"She didn't want you to see her again," said the old man. "She made me promise to nail it up; she made herself ready beforehand."

The flowers were blooming on the walls, and the plain furniture ranged in order.

"Was there any message?" asked Frederick.

"Nothing, sir, 'cept her love for the lady, and would she take a few slips from the plants, 'cause she'd like to think they was blooming in your house. That's all, sir."

Reverently the burden was lifted and carried out to a spot

among the trees, where the grave stood ready. Then the young clergyman read the burial service; "earth to earth, ashes to ashes," and Elizabeth's hand threw in the first clods. Before the grave was filled, she gathered all the flowers and dropped them down, so that the coffin-lid was buried in blossoms. Then the earth was restored to its place, and the ground smoothed and sodded; "No stone, no mound," the solitary woman had said, and her wish was fulfilled. A few weeks more, and no one could trace the outline of the grave in the fresh, spring grass.

Taking with them the flower-slips, the two sailed away, leaving old Kit in charge. Long they talked of the dead as they sailed back over the cold lake.

"I think," said Elizabeth, "that she took the name of that Georgia mountain, and the people about here misunderstood it and called it Jonah."

"Very likely," said Frederick; "she probably thought it best not to correct the mistake. Yonah—Jonah; yes, they are much alike."

"Poor soul, she is at rest now," said the young wife at last. "But, after all, did she do right?"

"Who can tell?" answered Frederick, gravely. "She gave her life for the sake of those she loved. If the sacrifice was mistaken, it was none the less heroic."

This was Miss Jonah's funeral sermon.

The wind was adverse, and the afternoon was darkening into night, as the sail-boat glided on toward Sandusky Bay.

"See, there is the range shining out," said Elizabeth, looking back; "old Kit lights it now."

Another turn, and Ballast Island disappeared.

The Fall of the Lighthouse

Frances Ward Hurlbut

THE GRANDMOTHER and narrator of this story is Emily Ward, the sister of Eber Ward, a pioneer Great Lakes iron manufacturer, steamship owner, and keeper of the Bois Blanche Island Light from 1829 to 1842. Like Woolson's "Ballast Island," Hurlbut's story portrays the courage required by early lakes lightkeepers, courage equal to that of the mariners who depended on them. Here, Emily tells of saving the lamps and lenses from the light before it fell into Lake Michigan during the January gale of 1838. Whether this story is more fact than fiction is less important than the picture it gives of a young woman, alone except for her adopted child, who felt responsible to save what she could so the lighthouse could be rebuilt. The equipment she rescued was a combination of lard-oil lamps, lenses, and reflectors that gave only a weak beam compared to the Fresnel lenses installed later, yet in the wild darkness of the Straits it would have been a welcome sight to men who had once sailed without it.

"IT WAS A WILD NIGHT when the light-house fell," said grandma, as she picked up a child's stocking she was knitting. "Father had gone over to Mackinaw two days before, intending to come back the day he went; but a storm had arisen that prevented his getting back, and instead of decreasing it had increased, until in the afternoon it was blowing a perfect gale.

"The light-house had originally been placed too near the water, and the encroachment made by the winds and the waves, since it was built, had brought it much nearer, so that now every heavy storm was full of peril for the old light-house.

"My father had long anticipated the day when some extra heavy storm would sweep the waters around its foundation, loosen it, and beat its stanch tower until it should fall; and now that day had come.

"Bolivar and I were alone in the house, and there was no one on the island but the Frenchman, who was a great coward, and his Indian wife.

"Our house was very near to the light-house,—so near that if it should fall a certain way it would fall upon the roof,—which made it a very unsafe shelter for us.

"It was a day of great anxiety; for if the light-house should be blown down, its great light would be put out, and I shuddered to think of what might happen to the vessels and their crews and passengers.

"And Eber was on the lake; and what if his boat, storm-driven, should look for that friendly light and not find it? My heart was like lead as I looked out upon the boiling waves, and the roaring wind, and the driving clouds, and thought of him. So I would not take down the lamps until the very last moment.

"Early in the forenoon I had seen that the water surrounded the building, and later on, as the storm increased in violence, every great wave would dash itself to foam against its brawny sides.

"Above five o'clock I saw that if I was to save the lamps and the great reflectors I must begin at once. So putting a warm hood on my head to protect it from the rain, I started, first telling Bolivar not to stir from the house, but to stand at the window and watch for me.

"The poor child burst into tears and begged me not to go, but I thought it was my duty to save the government property.

"I had no sooner got out of the house than the wind, with a sudden dash, nearly took me off my feet, the rain half blinded me, and the spray wet me through; but I ran quickly, and in a moment was in the light-house, climbing its hundred and fifty steep steps with all the speed I could. When I reached the top what a magnificent sight met my gaze!

"Whoever has stood on a perilous height, and seen the mad waters leap and roar and dash with all their mighty force against the frail structure that supported him, can imagine the wild exaltation of soul that filled me through and through to the exclusion of all fear.

"It seemed as if then, indeed, God, in his majesty, was sweeping the earth and the seas, and I felt that I also was part of the great universe that existed under that awful power.

"I had but little time, however, to indulge myself in these thoughts, for every wave made the whole tower reel. It took all my strength to carry those great lamps and reflectors down the winding stairs; and sometimes when I would stop to take breath, and would hear the beat of the waters and feel the shock it gave the tower, it would give me a momentary spasm of terror; but it would be but momentary, for my work must be done, and I had no time for fear.

"I think I climbed those stairs five times before I got everything movable down, and each time Bolivar would implore me, with tears streaming from his eyes, not to go again,—that I would surely be killed."

"Oh, grandma!" said one of the aunties, "I don't see how you dared to risk your life in that way."

"Oh," said grandma, "you see I wasn't hurt. When people are doing their duty they are not apt to come to much harm."

The children looked at each other, as if they could see that grandma did right, but that it was an awful thing to do.

"Well," pursued grandma, "after I had got everything down I changed my wet clothes for dry ones, and we ate our supper, and then took our places by the window to watch for the light-house to fall.

"I told Bolivar that as soon as I said the word we were to leave the house and go back into the woods, and that when the time came he was not to speak one word, but hang on to my hand tight and follow me. He said he would.

"We had not long to wait. The night had come; the rain had ceased, and the moon gave such light as scurrying and wildly driven clouds would permit. Suddenly we saw a long zigzag line run from the tower's base to its top. I said to Bolivar, 'Put on your overcoat and hat,' and I put on my warm shawl and hood. Still we stood by the window; another line shot up and around, and the tower tottered.

" 'Now,' said I, 'Bolivar come!' He took my hand, and we went out the back way, shutting the doors behind us, and ran for the woods, a few rods off.

"We had scarcely got there when, with one mighty crash, down went the huge pile of masonry, and the waves washed over the place where the light-house once stood.

"We could see that the house had not been injured; so with thankful hearts we went back, and Bolivar was soon in bed and asleep.

"But I could not sleep for thinking of the ships that were in peril, and especially of Eber; and tears that I could not restrain wet my pillow that night and succeeding nights."

"Was any one lost?" inquired Portie.

"Oh, yes," said grandma; "it was one of the most awful storms ever known on the lakes, and many ships went down and many lives were lost; but no one was lost near Bois Blanc, or that I knew personally.

"When father got back he was glad to find us alive; for he had been afraid from the first that the light-house would fall."

Geraniums

Dean Eltham

TO MOST LAKES SAILORS today, the lockkeeper is often a disembodied voice on the radio, telling the captain to tie up and wait for the lock to clear or giving him clearance to proceed. Communications are usually brief, professional, and anonymous. But this story, set on the Lachine Canal at Montreal near the turn of the century, gives an idea of how it once was before we all became strangers. Eltham describes the ending of an era, not only between lockkeepers and captains, but of shipping on the lakes, the time when ships were growing ever larger and the small shipowner could no longer compete with the rising corporations and their mammoth steel freighters that could carry a cargo faster and cheaper than anyone had imagined. This is a story of the death of dreams, of Captain Savage's dreams of becoming a wealthy vessel owner, of the lockmaster's fantasy of a comfortable retirement home to call his own. It is also the story of an unlikely friendship between two men who both discovered that to grow old is to feel outmoded, and how they, with their different ideas of home, tried to preserve what they valued. There are no storms in this story, no dramatic rescues, but it is as careful a study as one is likely to find of the difference between men who spend their lives in a ship and men who live ashore.

ANTHONY GREEN, lockmaster of Number Two on the Lachine Canal, watched with something akin to malice in his usually good-natured eyes, as the *John L. Savage* nosed its vast wooden hulk into the western lock. Vast, indeed, for a lake freighter in those days when the New Victoria Bridge was but two years old, and side-burns were the essential badge of respectability.

Anthony hid his admiration of the new vessel behind a wide placid face that was lined and interlined with tenuous hair-like purple veins. Taking his pipe from his mouth, he peered belligerently up into the wheel-house of the ship. Yes—John Savage himself at the wheel; though so preoccupied with the engine bells that he was oblivious to the lockmaster. Anthony snorted and waddled off indignantly to the stern of the vessel. Hah! Just as he thought. The upstream gate would only just take her. And even at that her stern projected over the gate which Anthony's men were closing in on her. His attention was suddenly averted by the blistering curses that emanated from the cupped hands of the rugged figure leaning over the ship's bridge.

Making his way forward, Anthony could not help noting the alacrity with which John Savage's deckhands snubbed her to the "niggerheads." John Savage: the same this year as last, now and ever shall be, thought Anthony; feared for his blasphemous temper by every deckhand from Fort William to Victoria Basin; owner of a few grain boats that had an uncanny habit of paying their way and enabling John to add to them occasionally. The *John L. Savage* was his latest and by far the largest.

Anthony snorted again. Here, at least, was one individual whom John could not intimidate. And the vindictive light in the lockmaster's eyes increased as he thought of the letter he had received a month ago from the Department of Canals, reprimanding him for the complaint of a lake captain—John Savage, by gum—who had been obliged to wait fifteen minutes till Anthony's men returned from an errand which had led them to a benevolent friend whence they returned with two wheelbarrows full of geraniums with which to embellish the lockhouse garden.

As Anthony came abreast of the bridge, he took his pipe out of his mouth, spread his stumpy fat legs to brace himself for the blast he was about to deliver at John, and dug his chubby fists into his paunch like a scandalized charwoman. But John was still busy casting insulting aspersions on the ancestry of his deckhands. So Anthony spat contemptuously at the new paint of the vessel and waited impatiently, meanwhile sweeping John up and down with scornful glances. Unfortunately, he could not see the blazing anger in the keen blue eyes under the visor of John's cap.

Suddenly the skipper straightened up, turned a scorching gaze on the lockmaster and pointed a quivering finger at him.

"I seen ye. I seen ye. Spit on my new ship, would ye, ye fat old trollop? Fire an' water! Go back to yer geraniums, Auntie—" scathingly.

Yes, John Savage had laid that complaint, by gum, decided Anthony with conviction, though his jaw sagged before the withering invectives that followed. Dang the man! Every time John came through, he had something to badger the lazy good-natured lockmaster with—had been doing it for years till it came to be as much a part of the cruise through the canal as the buoys up above the rapids. And he would have missed taunting Anthony just as much as a buoy that had broken loose from its moorings. It was John, of course, who had labeled him "Auntie." And now every lake captain cast the jibe at the matronly custodian of Number Two.

Anthony recovered his speech at last and shook his pipe at John, retorting in his ludicrous high-pitched soprano: "Now, looky 'ere. I know who laid that complaint agin me . . . Shet up, will ye?" John had not finished by any means—had merely paused for breath.

"I'll have ye know that this vessel's the biggest freighter on the lakes and not to be belittled by any lazy lubber like yew."

"Yes?" Anthony was exasperated and a bit befuddled so that he was unable to keep to his subject. "Ye'll build 'em so big some day that ye'll not get them through the lock. 'Er buttocks is almost 'ung up on the upper gate now," he shrilled, pointing upstream with his pipe.

"I ain't buildin' 'em any bigger, ye old fool, till they makes the locks ter fit. In fact, I ain't buildin' any more just now. For they's a few about the lakes as ain't payin' their way. I'm goin' to buy instead o' build from now on—an' buy cheap, too. See, Auntie."

"Huh! Now looky 'ere, I aint agoin' to be put off. About that complaint . . . d'ye 'ear? . . ."

But John heard a hail from the bow instead and turned away to the wheel-house, smiling to himself at having satiated his obsession—that of baiting Anthony. The gates were clear, the hawsers loosened and the deckhands were clambering over the bulwarks. John stretched a hand to a lever and a bell tinkled afar off in the bowels of the ship. Slowly she moved out of the lock, leaving Anthony's grudge unrequited.

Clear of the lock, John caught sight of his own reflection in the wheel-house window. The rugged, clean shaven features and audacious eyes pleased him—a personable rogue, to be sure. And there was a woman in Montreal much less pudgy than Auntie—oh, much less pudgy.

It took far longer to unload the small freighter of those days than it does to empty the largest steel-clad grain carrier that sails the lakes to-day. And by the time the *John L.* had secured a return cargo, several days had elapsed.

Coming into Number Two again, John looked for Anthony Green to deride as usual. But the lockmaster was nowhere to be seen. A mean-looking rat of a man officiated in his stead.

"Where's Auntie?" asked John.

"Suspended."

"What for?"

"Dunno, 'cept someone laid a complaint agin him. Second time. Don't get a third in the service."

"Gone fer good?" John's tone was almost querulous.

"Dunno. Ain't completely fired yet. Jus' suspended,"

answered the newcomer impatiently, obviously unwilling to discuss the matter any further.

"Fire an' water!" stormed John.

They talk about that trip of the *John L.* to the head of the lakes yet. No one before or since has ever beheld its skipper in such a sustained tantrum. His deckhands turned pale under leathery countenances before the torrent of abuse that belched from his churlish lips. And it never ceased all the way to Fort William and back again. In fact, when John beheld the rat-faced man still in charge at Number Two, it increased if anything. Twice running he had been done out of baiting Anthony!

Now John knew "a feller who knew a feller" in the Department of Canals; and the letter that he wrote was as choice a specimen of blasphemous coercion as anyone would care to see. Of course, he was in the way of becoming an influential owner some day. And the shocking phrasing must have been ignored in the Department . . .

One evening John wandered aimlessly down his gang plank at Montreal, and by the fitful yellow gleam of lamps picked his way more or less carefully among bales, hawsers and stanchions that encumbered the space between the freight sheds and the quay's edge. Shambling over the cobbles on Commissioner Street, he made for the sociable atmosphere of the Nautilus.

Now the keeper of that tavern must have been a subtle humorist, else he had never hung up the sign *"Ne blasphèmez pas"* and under it in terser English "Don't curse." No man who plays host for many years to seamen could have been otherwise and conceived the sign in the first place. John showed his wholesome appreciation of the joke by greeting Anthony Green across the smoke-fogged taproom with bristling oaths.

"So ye been stealin' the government's lumber, have ye, ye big tub o' lard? Nice business for a respectable woman, ain't it, Auntie?"

"Ye—ye—" shrilled Anthony, beside himself.

"Or was takin' in washin' and neglectin' the government's business?"

"Ye know right well what it was . . ."

"Me? How should I know?" scornfully. "Nice thing to be draggin' the name of an innocent lake captain into your nefar'ous schemes! Nex' thing I know, ye'll be blackmailin' me—suin' me for breach of promise or the like. For the life o' me I could never understand where they got such a baggage for Number Two."

"They washed out the complaints, they did!" screamed Anthony, goaded to such extremes to vindicate himself that he almost forgot to confront John with the charge of tale-bearing. "Got a letter this mornin' reinstatin' me." John betrayed nothing of his elation or of the part his letter had played. "And all your bellyachin' to the Department didn't do no good after all."

"My bellyachin'! *Aun*-tie!!" For a moment Anthony was given to wondering whether he had done his tormentor an injustice. But when John dramatically covered his face with his hands and wailed in mock anguish, "To think—that after all these years you would suspect *me*. Oh, this is too much!"

Anthony's purplish face turned a sickly mauve before the raucous laughter. With his paunch undulating at each jerky step, he attempted an impression of courtly disdain as he deserted the tavern. But what chance has a fat man of being taken seriously?

As he made his way over to Notre Dame Street to board a horse-drawn tram-car, he was pitifully uncertain as to whether his exit had been ridiculous or dignified. Though of one thing he was more certain than ever. John Savage, by gum. Him it was who had squealed. And as the quaint little horse car rumbled along, the indignities that he had suffered at the hands of the iniquitous John so occupied his mind that he absently knocked the red hot dottle from his pipe to the straw-strewn floor, and drew for his carelessness a sharp reproof from the driver. Anthony sighed. A cruel and unsympathetic world.

And so, for years, Anthony nursed his grudge and endured the sarcasm and taunts of the skipper of the *John L.* What else could a mere lockmaster do to tie the score with a man who became annually more prosperous and influential? First thing Anthony knew, John Savage would be retiring to an office to direct the affairs of his rapidly increasing fleet. Then, reflected Anthony sorrowfully, there'd be nothing but morose brooding left for himself instead of the revenge he forlornly hoped for.

But Anthony reckoned without the disposition of Fate and the short-sightedness of John Savage. The sad-faced disillusioned men who sold their wooden bottoms to John woke up one morning to the tune of gossip from Ottawa that the canals down the lakes were to be deepened by four feet; and the locks doubled in length. It was not many months before John came to recognize a good many of those men in the host of dredging crews that cluttered up the canals. But apart from cursing them frantically for the delays they occasioned, he was anything but perturbed at the new developments. Bigger ships? You're . . . right! And he'd build 'em when the time came. But that was a long way off yet, according to John.

A month or two after the deepening of the canals was completed, the *John L.* sailed into the western lock at Number Two—sailed in, mark you—and with oceans of room to spare. For once, John forebore to seek out the obese Anthony. No. By the time he had castigated his deckhands into feverish activity, he sauntered to starboard to take a look at the monstrous steel-clad freighter that could only just squeeze into the enlarged eastern lock. A scowl settled on his face. Curious, he sought her name—*Gotaland.* When she steamed out, he re-read the name on her stern and under it, "Stockholm."

Anthony had been standing back, directly amidships of the *John L.,* secretly gloating at the sorry comparison that it made with the foreign vessel. He came over to the bridge.

"And what do ye think o' that?" he piped, jerking his thumb toward the *Gotaland.* John, who was thinking furiously, momentarily ignored the voice behind him. At last he crossed the bridge to where Anthony stood.

"What's she doin' up here?" he asked soberly.

"What d' ye think—fishing for sardines?" answered Anthony, thinking he had John on the raw at last.

"Now look here, y' fat porpoise, I'll have yuh reported to the Department unless y're more civil to a skipper."

"No offense—no offense," mumbled Anthony. John was still the mightiest power in lake shipping and Anthony wouldn't risk running foul of the Department again. "She's been trampin' the Baltic an' thereabouts," he vouchsafed. "Brought over a cargo o' sardines and matches. An' now she's goin' up fer pulpwood."

"H'm," remarked John grimly. "I suppose we'll have a lot o' lousy Swedes stealin' our bread an' butter right under our nose now. A fine idea—deepening the canals! Ach! A fine idea for a lot o' blasted foreigners. Fire an' water!"

When John learned in the taverns in Montreal that a big corporation had ordered two steel bottoms laid down, he began to think more furiously than ever. Sell his wooden ships? Where? Nobody with any brains would buy them, what with the writing on the wall. And there weren't any brainless skippers left. Ironically enough, they had sold their ships to John! Maybe he could sell them to the coal companies that shipped across Lake Ontario. Even take a loss on them, and start anew with one or two of these mammoth lake boats that were mooted. But the coal companies wanted to sell theirs, too. The market was glutted with obsolete craft.

One by one the new ships came up the lakes. Great steel hulks that made John's puny fleet look like that of the Lilliputians. It took four of his vessels to carry the same tonnage as one of the new; and gradually the freight brokers came to shake their heads and smile commiseratingly, when, for the first time in twenty years, John had to beg for a cargo.

With the post-war depression, he was forced to beach three of his oldest craft, leaving them to rot in the mouths of muddy creeks. Tied up to a dock, they ran up wharfage accounts like wantons, till grim lines crept into John's face and settled there. And the windows of the wheel-house of the *John L.* mocked him constantly with a drawn visage topped by scraggy whitening hair.

Then he learned of a huge construction company that was about to operate sand and gravel concessions in the Lake of Two Mountains. They gave him a temporary contract, which he accepted with bad grace for two reasons. They told him that his contract would last only as long as it took the shipyards to deliver a fleet of steel scows. Jumping Christopher! Everybody bitten with the same bug? The second and crowning blow came when he nursed the *John L.* up to a dredge that screamed and hissed, and gobbled great scoops of sand and gravel out of the depths only to spew the slimy mass all over his decks. He almost tore his hair out by the roots.

Anthony saw him frequently now. For it isn't a long cruise from the Lake of Two Mountains to Montreal. Anthony, grown more ponderous than ever, was due to be pensioned off soon and was inclined to be garrulous about it. He was likewise inclined to be a little more self-assertive toward John, especially since a morose taciturnity had settled on the latter during the last few years.

But on the last voyage of *John L.* from the Lake of Two Mountains, John turned a stream of lurid rhetoric on Anthony that would have caused a buccaneer to stop his ears for shame. His contract was ended, his account with the construction company overdrawn, all his vessels scrapped except the flagship, and it due to be warped into a quay for the last time.

When Anthony heard its whistle, he was contemplating the scene in the late afternoon sun, remembering days when green fields flowed back from the canal, which today was the bottom of a canyon whose walls were towering mills blackened by the pall of smoke from spindling red stacks. Here and there a blast furnace gushed green and yellow flame against its dusty cowl, disseminating sulphurous fumes which wove in among the black smoke like diaphanous yellow scarves. Another whistle— a deep throaty roar—told him that an upbound freighter was also demanding his attention. He saw that she was coming up light, this great black steel amazon. Her bow was high and her red belly thrust lewdly upward as though greedily seeking the last rays of the sun. High above her in the clean blue sky hummed a plane, flashing in the sun as though proudly aware of its rare freedom.

Anthony turned to look at the *John L.* and shook his head. Forlorn indeed she seemed. Shorn of all her former pride. None of the *Temeraire* about her. And Anthony could not help frowning as he saw the sullen attitude of the crew. He blinked, unbelieving, when he saw one of them actually turn and scowl at John's vituperative commands. Poor old John. Despite his tenacious efforts to drive his men in the classic tradition, the raised eyebrows and drooping mouth betrayed the despair which had seized him. Better let bygones by bygones, thought Anthony. Go along and have a shot at consoling him.

"Got my papers this mornin', John," he began in his friendliest manner. "Pensioned off, I am. Kin drop out anytime I like now. But I got to have somethin' to do . . ."

"Why don't ye join a circus then, Auntie?" innocently.

"What for?"

"Get ye a job in the side show as the fat lady." John guffawed loudly.

"All right!" piped Anthony, scandalized. "I was only tryin' t' be decent to ye in yer advers'ty. Out o' the goodness o' me heart. I'm sorry to have to say it," he concluded with exaggerated hautuer, "but it's just what I'd expect from a feller as would betray me to the Department." Anthony turned his back and walked away from the fuming skipper.

"Well, y' dirty old baggage, y' lyin' old witch," stormed John. "Go get ye a piece o' land and tiddle about with geraniums fer the rest o' yer life. And mind some wicked sea captain don't come along an' marry ye an' drink all yer pension. Me betray yeh? Why, y' . . .!" And until the *John L.* moved out of the lock, Anthony's ears tingled with the epithets which followed him about.

"Cap'n Savage is right, Mr. Green," remarked the man who was due to take over Number Two from Anthony. "He didn't have nothing to do with them complaints. Remember Rat Nelson as was fired from the service for sellin' the timbers we took out of the old lock?" Anthony nodded. "Well, he it was who squealed on you. He was after your job. I knew it. But I was only a kid then and scared of him. Clean forgot about it till you and the cap'n was arguing about it just now."

Anthony was staring absently at the stern of the *John L.* as she moved out. Had he been nursing an unjust grudge against old John all these years? Well, the old fool needn't have been so testy about it. Why hadn't he told him years ago?

"Are ye sure about that?" he asked.

"Absolutely. What's more, I heard him cursing the cap'n, behind his back of course, about some letter the old man had written to Ottawa to get your job back again for you."

"Eh?" asked Anthony, dumbfounded.

"Yes. Seems he was the means of getting them complaints washed out for you."

Anthony swore an appreciative oath and cast a sorrowful glance after the *John L.*

Still brooding on John, he went down to the docks toward dark. These days he traveled in a clanging electric car and had almost forgotten the old straw-strewn horse cars. The Nautilus had changed but little, however, except that now it was crowded with men from all ends of the earth instead of mostly English and French-Canadians as in the old days. Cockneys and Swedes, Italians and Cubans filled the long tables, elbow to elbow. Seven days between decks and seven days in port taverns; and they looked it.

Anthony grunted as he sank his bulk gratefully into a cor-

ner seat, and smoked away stolidly, watching the swinging doors
for John. He was momentarily unaware of several pairs of scowling eyes, turned furtively in his direction from a group of mur-
derous-looking deckhands in an opposite corner. When at last
he gazed absently at them, they seemed to cringe and whisper
among themselves, till, one by one, they gulped down their beer
and slunk out.

Anthony blinked. He had recognized some of them as coming from the crew of the *John L.* It took quite a few minutes for
a suspicion to generate in his brain. But suddenly he stood up,
finished his beer, and waddled out across the cobbles to the stone
wall that enclosed the freight sheds and gaunt elevators. Cold
blue arc lights helped him to pick his way over the tracks. At
that he had to move uncomfortably fast to escape being run
down by an electric train. It had the effect, however, of stimulating his imagination. No use looking for him near the elevators. Now where were the slips that the construction company
used for its sand dumps? Up river to be sure. Anthony sighed at
the thought of the walk and plodded on doggedly. It was pitch
black beyond the passenger docks and he went warily. But in
spite of all his care he tripped and fell over a body prone in his
path. Sitting up and puffing digustedly, Anthony was startled to
hear a moan that was half a snort, nearby. He reached out his
hand and encountered a face. His hand came away damp. Striking a match, he discovered John, his eyelids flickering and an
ugly cut over his temple. The skipper struggled, raised himself
on his elbow; and Anthony slipped an enormous arm under his
shoulders, lifting John into a sitting posture. John swore loudly
and mournfully.

"Them deckhands, Auntie. I didn't have enough to pay
'em off." He felt his pockets. "They swiped me watch even.
Hell. An' all I got left is a boat what nobody'd buy even fer
firewood." He struggled again, and with prodigious effort
Anthony got him to his feet.

"John, I'm sorry fer blamin' ye." There was a shrill quaver

in Anthony's voice. "I just learned about the letter ye wrote fer me."

John ignored the inference by asking, "How did ye know I was beat up?"

"I didn't. But I seen them deckhands o' yourn in the Nautilus. An' when they seen me, they skulks off. I suspected somethin' was up. So I came along lookin' fer ye."

"Thanks, old lady," said John. Anthony winced at the term; but he was willing to forego an argument in view of the honest appreciation in John's tone.

"Better get back to yer ship, John an' take it easy. I'll help ye."

"All right. Damme! But I can't give ye a drink even. Me cabin's bare."

"I'll bring ye some from the Nautilus then."

"H'm. Think I cud walk over meself in a few moments. Feel better now. Come on." It was a command and Anthony found that there was no use in expostulating with the old firebrand.

Once inside the hazy atmosphere, John was himself again. And his eye roved dangerously about, as though seeking his assailants.

Anthony, sitting across from him, viewed this warlike show with sorry skepticism, well aware that John was no match for that hard-bitten crew. But the lockmaster's attention was distracted. For over in a corner, a haggard-looking cockney oiler with a filthy Turkish towel swathed about his throat for a scarf, was wailing out a song. Drunk with beer and sentiment, crocodile tears streaked his grimy cheeks as he strove to drown out a crony who was sprawled across the table babbling "Annie Laurie." The cockney drew a look of injured pride from his mate as he victoriously subdued him with "Silver Threads Among the Gold." Anthony turned to look at John's head. No golden hairs there. In fact the old boy's days were done. His fingers trembled as they reached for the glass; and despite his belligerent air,

Anthony saw that the raised eyebrows, the drooping mouth and thin white hair gave him the lie.

"John, what're ye goin' t' do, now that yer contract's finished?"

John's shoulders sagged slowly and he stared with melancholy eyes at the floor.

"Don't know," he said mechanically.

Timidly Anthony broached a thought that had been brewing ever since he had seen the *John L.* steam out of the lock at sunset.

"I got a bit o' land ten mile down stream, John. A sizable creek runnin' into the river. We cud—er," he was hesitant about going on, but John prodded him. "Well, we cud have a tug tow her . . ." he hated to name the *John L.* and his tone was almost reverent—"up into the creek, an' live on her fer the rest of our days. I'll dig a bit o' garden fer taters an' so on," he added with a weak smile.

They argued about it till the doors of the Nautilus were bolted behind them, argued all the way to the *John L.* and up to the bridge, even under the smoky swinging oil lamp in John's cabin. Anthony finally gained the ascendancy, chiefly because the impoverished skipper's prospects were so bleak that it was either that or starve.

"I owe it to ye, John. But fer yer letter I'd never had this pension. And I've more'n enough fer towage."

"More" was a scanty margin. But it tided them over till the next installment of the pension.

The *John L.* was beached in the creek and Anthony's truck garden well started when he discovered a curé in a village hard by, who was anxious to give him a few geranium slips. And John, coming back to the ship one day after a fit of restless roaming, found his ship deserted. Anthony gone to the village in all probability. John climbed to the bridge and stopped, staring horribly at the sight of the windows of his cabin. There, nailed just under the ledges, were some window boxes, and in them . . .

". . . A'mighty! Geraniums!" snarled John with madness in his eyes. He kicked savagely at one of the window boxes and scattered its earth and stones over his decks. "Sand and gravel!" he muttered weirdly. For some moments he stared aft, unseeing. Better to take her out to sea and sink her, he thought. "Fire and water!" No crew, no money to give her a decent grave and save her from the taunts of a jibing world. Next thing he knew, Auntie would be tying pink bows on the handles of the foc'sle doors, primping her like a simpering old strumpet. "Fire and water! . . . fire!" He peered about artfully. Seeing no sign of Anthony he went below. And when he emerged, a quarter of an hour later, a wisp of smoke followed him out of the companionway.

Up in the village the curé was showing Anthony a new scarlet geranium, when he clutched the latter's arm excitedly.

"Look!" he cried, pointing to the river.

A billowing mass of oily black smoke swirled skyward on the crest of a thousand vicious red tongues.

Anthony did not wait to say adieu. Puffing and grunting, he made for the *John L.* as fast as his enormous legs would carry him. But there was no hope of saving it. It was a seething furnace. John? Anthony's paunch quaked with fear. And his eyes filled with anguish till he caught sight of a bare-headed figure half a mile off, shoulders hunched desolately, striding in the general direction of Montreal.

Two tears rolled down Anthony's fat cheeks as he retreated before the terrific heat and saw, through the wavering smoke, a steel freighter inexorably plowing its way up the river.

"The *Edmund Fitzgerald* in Storm, November 10, 1975." (Edward Pusick; courtesy Shipwrecks Unlimited, Marquette, Michigan.)

White Squall

They're sailing on the northern star
Well off the western shore,
November seas break on her deck
And 'long her bulwarks roar.

The wind hauls north and bares its teeth,
And mountainous grow the seas;
They wash across her slanting decks,
And on her riggin' freeze.

"The Schooner *Thomas Hulme*"
Traditional Great Lakes Song

Getting Bounty from the English

Menomini Story Collected by Leonard Bloomfield

INDIAN BIRCHBARK CANOES have long been recognized as one of the most beautiful and most functional of Great Lakes vessels. Made of native materials and easily repairable on nearly any beach, they were also extremely light and portaged without difficulty, yet were capable of carrying cargoes in excess of four tons. Without them the Northwest could not have been explored so easily, nor could the fur trade have developed as it did. But for all their beauty and their usefulness, they were also extremely tender and liable to swamp in even a moderate sea. They were best suited to rivers and inland lakes, yet they were the only mode of transport for Indians and their often terrified white passengers on the open lakes. There are numerous traveler's accounts, beginning with the Jesuits in the seventeenth century, that describe long, painful days spent sitting absolutely still so the canoe would not ship water and sink.

Besides the fragileness of the canoe and the ever-present threat of water monsters like Missipeshu, many Indian tribes also believed that to drown was to have one's soul wander cursed, forever to haunt the place where one died, and to pass that curse onto one's children. It is understandable then that any voyage, particularly on the lakes, was taken with much trepidation, even after careful preparations had been made to appease the spirits. Those who embarked without proper rites—a fast, a black dog sacrificed to the water, some tobacco left on a sacred rock— were liable to die like those warriors who crossed too hastily after their enemies from Washington Island to the Door Peninsula and so were struck by a storm and lost, giving Death's Door the name it holds today. The story reprinted here tells of a voyage to collect bounty payments which probably began from a Menomini village on the Wisconsin shore and ended at the British garrison on Mackinac Island sometime before the War of 1812. Even today, in a technologically sophisticated sailboat equipped with radar, Loran, and automatic pilot, this is a taxing trip; we can scarcely imagine what it must have been like in an open canoe steered by the stars.

WHEN MY GRANDMOTHER was as big as this, being twelve winters old, then the people were summoned by the English, who wished to give them money and things to wear and things to eat. Then the Menomini made birch-bark canoes; four fathoms long were the canoes. And then, when they had completed them, they put into them their blanket-robes and their kettles. And then,—there were many children,—then all the children were put on board. Then four [?] grown people got in, to take along their children. Then all the Menomini, as many as were able, went along, all the canoes being launched at the same time.

    Then they started forth on their voyage. They did not see any land by which to direct their course; they observed the sun and moon: they went due east.

    When they were about to start, they made a great burnt-offering,[1] making prayer to the spirits of the water that they

---

1. The word, normally at least, implies tobacco as that which is burnt. [Bloomfield's note.]

might safely reach their goal and return. They were heard. Not once did the wind blow while they voyaged. For ten days they voyaged, all day and all night; the grown people who did the paddling slept by turns.

Then, from some quarter a wind did spring up; the water to some slight degree came into motion; the women grew frightened and wept. Then one man was given tobacco, a man who had performed a great fast and had seen a vision of the waters. He accepted the tobacco and made a speech, dropping the tobacco into the water. Then, when he had finished his speech, then they all sang: thereupon the wind stopped.

So then they again started to paddle. As they paddled on and on, when they had eaten all of what little provision they had on the way, then they would eat only a little salt. Thereupon they would drink water; in this way their hunger was stilled.

As they voyaged along, a wind came up. Of course, they were as good as dead, if the wind grew strong. So then they made four tiny vessels of birch-bark; and into each little vessel of birch-bark they set an insect, namely a louse: and then they placed those little vessels into the water. Then those little vessels tipped over; then were the children made to weep, so that they wept loudly: and then all the grown people spoke.

"Now they are all dead!" cried the women.

At that the wind ceased and the water lay quiet.

Then they went on with all speed, all of them paddling, that they might quickly arrive.

At last they came in sight of land; they had reached their destination.

When they had disembarked there in the Englishman's town, they were given plenty to eat, the Englishman giving them raised bread, pork, and all sorts of things. When they had eaten, they were at ease. Some of them did not eat any bread; they did not know what it was, or pork either.

On the next day the English gave them silver coins, such and such a number, giving a large sum of money to each and every one of these Indians, and giving them also garments, blankets, broadcloth, and all things.

So much did I hear my grandmother tell when I was little. That is all. "Unbounded-Space" was my grandmother's name.

The Deep Water Mate

Norman Reilly Raine

WHEN RAINE began work as a newspaper man for the *Buffalo Express* in 1912, the days of sail were nearly over. But Buffalo had its memories, and there would have still been wind-ship men from salt water looking for work who stopped at the first lake port they came to and signed on for a trip. Buffalo was a crossroads for men from fresh water and from salt, and their memories, stories, and brawls would have been colorful inspiration for a young writer. In this story of a voyage across Lake Superior to the Sault, Raine creates a classic confrontation between a tough, driving saltwater mate and a relaxed Great Lakes captain, between a man accustomed to enforcing discipline on long ocean voyages by brute force, and one who governs by respect alone. Holystoning the decks—scrubbing them down with a piece of sandstone, as the mate in the story attempts to force the crew to do—was a common practice in the navy and on larger saltwater merchant ships in the nineteenth century. Dana, in *Two Years before the Mast*, and Melville, in *White Jacket*, both make much of its drudgery. But it is unlikely that many lakes sailors on small schooners were ever forced to apply stone to deck on their hands and knees, for as Raines' mate discovers, they have more important things to do. Their casualness about sailing etiquette is not disrespect for their officers, but reflects the more tolerant attitude on lakes ships, where what mattered was not how clean the deck was, but given the storms on the lakes—here a classic Nor'Easter—whether one was a good enough seaman to save the deck to stand on.

THE BIG MAN in the pilot-cloth jacket, with the anchors tattooed on his thick sunbrowned wrists, tacked out of the traffic of the lake port's main street, and down toward the waterfront. There was an easy swing to his stride that hinted of rolling decks and foreign oceans, and on his weather-reddened face was the stamp of command. A deepwater man you would say, if you knew the breed, and a wind ship man to boot.

Passing through a region of railroad freight yards, elevators, and lumber mills, he came to the docks, snuffing the fresh lake air, his seaman's eyes resting with disparagement upon the vessels made fast alongside. They were typical Great Lakes craft, long in the waist and engined aft, with the navigating bridge stuck up almost on the forecastle head. Built by the mile, and chopped off in lengths, he thought: all guts and no backbone; good for their purpose, with plenty of cargo space, but ugly, and no use in a seaway. Still, what kind of a sea were they likely to have to face on these inland patches of landlocked water? He laughed shortly.

Consulting a scrap of paper he turned down along a lumber yard toward a nearby slip. He could see the lofty topmasts of a large three-masted schooner above the piles of sweet-smelling pine, and instinctively he noted the state of her top hamper. None too tidy, and with Irish pennants flying here and there.[1] If she was the ship he was seeking, and he got the berth he was after, he'd soon change all that.

The schooner's slender jibboom came into view, the headsails rumpled over the feet of the stays like a paperhanger's dis-

---

1. The top hamper is the ship's upper works or rigging. Irish pennants are fag ends of rope yarn or strips of canvas left hanging in the rigging.

carded overalls.[2] A nameboard, bolted to the ungainly bows, spelled *Juniper* in gold scrolls on a white ground. She was deep in the water; full below hatches, and with a deckload of heavy square-cut timbers that rose to the level of the poop and were secured by thwartship chains and turnbuckles.

The deepwater man crossed the plank that served as a gangway, his practised gaze taking in further details of her running and standing gear. Fairly sound, he decided, but sloppy; typical of the dishpan seamanship of fresh water. He made his way aft.

On the poop, two of the crew, interrupted in their task of washing down the paintwork of the house, were being entertained with a lively exhibition of the black bottom by a raffish-looking young man with curly hair, a bright smile, and a small mustache. He finished his turn, not at all abashed, then greeted the stranger. "Ah, there!" he said.

The big man ignored him and turned to the others.

"Is the master on board?"

They eyed him curiously. One said, "Eh?"

"Where's the captain?"

The bright young man became helpful.

"I'm the second mate. Anything you want?"

The deepwater man turned his level gaze upon him and the second mate's smile suddenly faded.

"Oh, the captain! Just a minute: I'll call him. He's below, changing his duds. Cap'n Sam . .! Cap'n Sam! Here's a feller wants to see you!"

There was no answer. He repeated the summons. After a time an equable drawling voice responded.

"All right, son: keep your shirt on. I'll be there, soon's I get into these danged pants. Don't want to give the gulls a treat."

Presently the owner of the voice appeared, a wisp of a man

---

2. A spar designed to extend the bowsprit, the jibboom spreads the stays on which the headsails are set.

with sparse gray hair, and a face as red and shining as a winter haw. There was a quirk to his lips, and shrewdness in his bright, bird-like eyes. He nodded to the stranger.

"Want to see me? Ye'll have to speak up. I'm a little deef."

"Are you Captain Coffin?"

"That's me. Samuel Coffin—gen'ally called Cap'n Sam . . . eh!"

"I'm looking for a berth. Heard you needed a mate."

The bright eyes crinkled.

"Sure do. Say, you're a salt-water man, ain't ye? What's your qualifications?"

"Master's ticket in sail. I—"

"Jest a minute." Captain Coffin turned to his men. "If you two boys are through massagin' that house ye can kill some more time by draggin' out the split standin' jib, an' havin' Charlie there do some stitchin' on it. Good fer toughenin' yer hands, Charlie, case ye tuke to dancin' on them, 'stead o' your feet. Come along below, mister, an' we'll get your pedigree."

The main cabin was roomy and comfortable, with leather-covered settees and chairs, and a few homey prints about the bulkheads between the ports; but it was none too tidy, and articles of the captain's apparel could be seen on the floor through the open door of his room. Mentally the deepwater man compared the place with other ship's cabins he had known, and fresh-water stock took another drop.

The old man waved him to a seat, and crammed a horny thumb comfortably into his pipe bowl.

"From salt water, eh?" he resumed, and his eyes were interested. "What are ye doin' in these parts."

"I was mate o' the bark *Firefly*, out of Singapore for New York and Halifax. We got caught in a squall among the Islands, down in the South Pacific, and she piled her rump on French Frigate Shoal. She's there yet."

"Whose watch'd she go ashore in?" Captain Sam interjected quickly.

"Mine. I'd just come on deck when she struck."

"Hmm! Got any papers with ye?"

He scanned the proffered papers painstakingly, then folded and returned them.

"Name's Hammond, eh? I see ye got a commendation from the Wreck Commissioner over that *Firefly* business. Papers look all right, too. I seen worse. What happened then?"

"I got to Vancouver and found orders from the owners, to come east to New Brunswick and take over another ship—the *Sumatra*; but I'm not wanted there till the end o' next month. I've never seen the lakes, and thought I'd try them out for a passage down. Yesterday's paper said your mate had died, so—"

Captain Sam nodded.

"He did—beyond recover. Died of over-fondness: women an' shellac. You a drinkin' man? Moderate, eh?"

He pondered for a minute, fingertips together.

"I ain't conductin' a Cook's tour exactly," he said drily, "an' prob'ly you'll find things different on the lakes from salt water. We don't raise no chanteys fer a mains'l haul, an' we don't have no flyin'-fish fer breakfast like that feller Dana tells about; but if you can do without them nautical luxuries for a spell the berth's yours." A queer wistfulness crept into his voice. "I'll be kind o' glad to have a man from salt water on board. Allus was interested in life on the ocean wave."

Hammond glanced at him sharply, but there was no guile in the old face; merely, the eyes seemed brighter—almost boyish. Captain Sam arose.

"We're bound down the lakes, sailin' tonight. So if you'll get your gear aboard ye can take that cabin on yonder side. Joab's in there at present havin' a nap. He's a melodious character, Joab is, though ye wouldn't think it to hear him now. He'll be out, time ye get back. He walked over and pounded on a closed cabin door. "Joab! Get up out o' that, ye lazy rascal! The new mate's aboard."

A grunt and renewed snores answered him. Captain Sam grinned, and read the question in Hammond's tightened brows.

"Joab? Oh, he's the cook. He comes aft an' lets me beat him at cribbage fer the privilege o' drinkin' my applejack. Him an' me's been shipmates fer years."

That evening the *Juniper* was snaked out of her slip, and put under sail. The night passed without event, and morning found her standing down Lake Superior with everything set and drawing well under a fair breeze. On the starboard beam, the Isle Royale coastline was a slender shadow of purple and jade.

The new mate, standing on the poop, watched with active distaste the crew's leisurely method of swabbing down under direction of the bosun. The latter was a Swede, lulled by years of fat inland living into forgetfulness of his harsher early days on the Western Ocean. He moved lazily about the decks, smoking an evil-smelling meerschaum and passing jokes in a tone of easy familiarity with his grinning men. Hammond observed their slipshod labors for a time, planning for them a sudden and drastic awakening. When Captain Sam appeared the mate asked if there were any holystones on board. The captain was mildly amazed.

"Holystones? What fer? Fer the decks?" He chuckled. "Bless ye, man, them planks don't need holystones. We ain't entertainin' no furrin potentates an' their dusky wives when we make port. The decks ain't like a yacht, I'll admit, but I seen worse."

Hammond turned on his heel, flushing darkly. "Damned bathtub sailors with an ole woman for a skipper," he thought, and his eye roved derisively over the smiling lake. As the day wore on the late mate of the skys'l-yarder *Firefly* increasingly realized the truth of the old man's words—that here he would find things different from salt-water ways. Accustomed to the hard discipline and unquestioning obedience of a crack deepwater wind-bag, he found it impossible to readjust his habits. Things annoyed him; the casual method of casting off and getting under sail the previous night; the flippant manner of that half-baked little sweep, the second mate; the presence in the cabin of the garrulous, hymn-singing old cook, Joab, who came aft for a yarn and a game with Captain Sam after dark and kept Hammond awake for half his watch below with a lugubrious rendition of "Now the day is over, Night is drawing nigh . . ."

From the start he was unpopular with the crew. They sensed his unspoken contempt, and although there was something in the bearing of the big, sea-toughened, wind ship man, with his bowed legs and formidable chin and great tattooed hands as he stood balancing easily on the poop, that effectually checked open expression of their resentment, they managed in countless small ways to gall him, until his gnarled finger joints yearned to manhandle them.

Captain Sam noticed the mate's scorn of his surroundings, but said nothing. In his chirpy way he seemed to extract a certain pawky humor from observation of Hammond's initiation into fresh-water ways, especially as he realized that on lake ships more modern than his own were standards hardly excelled by the smartest of ocean craft.

In his watch below, the mate was invited by the old man to inspect his cabin. The reason for this was plain when Hammond noticed the trend of the considerable library which Captain Sam maintained on shelves made fast to the bulkhead. The captain's face beamed with pride as he indicated the books, and the heaps of dog-eared magazines that cluttered one end of the settee.

"You ought to feel at home in here, mister," he said. "Them's all stories about salt-water sailin'. Kind of a hobby o' mine. Read ever'thin' I can get a holt of on the subject. Set down a minute."

He seated himself opposite, and drawing at his pipe plied Hammond with questions. The mate, insensibly flattered, narrated briefly some of his experiences and described in technical terms some of the blows he had weathered in remote seas. Captain Sam sat back, blue smoke wreathing his head, in the seventh heaven of contentment. It was clear that life on the rolling deep possessed for him much of the vital fascination that an adventurous boy would feel.

Hammond rose to go topside, after a terse and unvarnished account of bloody all-night fight off the China coast some years before, when a ship in which he was second mate had been attacked by piratical, fast-sailing junks off Bias Bay.

"It must be great to have seen an' actually lived through them things," said Captain Sam, with glowing eyes, "but ye must have had a purty good ship's company back o' ye. What say?"

They were on deck now, and the mate's eyes traveled forward along the timber-piled waist of the old *Juniper*, to where two of the crew were muddling through a wire splicing job.

"Yes sir," he made belated answer. "But they were seamen, all o' them, of course."

"Of course," echoed Captain Sam.

Hammond suddenly was curious.

"Have you never sailed salt water, sir. I should think . . ."

Captain Sam shook his head. His hand indicated the expanse of Lake Superior, blue and sparkling under the summer sun, the horizon smudged with the smoke of many steamers, the shoreline periodically etched with the tall chimneys of industry.

"No . . . I never even seen it. I been sailin' these here lakes for over fifty years. It ain't been very excitin'. I guess the atmosphere ain't right: no palms, nor coral islands, nor the like o' that. When I was a boy I used to dream of adverturin' some. But I had responsibilities at home, when the old man died. Then, later, I planned on mebbe havin' a trip to the Maritime Provinces. But here I am still. O' course, even on the lakes it comes on to storm purty hard, sometimes. I've had some close shaves that way myself—nothin' like what you'd get on the ocean," he hastened to add, "but purty bad in their way, especially in the fall. An' one time I was caught out in the ice in an early freeze-up, an' had two o' the hands froze to death an' the rest of us starvin' fer a few days. But they ain't adventures, strictly speakin'."

The mate's eyes took in the fresh green of the coast, the dimpled water, the great clouds reflected in the rippling surface of the lake. He thought of the cabin fare—identical with that of the men: fresh meat at all times, new-grown vegetables and fruit in season; the best of everything, and plenty of it; and he found it hard, indeed, to link it up with the perils and hardships that were part and parcel of life afloat as he had known it.

"It isn't very stimulating, is it?" he said.

"Stimulatin'? Well, no-o, it ain't." The old man sighed; then he chuckled. "I'm an old fool. After all, scratchin' a livin's stimulation enough fer most men, an' this ain't such a bad way o' doin' that. I seen worse."

The *Juniper* was an old vessel, worn with years of knocking up and down the thousand miles of the Great Lakes. She was clumsy, and a poor sailor except with a stiff wind on the quarter, when she would snore along at almost six knots to the great delight of her crew, her ancient timbers groaning, and her worn gear chafing and threatening to come adrift. But Captain Sam made her produce whatever was in her, and never an ounce of wind was spilled.

The afternoon of the second day she was slapping along, heeling before a good breeze, with the vivid reach of the lake to port, and off to starboard the verdant coastline of Keweenaw Point. The mate was on the poop when a deckhand named Grost, a big, pot-bellied, untidy fellow with an ugly jaw, passed aft to take his trick at the wheel. In deepwater parlance Grost "spit brown"; that is, he was an inveterate tobacco chewer, and had a perpetual dribble down his stubbly chin. Hammond had noted his lubberly habit of discharging this liquid cargo about the deckload and the forecastle head; and if his aim in the general direction of the lake went astray he did not seem greatly to mind.

The man now gave his belt a hitch, took the wheel, and

covertly eyeing the mate relieved his facial muscles of their strain. Hammond, at the poop break, turned just in time to see the brown fluid bespatter the deck. He crossed the deck at a bound, eyes blazing at this cardinal deepwater sin.

"You lousy Port Mahon baboon!" he roared. "What the devil do you mean by that?"

The big sailor's gaze roved over him in insolent appraisal. He dropped a ham-like fist from the wheel and clenched it.

"Kind o' finiky, ain't you?" he said cooly, and spat again, just missing the mate's foot.

Hammond summoned the second mate who was enjoying it all against the rail.

"Take the wheel," he said quietly.

The second mate's glistening smile disappeared.

"Hey!" he protested. "I ain't supposed to . . ."

"*Take the wheel!*" the mate repeated in a Cape Horn voice.

The other obeyed with alarcrity.

As Grost's hands left the wheel the deepwater man stepped in, corded muscles bunched, and smashed him with both fists. The other was a vicious fighter with plenty of weight and courage, but he was no match for the mate, who was built like an oak, and had a reputation as a man-killer in the forecastles of tall ships. When he had beaten his man into submission, which did not take long, Hammond, stemming a cut lip, sent him for a bucket and a swab and made him clean up the mess.

"Give me time, and I'll make sailors of some of you yet," he promised grimly. "Get back to the wheel, you slut!—and when your trick's done you'll lay aft and swab your trademarks off the forecastle head!"

Captain Sam, attracted by the stamp of feet overhead, reached the deck in time to see the last of the fracas. He did not interfere, but his lips went tight, and there was a hard light in his eyes that seemed to add inches to his stature. He waited until the deepwater man moved out of earshot of the man at the wheel, then he approached him.

"I'm makin' allowance for your peculiar point o' view, mister," he said, striving to keep his voice down, "but in future, keep your hands off the men. Bucko mates went out o' style on the lakes years ago. I got other ways of disciplinin' the hands when they need it, and they don't need no kicks to make 'em do what's wanted."

Hammond's voice thickened with astonished rage.

"Did you see what he did, sir?" he demanded. "Spat on the poop—the swine!"

"Well, 'spose he did? A mite o' tabacco juice won't sink us. It's hard to pass up, accordin' to your lights, but ye have to overlook a lot o' things on fresh water; an' ye can't beat up deck hands these days. They'll have the law to ye if ye do."

The law, for skelping an impudent seaman! All the traditions of the mate's briny past boiled up in him. By a mighty effort he controlled himself.

"Very good, sir," he rasped. "You're the master, o' course, and I'm here to obey your orders. But if I fail in my duty as mate, with this pack o' hay-raking tomcats, ye needn't call me to book!"

"Ye won't fail, mister, if you're willing' to learn somethin'. These fellers work in factories all winter, and there's not much chance to make real sailors out of 'em. They ain't such bad boys, at that, as ye might trouble to discover. I seen worse."

Hammond paced the deck in tight-lipped silence. He was fed up with Great Lakes ships and their lily-white ways; manned by factory hands and circus roustabouts who didn't know square sennit from Barney's bull. He thought of seamen he had known—every hair a rope yarn, and blood of Stockholm tar, as the old saying goes. Nostalgia gripped him. Back to salt water, where a ship's officer could call his soul his own!

Toward evening the breeze freshened. The sky was a pale green that deepened to vivid emerald in the east, casting an eerie light over the darkening water. The old man came on deck with his pipe, and sniffed.

"Goin' to have some wind presently," he told the mate. The *Juniper* rolled deeply, and the water boiled up the lee rail. "Better send a couple of hands along and give an extra twist to them turnbuckles on the deckload."

Hammond was relieved, and went below for his supper. When he returned to the poop the wind had dropped, and the lake was a dead flat clam. The *Juniper's* big sails shook thunderously. Soon, catspaws came stealing over the smooth expanse. Wind lanes appeared, riffling the water. The wind arrived from the northeast in sudden vicious puffs which soon melted into a steady blow, rapidly increasing in strength. There was no afterglow in the sky, and slatey scud obscured the early stars.

After a bit, solid water rapped the *Juniper's* ungainly bow and cascaded aft along the heavy deckload. Ahead, the dark bulk of Caribou Island showed for a brief space, then was swallowed in a driving squall, accompanied by rain.

The mate glanced aloft. "Ease her a bit," he told the man at the wheel. The bow responded and the strain decreased. Plenty of time to take in sail.

Captain Sam appeared at his elbow, with the mate's oilskins and sou'wester on his arm. The old man himself was clad for weather.

"Better get inside 'em, mister," he said. "The lake's goin' to kick up nasty after a bit, an' ye'll need 'em."

Hammond thanked him perfunctorily, but ignored the advice. Inwardly, he snorted. A sea kick up nasty on this bloated millpond!

It was now quite dark. Captain Sam put his head into the wind and crossing to the weather side clung to the mizzentopmast backstay,[3] smelling the wind and peering into the gloom for a sight of Caribou Island. Ahead, was rain and pitch blackness. A wild night.

---

3. Backstays are ropes or wires that support the masts against the forward thrust of sails. A mizzentopmast backstay supports the top section of the mizzen mast.

Presently he returned to Hammond. "We're in for a real buster," he shouted above the rising scream of the wind. "Did ye sight Caribou before dark shut down?"

The mate gave him the bearing, and he glanced in the binnacle.

"We're all right so far's that's consarned then," he grunted. "Bring her up a bit more an' we'll get some sail off her."

At midnight the *Juniper* was battering into an enormous head sea that smote her old hull until she quivered from trucks to keel.[4] The combers mounted over the bows like hungry, gray, white-maned wolves and round aft along the deckload to fetch up with a smash and a cloud of blinding spray against the house. Hammond long since had donned his oilskins, and with the action discarded one or two notions respecting the power of Lake Superior sea when pushed by a force-ten gale. Used to the long, regular, surging ocean billows, he was first amazed, then disconcerted at the pounding power of the lumpy chop that seemed to flop aboard from all directions out of the belly of the night. It was like nothing he had experienced. He ventured a remark to Captain Sam through cupped palms. The reply was snatched away by the wind, but he caught the words: ". . . seen worse!" "Lord!" he thought, and wiped his rain-beaten face, conscious of a vague surprise that he tasted no salt on his lips, until he remembered. By two o'clock in the morning the wind had increased to hurricane force.

Captain Sam, forced to seek shelter for his frail body against the strength of the blow, remained unperturbed. Unlighted pipe between his lips he made himself as comfortable as possible in the lee of the house, darting out at intervals for a word with the mate whose burly form hovered constantly near the wheel. Lifelines had been rigged along the deckload from the forecastle, but every trip along its length was a gamble, with

---

4. A truck is a wooden cap on the top of a mast.

death holding most of the tricks. Insensibly, in the midst of the welter of pounding seas and the clamorous shriek of the wind through the thrumming cordage, Hammond became aware of a high shrill note as of someone singing. His head jerked up as the skinny frame of the old cook, clad in oilskins many sizes too large for him, rounded the house and staggered across the poop lugging a heavy covered pail and singing at the top of his voice:

"Fierce was the wild billow, dark was the night:
Oars labored bravely, foam glimmered white—
Have some hot coffee!"

He dipped it out in a granite mug and handed it first to the mate, then to the wheelsman, whom the mate relieved while he drank it.

"Trembled the mariner; peril was nigh—"
the quavering old voice went on.

Captain Sam jumped out of his shelter and shouted at him.

"Get away down below, ye old scamp! D'ye want to be swept overboard?"

Joab waved him off, and started for the break of the poop. Before anyone could prevent it he was on the deckload. He turned, yelling indignantly, "Don't ye want the boys to have none!"

The streaming night closed in on him as he made his precarious way toward the forecastle.

"Then said the God of Gods, 'Peace, it is I' "
The words came faintly aft on the breast of the wind.

Suddenly a sharp twisting crack ripped out of the blackness for'ard, followed by a muffled tumbling roar that vibrated through the clamor of the storm. The *Juniper* lurched to starboard and a gigantic sea thundered along the deckload. It was lipped with swishing white, and in the half-phosphorescent glow of the crest a great square-sawn timber twisted like a match before being whirled astern. A mountain of solid water leaped over the poop.

"Look out!" Hammond roared, and jumped for the wheel

to help the man wrestle with it. They were swept off their feet but clung desperately to the kicking spokes, reinforced, when the sea was past, by Captain Sam.

The young second mate, drenched from head to foot, emerged with white face and staring eyes from the boiling flood. He staggered over the mate and grasped his big shoulder with frenzied fingers.

"Joab!" he screamed. "He was caught in that!"

His body shuddered convulsively. For a moment he appeared to hesitate, then like an arrow he darted for'ard.

"Come back you fool!" Hammond shouted, but the second mate was gone after the old cook.

A second grinding crash came from somewhere between poop and forecastle. The tortured *Juniper* lurched again—terribly; and when she recovered her decks were canted far beyond the angle created by the wind. The mate's stout heart hammered at his ribs. The deckload had shifted.

Captain Sam was at his side. "I know," he shouted. "Get the rest o' the hands aft!"

It was unnecessary to summon them. They came streaming out of the blackness, soaked, dishevelled, wild-eyed for the moment.

"Where's Joab? Where's Charlie? Are they with ye?" the old man roared, but dumb looks and head-shaking answered him.

Darkness hid the sudden twisting of Captain Sam's lips. He clamped his teeth on his pipe, half-full of wet tobacco, biting into the tough stem.

"Get them gripes off the boat," he directed presently. "We prob'ly won't need it, but it's as well to be ready. We're in a fix, but I seen worse, an' I guess you have too, Mr.—"

"*Hang on all!*"

The deepwater man's mighty bellow assailed their ears. The hull of the *Juniper* rose as though lifted by a titanic hand. She rolled to leeward—farther—farther, until the white water roared over the bulwarks. From for'ard rumbled a cascading thunder of sound. The lofty topmasts swung in a wide lateral arc.

"*She's going over!*"

Heartbeats stopped as the warning cry went up. The great booms jerked and kicked like insane things at their splitting crutches. Another immense sea swept the poop, and the *Juniper's* company, clustered like ants on the weather of the sharply tilted deck, fought desperately for a stable grip. The list increased. The *Juniper* was on her beam ends.

The deepwater mate, cold and resourceful in emergency, thought fast, and made a decision. After all, he owed Captain Sam something. In a lull before the next murderous comber he grasped the arm of the man nearest him, and shouted in his ear. The fellow obeyed, and they crept aft to the cabin companionway. With infinite difficulty they got inside and below, guided by the smoking lamp that hung bumping at the extreme limit of its gimbals. The main cabin was flooded, and loose articles of gear swashed to and fro. The great timbers of the deckload were holding *Juniper* down as in a vice, but the mate knew that if they were released she stood a chance to right herself. He was looking for an axe. He found one—a fire axe—in its rack on the after bulkhead, and passed it back to his companion. As he did so he saw the man's face for the first time. It was Grost, his tobacco-chewing adversary.

"I'm going to clear the deckload, but I need help," the mate told him. "We may both get snuffed out, but it's the ship's only chance. Are you with me?"

Grost's ugly jaw tightened. He spat brown into the flooded cabin.

"Sure," he grunted. "Let's go!"

They regained the poop and made their dangerous way for'ard, freezing to the weather rail once they were clear of the house. Hammond made a length of line fast to his waist, passing the free end to Grost with instructions to haul taut and help brace him as he struck. Opposite the mainmast Grost took a turn about his own body and passed the end through a ringbolt for purchase, and the mate moved like a molasses-trapped fly down the sheer slope of the deckload. They waited desperately, clinging to breath as they were engulfed in a shouting sea. Hammond dropped still farther, fumbling with his toes for a foothold on the uneven surface.

He found it, with one of the chains under his heel. "Haul taut!" he roared, and Grost braced himself. Hammond raised his axe and swung. Once—twice—the bright blade flashed in the dark, steel against straining steel with all the weight and power of the deepwater mate's tremendous muscles behind the blows. There was a crack, a metallic *pung* and the chain parted, the massive timbers rolling free in a sonorous cataract of sound. Held only by the straining muscles and thick body of the sailor, Hammond swung for a second between life and death; then a quick heave dragged him free of the hurtling sticks and he bumped against the sharp pitch of the *Juniper*'s deck.

The gallant old vessel, free of her burden, swung around in the trough of the sea and jerked like a fallen horse, striving to clear her masts from the clogging water. Again a terrific cracking split the night as she rose superbly to the strain. Something was bound to give, and the *Juniper* rolled sickeningly back to an even keel, totally dismasted.

Helped by eager arms the two regained the poop in time to become aware of a new manace. The parted masts, held to the ship by stays and rigging, began a relentless pounding against the vessel's side. Like colossal rams the huge spars were battering the *Juniper* to pieces.

Captain Sam, his cold pipe still between his teeth, ranged alongside the mate.

"Ye done noble," he shouted, "but she won't stand this long. We'll have to cut adrift from the wreckage."

"That won't serve," Hammond told him. "The wind is driving her right down on it. We'll try it if you like though."

More axes were secured, and the crew, dodging the sweeping seas, worked like fiends along the lee rail, parting the strands that held the tangle of wreckage to the vessel's side. It was as the mate had said. The force of the wind pressed the *Juniper* upon the hammering spars, and she was commencing to break up.

Captain Sam's voice was calm, almost casual, as he made his heart-breaking decision, but the mate was not deceived.

"Get the boat swung out," the old man said. "We've got to leave her." He turned his suddenly-lined face east, to where a faint streak of rose divided the horizon from the night.

The *Juniper*'s crew were not a very seamanlike crowd in their handling of the boat. They bungled the job badly until the mate took hold; but, somehow, the deepwater man found nothing to criticise. And even he made a slip that brought a grim smile to the old man's lips as he strove for his balance on the reeling poop.

"What about fresh-water breakers for the boats, sir?" he had asked.

Captain Sam dodged a swishing sea, and jerked his thumb after it.

"Help yourself, mister," he said. "There's plenty for all."

Daybreak unveiled a wind-shot expanse of tumbling gray water as the *Juniper*'s boat dropped from the davits. The mate noticed with some astonishment that before leaving the poop Captain Sam had made one end of a coil of light but stout line fast to the quarter-bitts, and had tossed the remainder in the bow of the boat. The old man was the last to leave the vessel, sliding awkwardly down the falls. He waited for a rise, unhooked the block, and instantly the boat was gripped by a sea and whisked clear.

"Out oars," Captain Sam commanded. "Mister, you'll take the helm for a bit. Now then, boys, bend to it!"

Clumsily, the inexperienced crew pulled away. Daylight was increasing rapidly, and the mate now saw the purpose of the line which still connected them with the *Juniper*, and which Captain Sam was paying out from the bows as the distance increased. The abandoned hulk was in clear view, battered by smoking seas, and the thud and crash of the sundered masts against her ribs was audible above the tumult of wind and water.

Captain Sam gave his line into the care of a man in the bows, with instructions to belay when he gave the word. Then he clambered aft into the sternsheets. "Belay!" He sang out, presently, and the boat's head swung around, riding to a long painter with the wreck of the *Juniper* as a sea anchor. By occasional manipulation of the oars the boat was able to take advantage of the shelter afforded by the hulk against the menacing seas. Over the stern they could make out the loom of the land.

"Aren't you going to make for the beach, sir?" the mate protested. "The *Juniper*'s done for, and it's not above four or five mile—"

"No, mister," Captain Sam answered doggedly, sucking at his drowned pipe. "I ain't. Chances are a hundred to one the *Juniper*'ll founder before this blows itself out—though, accordin' to the look o' the sky that won't be long either. But so long as one stick of her holds to another I'm still master of her and responsible to the owners—and I'm goin' to hang on!"

"But—"

"But nothin'!" and for the first time a trace of acerbity crept into the old man's tone. "I ain't agoin' to make shore an' then watch some steamer, mebbe, pick up the *Juniper* an' tow her into the Soo for a nice fat salvage. If she's towed in, I'll be aboard, an' so will my boys here. You know best about salt-water ways, but fresh-water men stand by their ships till they go under. What say?"

The deepwater mate did not resent the thrust.

"I said, sir," he answered slowly, "that we have no lessons to give you. I may not be much as a fresh-water mate, but I'm sticking with you, and proud to do it."

The old man instantly relented. He reached over and his old fingers closed about the mate's huge biceps.

"Who said you wasn't much of a mate, son?" he said. "I seen lots worse—but I never seen a better!"

The Survival of the Fittest

Morgan Robertson

AS THE TWILIGHT of the sailing era fell over the lakes, many ships were still seaworthy but too small and slow to be profitable except as barges towed behind a larger, swifter tug. With their topmasts cut down, the once-proud wind ships trailed up and down the lakes at the end of a rope, a common sight at the turn of the century. The grave danger was that if the rope should part the tow had difficulty propelling herself with her stubby masts, and so she was at the mercy of the waves. This is the story of one such occurrence, a tour de force description of an untutored mechanical genius with no sailing experience who discovers how to jury-rig an abandoned barge to avoid being wrecked.

Heroic adventures of this type have long been a staple of maritime fiction, although most are set on salt water. One of the more famous is *The Sea Wolf* by Jack London, whose career began as Robertson's was ending. Both writers subscribed to the late nineteenth-century idea of Naturalism, a literary philosophy based on the biological determinism of Darwin—the survival of the fittest—and the economic theories of Marx. But Robertson was more seaman than artist and so he pays particular attention to the mechanics of sailing. Since he was the son of a lakes captain and had qualified as a saltwater mate, the technical terms he takes for granted most modern readers will not recognize, making "The Survival of the Fittest" a demanding story. Nevertheless, it is worth a little effort, for it portrays aspects of sailing still relevant in a manner as absorbing as that of Dana or of Melville.

HE HAD STARTED life at sixteen on a small farm in Ohio, had won the heart of the farmer's wife by putting new life and ambition into the disabled old clock during her absence, but had incurred the wrath of the farmer himself by taking apart the threshing-machine, which showed signs of wear and which he had sincere intentions of mending. A sound beating caused a vacancy on that farm, and filled a corner of a freight-car with a small boy bound for the West. He never reached that ever-receding section. Hunger brought him out at a small town and compelled him to beg; and finding this means of livelihood easier than working, he continued at it, and developed in a few years into as picturesque a "tramp" as ever enlivened rural scenery.

He was not vicious, only ignorant and lazy. Sometimes, to relieve ennui, he would work for a few days, but only at labor that brought him into contact with machinery. He was a born mechanic; but this expresses all. He knew by intuition things that successful civil and mechanical engineers would be glad to acquire after years of study, at the same time possessing none of the balance of mind that makes us respectable. He had a bulging forehead, with ears set well back on his head. A phrenologist, examining such a head, would have described it as showing large imitation, hope, form, and weight; abnormally large causality, comparison, and constructiveness; but sadly deficient in continuity, combativeness, destructiveness, firmness, acquisitiveness, and approbativeness.[1] With a little energy he could easily have earned at least the title of "Jack of all trades," but even this was

---

1. Phrenology was an eighteenth- and nineteenth-century philosophy that attempted to prove intelligence and character could be detected from skull formation.

beyond him. In short, he was a happy-go-lucky vagabond, with an ever-increasing repugnance for work, and an ever-decreasing community of interest with his fellow-men.

He wandered to New York, and stood with a crowd watching the ascent of a large safe, which men were hoisting by means of a wagon-winch to the upper story of a high building. A man stood on the safe, guiding it. People passed underneath, indifferent to danger, and no one but our "tramp" noticed a slight movement of the rope, just above the wagon, followed by a quick untwisting, as a strand parted.

"Stop!" he yelled, "the rope's breaking."

"'Vast heaving!" roared the foreman. "Stand from under! Jump for a window, Tom—jump for your life!"

People scattered to the middle of the street. Among the first were the foreman and his men. The man on the safe frantically climbed the tackle to reach a window just above him. The two remaining strands of the rope quivered under the strain, becoming fuzzy with the ends of yarns that had broken and were forced outward, while the broken strand showed its spiral bulging six feet above the place of fracture. Then the tattered idler on the sidewalk made some very quick movements. Seizing the end of the rope from the wagon, he pulled about eight feet twice around a nearby lamp post, over and under itself, thus hitching it. Jumping to the wagon with the end, he tied it to the straining rope as high up as he could reach, then sprang to the ground a second before the overworked remaining strands snapped. Down came the heavy safe a foot or so, and the reinforced rope sang under the sudden tension, the man above barely held his grip on the tackle, and the lamp post was bent and nearly wrenched from the ground. But the hitch did not slip.

The foreman and his helpers came back with some new ideas. The rope, or rather two ropes knotted together, now led straight to the doubtful lamp post. Hitching another rope above the first knot, they hove on it, bringing the strain on the winch, and the danger was over.

"Where is that tramp?" asked the foreman. "He's a sailor. I've been there, and know the signs. He's passed a clove hitch on the lamp post and a rolling hitch on the fall. I'll give him a job."

But the "tramp" had gone.

At Buffalo he fired a stationary engine, on trial, but displayed so keen an interest in the engineer's own work as to lose the job. Later, inspired perhaps by a fleeting self-respect based on his late usefulness, he secured another, this time as engineer. The employer was suspicious at first of the ragged, unlicensed aspirant; but he talked glibly of grate surface, eccentrics, valves, pistons, etc. (words picked up in his last service); no other applicant appeared, and the engine must run; so he was accepted.

Instinct, mechanical and other, is inherited knowledge, and the fact that a correct estimate of the tensile strength of red-hot boiler iron in contact with cold water did not form a part of this man's genius was due, no doubt, to the antecedent fact that none of his ancestors had experimented in this line: Indeed, few who so experiment live long enough to transmit to descendants, in the form of instinct, this acquired knowledge. On the second day he sailed over two fences amid a cloud of hot steam, while the shattered boiler went the other way.

He was picked up scalded, disfigured, and unconscious, and sent to the hospital, from which, in three months, he emerged blind in one eye, minus an ear, and with his whole right side shortened and weakened. On a stormy December morning, hungry and cold, he shipped deck-hand on a steam-barge, the mate taking on the forlorn applicant for the same reason that had influenced his last employer: no other appeared. He scrubbed decks, scoured paintwork, and helped trim sail as the shifts of wind demanded, while the steam-barge dragged herself and two tow-barges up the lake. He soon understood the proper angle that sails should bear to the wind and the resultant force exerted on the vessel. He helped the second mate splice a rope, and knew how before the job was half done. He had seen the rudder at the dock, and now explained to his fellows the action of the slanting blade on the water. Scrubbing paint on the bridge, he heard the captain say to the mate: "Pull up the center-board; she gripes"; and being sent to help, asked the good-natured second mate what the center-board was for, and what griping meant. The second mate explained: the center-board was a movable blade in the bottom to keep the boat from drifting sideways, and "griping" was the carrying of the rudder to one side from the uneven pressure of the wind.

By the time he had assimilated this nautical lore the boat had reached Point Pelee, near the head of the lake; and here, as though misfortune were still "camped on his trail," he fell overboard.

"Man overboard—rouster!" yelled the second mate.

"Which one?" asked the captain, as he rang the stopping-bells.

"The blind one—the cripple."

"Let the tow pick him up," growled the captain, ringing full speed to the engine. But as a salve to his conscience he blew a few short barks of the whistle, to signify to the barges behind to "Look out."

Our hero, fathoms deep as he thought, barely escaped a blow from the propeller as he was sucked under the quarter, and came to the surface half the length of the tow-line behind. Being no swimmer, he gasped once and sank; then arose, only to be beaten under by the bow of the oncoming tow-barge. When next he appeared, it was behind the first tow-barge, and the second, approaching at a seven-knot speed, was almost upon him.

"Help!" he gurgled. But no one heard or saw him, although a profane but humane second mate was periling his position and blackening his soul with loud, blasphemous objurgations to the barges, and vows of legal vengeance on his superior, the captain, as he peered aft from the steamer's taffrail.

Just as his head disappeared, the outer bobstay of the second barge struck him on the shoulder.[2] He grasped it. Tearing through the water made it hard work to pull himself up; but he got his head out, and rested; then, inch by inch, he dragged his crippled body up the pair of iron chains to the bowsprit and thence in-board to the deck, on to which he tumbled an unconscious heap. He was carried below, stripped, and brought to with much rubbing and copious draughts of whisky; but not being used to this stimulant lately, he relapsed into a stupor.

That night it snowed so hard that the men steering the tow-barges could not see the steam-barge ahead, and the captains and mates took turns at standing in the bows, and, guided by the trend of the tow-lines, bellowing "Starboard," "Port," and "Steady" to the helmsmen. The captain of the steam-barge, too sure of his position to anchor, yet not sure enough to go ahead without sounding, slowed down, took a cast of the lead, and went on, without being able to see through the snow the position the second of the tow-barges had reached. She had crept up on the first barge, but had given her a wide berth; and now, when the tow-line tautened, it bore at right angles—to port.

"Hard a-starboard!" sang out the mate of the second barge, as he saw the hawser lift from the water.

It was his last speech. The terrific strain broke the iron casting on the bow through which the hawser led, and the mate, standing on the port cat-head, was struck in the legs by the sweeping recoil of the heavy line and swept overboard.[3] He did not rise. Ropes were thrown out, but the relentless power at the other end of the tow-line carried them away from the spot; the loudest pair of lungs could not penetrate that thick snow; and the mate was given up.

---

2. A bobstay is a length of chain or wire running from the bowsprit to the stem.

3. Catheads are heavy timbers projecting from the bow to hoist and stow anchors.

The old captain, much shaken, took the mate's place at the bow, noting, despite his horror, that the port jibboom guys[4] were torn from their fastenings by the tow-line, which now bore a little forward of the beam, showing that she was straightening up to her course. The tow-post creaked and groaned with the unfamiliar side-strain, and she came around, slackening the tow-line with the increased speed acquired in the wide sweep. Then she swung the other way, the strength of the helmsman, a mere boy, not being sufficient to steady her.

As the tow-line tautened, leading now off to starboard, though the brand-new rope held, the rotten tow-post, weakened by its wrenching, did not. Breaking at the deck, it crashed over the bow with the line, catching and carrying away the port bowsprit-shroud as it went;[5] and with her momentum and the wheel still to port, the barge swung around, lost headway, and, pointing her nose to the north shore, drifted to leeward, with all the rigging of the bowsprit and jibboom gone on the port, or weather, side.

The much-wrought-up old skipper, who had barely escaped the flying tow-post, sprang to the rail and screamed his curses on the steam-barge. "Think I'm goin' t' anchor, do ye? Anchor in this passage—an' wait for you t' take a night's sleep at th' dock 'fore ye come back? Not much! Ye've carried 'way my head-gear, but I'll find a better place—'f I run t' Buffalo—How's her head?" This to the wheel.

"Nor' by east, sir."

"Bring her east by south, half south, when she'll come. Give her the stay-sail, boys."[6]

This sail was loosed, hoisted half up, and lost in the thick

---

4. The jibboom is a long spar used to extend the bowsprit. Guys are the tackle used to give it lateral support.

5. Bowsprit shrouds are standing rigging that runs from the outer end of the bowsprit to the bow to provide lateral support to the bowsprit.

6. A triangular sail hoisted on a stay, known as a fore staysail.

maze to leeward as a sudden puff of the increasing gale blew it to pieces.

With decks awash as the seas boarded the weather rail and spilled out of the lee scuppers, and in that blinding snow-storm, the flakes of which were attaining a needle-like sharpness, the gray old skipper was more than ever resolved not to anchor in a dangerous channel, and his men began rigging preventer guys to the bowsprit, for head sail must be carried to bring her before the wind.[7] The boy was told to drop the wheel and lend a hand. The darky cook was called and sent out on the bowsprit with the rest, as they endeavored to hitch a heavy hawser around the end of the spar. It was icy cold. The waves made hungry licks at their legs as they worked, and their fingers were numb, and the ropes and spar slippery with ice; but they completed the task, and had started in when one of those vicious Lake Erie seas, the first of the three which travel in company, lifted up to windward, a gray, nearly perpendicular wall.

"Look out!" cried the captain; "hang on!"

When the sea had passed over and the captain had straightened up, he saw one dark object clinging to the icy gear under the spar, while from the blanket of snow to leeward came gurgling cries. Then, as the next sea crashed over the bows, he heard: "Help, Cappen!" as the cook also was swept away.

Unable to save them, and trembling with horror, the old man crawled aft and went below, where he buried his head in his hands on the cabin table. "Great God!" he groaned, "all gone, every man; and all in half an hour!"

He sat there, wet, lonely, and miserable, until daylight shone in on him; then he remembered the deck-hand in the forecastle, and started forward to arouse him, if he too had not died in the night.

---

7. Preventer rigging is temporary rigging used to back up the standing rigging during heavy weather. Headsails are jibs and staysails raised at the forward end of a vessel, here on the bowsprit and perhaps the foremast.

It had stopped snowing, but the snow was replaced by the drift from the sea, which, freezing where it fell, had already encased deck, rail, and rigging in a coating of ice. It was slippery walking, or, rather, creeping, for an old man of seventy, with the craft rolling both rails under, and it is no wonder that an incoming sea swept his legs from under him, bringing him down with a thud on the icy corner of the forehatch.

He groaned with the sharp pain in his back, but could not rise. His legs were useless; so he hitched and crawled as best he could, and in time reached the forecastle-hatch, where he called—called until his voice grew weak, then gasped his prayer for help, while the man below slept on, and did not waken even when the masts crashed over the side.

It was high noon when the sleeper opened his eyes—on strange quarters, with an icy ladder leading up to a square of light, blocked by a gray face fringed with icicles, on which death had stamped the agony of its owner's last moments. He shivered with cold as he turned out. His clothes, nearly dried by the now cold stove, hung on the pawl-post,[8] and he dressed himself, with many upward glances at the grewsome thing above. Then he mounted the slippery ladder, shutting his eyes as he neared the staring face, and not opening them until he had climbed over it and floundered on to the deck beside the body, covered now, like the deck itself, with a frozen mantle.

He made his way aft, and called down the cabin door: "Anyone here?"

Hearing no sound, he descended, and opened all the state-room doors, but found no one. His hunger brought him to the galley, where he partook of some food, and then returned to the deck. It was a situation to appal the heart of even an experienced sailor. The vessel had once been a fine three-masted schooner, degraded later to a barge by sending down her topmasts.[9] Now she was a dismantled hulk, with ice on deck making a curve

---

8. Post connected to the capstan on deck.
9. The top section of her masts had been taken off.

from the rails in-board to where it raised in hummocks over the hatches. And on this dismantled, ice-bound hulk, rolling in the trough of the sea, somewhere on Lake Erie, he was alone with a dead man. This much he knew. Ahead and astern were two lines of blue, which he took for land. But no sail appeared to cheer him. As he stood in the companionway, sheltered from the furious blast, the memory of his fall from the steam-barge, his being swept under by the first tow-barge, and his painful climb up the bobstays of the other came back to him. But he remembered nothing more.

"Somethin' orful's happened," he muttered. "S'pose every-one got washed off—or, mebbe, they're in the boat; that's gone. Wonder what killed the man forrard? I've got t' do somethin'."

He noticed the thumping of the spars alongside, where they lay held by the rigging, and concluded to cut them away; they might knock a hole in her. An ax alone would do it. He looked at the frozen deck. Axes suggest wood-piles, and wood-piles suggest stoves. This inductive reasoning brought him to the galley, where he found a hatchet; and with this he chopped at lanyards and running-gear until the spars drifted away. The jibboom had snapped at the bowsprit end, but the bowsprit still stood; other-wise he would have had to cut through a chain bowsprit-shroud—a thing practically impossible.

He saved as much of the running-rigging as he could—not that he knew why; he had no use for it as yet; he obeyed an instinct—the same that impelled him to put the hatchet care-fully away in an oval-shaped hole in the after part of the cabin. As it was daytime he felt no nervous fears of the dead man forward, and crawled around the deck, inspecting what was left of her fittings. He examined a hummock of ice amidships, show-ing a black skeleton of iron. "Center-board winch," he said. Another pillar of ice enclosed the capstan; the steam-barge had carried these things. Creeping aft, he looked over the stern and discovered the rudder, ice-covered, but free in its movements, which a sailor would have known by the spinning of the wheel.

He was now wet with the drift and chilled through. He

went below, and in the mate's room found dry clothing, with which he replaced his wet rags. The captain's room furnished a good pair of rubber boots and a suit of oil-skins. While here he noticed a bundle of paper rolls, which he examined. "Maps," he said. He found the chart of Lake Erie, and for the first time in his life valued a much-neglected accomplishment: he could read.

A cursory glance showed him a long, bag-shaped outline of coast, with Buffalo at one end, and other cities, most of which he had visited, marked on the edges. In one corner was a circle, filled with numerous interlocking stars, which he could not understand. He put the chart away, and, clad in his warm, protective clothing, returned to the deck, where he did an hour's hard thinking and experimenting.

"She don't lay even in the holler of the waves," he said. "Why?" He thought of the center-board. "She drifts sideways, an' if the board's down it makes a point, kinder, an' she'd hang on it. If it's forrard o' the center, it'd hold that end to the wind a little. I'll see."

The rubber boots gave him good sea-legs. He went to the center-board winch, measured the distance forward and aft with his eye, and returned for the hatchet. As he took it from the hole in the cabin, he saw a curious, whirling disk inside, which, when it had ceased it gyrations, resembled the diagram on the chart. He had never seen or heard of a compass, but the letters, E, S, and W on the edge of the disk, and the fact that it retained a steady position independent of the yaws of the vessel, were data for later deductions.

He chopped the ice from the winch, and roughened it under his feet, then, little by little, with his feeble strength, hoisted the center-board. A man can lift a great weight with a worm-geared winch. Going aft, he proved his reasoning; she lay plumb in the trough of the sea.

He chopped the ice from two large, octagon-shaped boxes, abaft the stumps of the fore and main masts, and looked in.

They contained heavy hawsers, tackles, etc. He noticed the heavy, cross-plank construction of the covers as he replaced them. A barrel was lashed to the fife-rail around the stump of the foremast. [10] Chopping into it, he found salt, and remarked that where he spilled some on deck the ice crackled and melted to water, which did not freeze again. Then he went aft, and puzzled over the action of the compass, which, not being governed by purely mechanical laws, was beyond his comprehension. But he divined its scope and utility, and out of his environment of screaming wind and heaving water evolved a plan of salvation—apparently so wild, so baseless and hopeless, that no sane seafaring man, hampered by experience, would have considered it for an instant. But this man was not a sailor; he was a mechanic, heaven-born.

"She's driftin' 'bout as fast as a man kin walk," he mused. "If she'd point with the wind she'd move faster. How kin I make her? More pressure on one end or less on the other; a sail forrard 'ud do."

The foremast had broken about ten feet from the deck, and the boom and gaff, [11] with the foresail furled to them, lay with the jaws in place on the stump and the after ends frozen fast to the ice in the scuppers. The main and mizzen masts had snapped at the deck, and everything pertaining to them was overboard except what he had saved of the running-rigging. Forward, from the bowsprit end, descended an immense icicle, the accretion of ice to the jib-stay, broken aloft and hanging down, while on the bowsprit lay the furled jib—an elongated cone of ice: a solid mass with the spar. [12] He shrank from attempting to chop loose and set this sail to the stump of the mast, and considered the alternative: less pressure aft; he could rig a drag.

---

10. Fife-rails were semicircular rails built around the base of the masts to hold the belaying pins with which the sail halyards were secured.

11. A gaff is a spar that spreads the head of a fore-and-aft sail.

12. The jib-stay is rigging that runs between the foremast and the bowsprit; here it is broken and hanging down and the jib is furled and frozen to the bowsprit.

His ideas were crystallizing. He searched for and found a well-equipped tool-chest, and spent the rest of the afternoon chopping from the icy deck the ropes he had pulled in—coiling them, or, rather, crushing them, in the cabin, where he sprinkled them with salt from the barrel. Then, building a fire in the stove, he cooked and ate his supper, first bringing all the ropes'-ends into the galley to dry.

By the light of the galley lamp he studied the chart, but could make little of it except that he was somewhere on a line, midway between the shores, which he creased with his thumbnail from Buffalo to the head of the lake. If he could get her before the wind and steer, and the wind should shift, he might make one of the ports on either shore; and in case the wind held as it was, he could not misss Buffalo, for the compass told him the wind was blowing him there. He schemed and planned until sleepy, then "turned in all standing."[13]

Morning showed more ice on deck and a slight change to the northward in the wind, which had been due west, but no lessening of its velocity or of the bitter cold. After breakfast he went to work. His ropes were now pliable and the ends dry. With an auger he bored four holes in the rim of one of the heavy box-covers, into which he inserted the ends of ropes, making a bridle such as boys put on their kites. Weighting one side with a heavy piece of iron, he fastened the end of a hawser from the box to the bridle, and pushed the contrivance over the stern, paying out the line as the vessel drifted away from it. When about a hundred feet were out, he made it fast to the quarter-bitts (a strong post), and watched the effect as the line tautened. It certainly did bring the stern to the wind, but not enough to give the craft headway. He rigged the other box-cover as a drag on the other quarter, and had the satisfaction of seeing the craft pay off and go staggering through the water, and, though yawing right and left, keep a general direction eastward. He hurrahed

---

13. Fully dressed.

his delight, and took the wheel, but found that he could make no improvement in the serpentine wake the barge left behind her. Deeply laden and weighted with ice, she now shipped every sea over the stern, and to escape them he went below, satisfied for the time that she was going somewhere at a fairly good rate. Had he been successful at the wheel, he would have cut away the drags to increase her speed, but he feared to. Could he put sail on her, and increase her speed with the drags still out? The sound of the drag-ropes, straining on the bitts, gave him an idea of power that he could use—power beyond the strength of a hundred men.

Up he came and surveyed the ground, inspecting first the jib. It was covered with six inches of solid ice. It would be too dangerous to climb out there and chop it loose. Besides, when set, it would show little surface, and would only help to keep her before the wind. He needed a mast and a larger sail. So he inventoried his material. The furled foresail was there, with a good boom and gaff; the boxes were filled with strong hawsers, and on top of the coils were tackles, small line, and deck tools; he had a cabinful of running-gear, and, counting the pulley-blocks in reach, found himself possessed of four large double and three large single blocks, all shackled to their places. With salt, hatchet, and tools he disconnected these and carried them below.

The forward hawser-box was in his way, and he emptied it, coiling the lines in the cabin. Disdaining to chop it clear of ice, he merely scored a rough groove, knotted a heavy rope to the box, and, leading this aft, hitched it to one of the drag-lines—with the same knot he had used in New York—and slacked away. The surrounding ice crackled, split, and went to pieces as the heavy box bounded from its bed and rolled about the decks. A friendly sea carried it overboard, and he cut it adrift. He spliced ropes for tackles—and an able seaman could have spliced no better, though, possibly, more quickly; for sailors are made, not born, like poets and mechanics. He chopped ice and manipulated tackles—with the drag for power—and by noon had the heavy boom, sail, and gaff on deck, and two holes sunk in the solid bed of ice abaft the stump to receive the jaws when his mast should arise. Salting his work as he left it, he labored on, perspiring with his efforts, and drenched by the merciless seas which boarded the craft amidships. His clothing stiffened with ice, but he worked with an energy new to him. Was it love of life or love of mechanics that impelled him?

Late in the afternoon he first felt hunger, and surveyed his work before going aft to eat. The sail was cut away and lay on deck—a frozen cylinder, lashed to the rail. Not wanting the gaff, he had sped it over the side by clever handling of ropes and drag-lines. The boom lay nearly amidships, with the middle of a brand-new hawser knotted to its after extremity, the ends of which, equally cut to the length of the boom, he had secured to two strong iron rings in the rails, one each side—stout shrouds for his new mast. A strong tackle led from the end of the boom to the jagged head of the mast stump. Another from the same end led to the bows, hooking into the still intact bull's-eye of the broken forestay. The first was to lift his mast until the other could act, which would then complete the work, and, when the mast was up, act as a permanent support from forward—a forestay. A single block, with a long rope pulled through, was secured to the under side of the boom, close to the end. Although he might not have named it, this rope was his halyard—to hoist his sail. His fertile brain had worked in advance of his crippled body; he had lost no time in planning the next step.

After a hurried lunch he studied his drag-line—his power. Could he lift that mast with one drag? He knew nothing of foot-pounds, horse-power, or mechanical equivalents, but "guessed" that he could not. So, knotting the ends of both to his last hawser, he threw them overboard, and soon had both drags straining on one rope—a doubling of power, but an unseaman-like waste of good manilla. He then led the falls, or hauling parts, of his tackles aft, and, hitching the one he was to use first to the drag-line, slacked out until it tautened. But his mast must go up straight as a jack-knife blade from the handle; it must not swing; he needed side guys to steady it. These he rigged from the end of the boom through two blocks hooked in the rails, hence aft to where he could slack away from two iron belaying-pins. Then he was ready.

First, inspecting everything, he payed out carefully, and had the satisfaction of seeing the boom lift amid a shower of crackling ice from the tackle, staggering its way upward, and jerking violently on the guy-ropes as it swayed back and forth. But they soon tautened, and, leading the drag-line across the deck, he slackened these guys alternately, paying out on the drags as he moved back and forth, thus keeping the spar comparatively steady. When the tackle had reached the slippery angle of forty-five degrees, he fastened the fall of the long bow-tackle to the drag-line, and soon got the weight of the boom on this. Then cutting the other way, he payed out roundly, fearing the guys would part from the merciless tugs they received as the spar, nearly on end, thrashed from side to side. But they held nobly. Soon the heavy shrouds tautened, and the new mast, describing a few jerky circles against the gray sky, settled itself, a rigid mass with the hull, held by its icy socket at the deck, aft by two hawsers to the rail, and forward by a strong four-part tackle to the bow. But he must secure this forestay, now depending on the uncertain tension of the drag-line. By the time he had done so darkness had almost arrived, and the ghastly mound on deck, looking ghastlier in the lessening light, sent him aft for the night. First, however, he salted his halyard, coiled on the fife-rail, and threw the rest of the salt on the frozen cylinder which he was to transform to a sail in the morning. Then dropping the tackles and deck tools down the stairs, he looked around the shortened horizon before following them.

The aspect had not changed. The same black-and-gray waste of wind-driven cloud and foam-crested sea met his eye; and yet he fancied the darker line of land to the southward looked larger. He went below, wet, benumbed, and exhausted, but feeling within him the exultation of a victor and the strange stirrings of a newly-aroused manhood. Dry clothes and supper refreshed him a little, and again he studied the chart. Reaching down the cook's rolling-pin and placing the chart on the floor, he knelt on it.

"Now, that circle in the corner," he said, "can't mean nothin' but to show the way the lake runs. That line on it marked E an' W means east an' west, the one crossin' it with S at the bottom means south, an' t'other end must mean north, o' course. An' that thing in the hole up-stairs is marked just the same an' allus points the same way—wonder why? Now, le's see.

"In the mornin' I 'spect she'll be pretty close to that shore." He placed the rolling-pin so that by ranging his eye he struck a line from Buffalo nearly parallel to the south shore, and touching it two-thirds of its length from that port.

"Now, I'll jess guess that in the mornin' I'll be somewhere near this line." He rolled his improvised parallel rule; it would not reach the compass diagram in the corner, and he supplemented it with the edge of the chopping-board, which he placed on the center of the circle and flush with the rolling-pin.

"Eight divisions o' that circle 'tween east an' north," he mused. "This strikes off 'bout two an' a half o' them. Two an' a half divisions north o' the east line. I'll remember."

His sleep was troubled. All night he chopped ice and poked frozen ropes through blocks too small for them, tied hitches that slipped, and spliced ropes that broke. Once he was up. The mast was still in place, and the drag still kept her before the wind. He could not see the compass, but the wind and sea were unquestionably milder. So he turned in again, and aroused at daylight to find himself within two miles of the shore, an angry surf showing, and the wind brisk from the north. But the gale was over.

The barge was heading straight for the nest of breakers, and he must do something quickly. A few moments of dazed thinking and he was awake and himself. With some small dry rope from the cabin he lashed the forward upper corner of the sail to the foot of the mast. He could not haul it snug to its place, but made it secure. Then with the ax he chopped one of the blocks from the rail, where he had left it, secured it to the mast, and, knotting one end of the halyard into the after upper corner of the sail, he passed the other through this block, and, leading it aft, fastened it to the drag-line, not by a hitch—both ropes were icy—but by a firm lashing of small line.

Before paying out to hoist the sail, he took his ax and made mighty dents in the ice which bound it. He chopped, hammered, and pried until he dared wait no longer; then he threw off the drag-line turns and chopped again, where most needed, as the sail shook itself loose and arose with a thrashing and crackling that was deafening.

He was driven away by the hurling pieces of ice, and ran to the drag-line. Taking a turn, he dubiously watched the sail ascend as he slacked out, not knowing as yet how he was to secure the lower part, until he noticed a ring worked into the edge which was just ready to slip over the side out of his reach. Making fast, he ran below, emerging with some small line and his best tackle, one block of which he hooked to this ring, lashing the hook, and the other to the ring-bolt in the starboard rail left vacant by the single block. Hauling taut, he secured the tackle, then, paying out more drag-line, brought the sail up.

It set beautifully, a picturesque leg-of-mutton above, but sadly blocked the deck with the unused portion below. It increased the barge's speed towards the shore, and he took the wheel to throw her round. She would not come; so, lashing the halyard to the bitts, with some misgivings he cut the drag-line. Then she answered her helm, and soon was clawing off that lee-shore as bravely as though carrying a complete equipment of spars, sails, and able seamen.

He found the course he had selected and held her to it, not steering true, but very well for a novice. When hungry, he dropped the wheel, rushed to the galley, and, coming back with some bread, found her rounding up to the wind. But she payed off when he put the wheel over, and, munching the bread, he steered on, watching for ports on the south shore.[14] He saw no signs that his judgment approved of, however; the wind was freshening and hauling back to its old quarter, and he resolved to go on; he could not miss Buffalo.

As night came on he reasoned out the necessity of light on the compass, and, investigating, found two lamps—one burned out, the other full—approachable from the inside of the cabin. He lighted the full one, and, returning to the wheel, found the vessel in the trough of the sea and threatening to roll her mast out. But it held, and he brought her back to the course, resolved not to leave the wheel again.

Darkness descended, and he steered by compass alone, as the wind freshened to a gale, and by midnight to a hurricane that at times flattened the seas to a level. His lame side ached; his blind eye, inflamed with cold, smarted as though torn with needles; but he bravely made his course good. The seas poured over and drenched him, and ice formed on his back and shoulders, descending as a curtain from the rim of his sou'wester. Working the wheel made his arms and breast perspire, while his feet smarted, burned, and grew numb as the water in his boots congealed. All but engulfed in a liquid world, he felt the torture of thirst until he bit ice from his sleeve. He talked to and about himself.

As the night wore on, the frozen dead man left his icy bed and flitted about in the darkness—beckoning. The wailing of the wind in the rigging of his jury-mast became the winter song of the kitchen chimney in his childhood home, where his mother had taught him to read. She came to him at times,

---

14. A vessel rounds up to the wind when she faces it directly, thus making no headway. She pays off when she turns until her sails are full.

during the lulls, when the seas would rise, and the terrible aching fatigue of arms and back would wring from him hoarse groans of agony; and she would stand beside him, pointing to the page of his book. But the printing on the page before him was the markings of a brightly illuminated compass-card, and her finger would seem to be a dancing, wavering lubber's point that swung unsteadily—far to the right, far to the left—and would not be still. Then would come a squall of the hurricane, when the seas would flatten to a milky froth, and the chimney song rise to a continuous screaming sound. But during these moments mother and dead man would go; for, braced heavily against the nearly immovable wheel, his tortured mind and body obtained momentary respite, and sanity came back.

A bright light flared out away on the port bow and went out. It appeared again and again. What was it? He did not know, but it cheered him. It passed astern, and another appeared to starboard. And so he steered on through the night, on the course he had chosen and remembered: northeast by east, half east.

A sleepy life-saver, patrolling the beach, saw a curious craft approaching port in the gray of the morning, making wild, zigzag yaws, as though undecided which shore to strike. He awakened his comrades and then the nearest tug captain, and having nothing better to do and with plenty of time, turned out all the tugs moored on his side of the river. Six puffing, snorting, high-pressure tugs ranged up alongside the shapeless iceberg floundering into port, their captains roaring out requests for a line to the disheveled creature at the wheel. A vacant stare and a backward wave of the arm were the only answer.

Gayly and noisily the procession passed up Buffalo River, and it was only after the leading craft had torn three vessels from their moorings; after passing the foot of Main Street, black with cheering men, and through the bridge, barely swung in time to save it, that the tugmen managed to get aboard and take lines. The barge was stopped just in time to save a canal-boat that lay in her way from a fatal ramming.

She was moored to the deck, where crowds poured aboard and passed comments. And her helmsman and navigator—where was he? In the galley, lighting a fire; he had earned his breakfast and wanted it. Newspaper men sought him and asked questions, which he answered between mouthfuls, mainly by a simple "Dunno." One brought him a looking-glass, into which he looked, wonderingly; his lips were shrunken and drawn, his face wrinkled, and his hair, which had been dark, was white as the crests of the seas he had conquered.

The captain of a wind-bound liner appeared and interviewed him. "He's not a sailor," he reported, later; "but he has accomplished the greatest feat of pure seamanship I ever heard of. I met that craft at the head of the lake three days ago. She must have been dismasted that night in the first of the blow. He told me how he found himself alone, rigged drags for power, put a jury-mast in her and struck off a course with a rolling-pin, and clawed her off a lee-shore, and sailed her down this lake in the wildest hurricane we've ever had here. Yes, sir, it's wonderful; but it's possible. And it's a salvage job, too; he'll get several thousand dollars."

But though every reporter on every paper in Buffalo hunted for him high and low, he did not put in a claim for salvage.

That night a south-bound freight train carried a wrinkled, white-haired, one-eyed "tramp," bound for sunnier climes, where ice and snow were unknown.

From *November Storm*

Jay McCormick

NOVEMBER STORM is the finest novel written about maritime life on the lakes. Set on the *Blackfoot*, a 400-foot self-unloader, it takes place during a summer and fall season in the 1940s, and tells the story of young Sean Riley, who has just buried both his parents and left his last link with the shore, his friend Whitey, to ship out as a deckhand. On the surface this novel is a classic story of a young man's coming of age, but *November Storm* is much more than that. In his carefully delineated portraits of the crew, McCormick has created a picture of life aboard a Great Lakes bulk carrier that has never been surpassed for psychological perceptiveness and realism of detail.

Captain Julius Starr is the master. Nominally married to a neurotic wife who refuses to leave shore, he is really wedded only to his command. But he is growing old and lately he has begun to realize that his days aboard his ship are no longer without number. Arch, his first mate, has no life apart from the ship and his driving ambition to command her, even though he does not feel equal to the task and envies Starr's quiet confidence. Between these two exists a quiet, submerged war into which the other members of the crew and the occasional passenger are caught up and revealed: Burgee, the old, crippled second mate in his last season who quotes all of Shakespeare except *Richard the Third*; Anchor Larson, a wheelsman who has orchestrated the death of a young deckhand in the bosun's chair because he raped a girl, but who has now realized that it is himself, the murderer, who is truly damned; and Stella, Captain Starr's wealthy, nymphomaniac, alcoholic mistress who sails during November so that she can vicariously experience the power and thrill the crew feel at overcoming the weather. Those who have not sailed may think that such a motley crew as this is the writer's fancy run wild, but no one who has spent time in the merchant marine will be surprised. Ships like the *Blackfoot* make a home for those who have none worth keeping on shore, and although sailors are often a quarrelsome lot, they are also tolerant of eccentricity because they all are bound together by the shared life of the ship. In this respect, *November Storm* is more realistic than most. The excerpt reprinted here is the last chapter of the book and begins as the ship heads out into that most typical of Great Lakes storms, a November gale. McCormick based the fate of the *Blackfoot* on that of the actual ship *Conneaut,* which was caught in the Armistice Day storm of 1940. But like all ships in all storms, this will be the testing of those who sail her, calling into question their fantasies of invincibility, reminding them of all they have to lose, and leading them to value most what they gain from each other: pity and compassion, friendship and respect, and finally the simple joy of being together to see another day.

ARCH WAS AFRAID. He didn't like the way the weather looked here in Milwaukee. The boat was nearly unloaded. Starr had said nothing about lying here at the dock until they could see how bad the storm would be. It was time to wake Starr up, but Arch hesitated to do so. Perhaps the storm would break before they were unloaded, and then Starr would have no choice. Arch didn't mind a blow. This was going to be more than just a blow. He had heard men from the Gulf tell about hurricanes. You didn't have hurricanes on the lakes, he tried to assure himself. That was the way it felt, just like they said.

The air was warm and moist, not like the cold November weather it should have been. It was hard to breathe. Arch knew it was not just him. He had seen the men on deck. They stood listlessly beside the deck engines. They sprawled on stools in the messroom. Everybody was tired, and it was hard to breathe. The saltwater men had said it was like this. The river smelled bad. The river always smelled bad in Milwaukee. Today it hung over the boat, a sour, unpleasant smell.

Arch looked almost wistfully at the riverbank a few feet away. It was going to be a hell of a storm. There were only a few feet between him and the land right now. He was tired. He felt as if he had never been anything but tired. Just go down the ladder and walk away. Let Starr do as he pleased. Arch slapped his gauntlets against his coveralls and went into Starr's office. He shut the door quietly. He did not want to awaken Starr yet.

The barometer said twenty-eight; five. It had dropped three tenths of a minute since noon. Arch set the marker needle down over twenty-eight; five. He hoped he wouldn't have to move it any way but up again. From Starr's desk he picked up the weather report and a yellow-colored message from the company. He read them slowly, as if they were messages to him, demanding his special attention.

The conveyor rumbled dull, a long way off. Not much more than a slow throb here in the quiet of the old man's office. Arch thought of the way it sounded in his own room. He looked at the plated handle and dial of the safe. He flicked ashes from his cigarette into the brass spittoon. Again he glanced over the yellow oak roll-top desk, then he went in the other room to call the old man.

"Cap'n," Arch said.

The old man slept in a nightshirt. He fought off the blankets and sheets as he slept. He was an ugly sight now, with the shirt twisted up tight under his armpits. His thin, dry, old man's legs stretched obscenely apart from the fat, hair-pale belly.

"Cap'n."

A snore broke into a phlegmy snort, and one angry, sleep-red eye looked down the bed at Arch. The old man turned over on his stomach, his head deep in the pillow. Slow, deep, dozing-off breaths again, until Arch thought he was going back to sleep. Suddenly, "What in hell you want?"

"Half hour, Cap'n."

"A'right." A snore.

Arch stood looking out the deadlight. He did not want to move. The radiator hissed suddenly, then clanked. Arch started and shifted his feet.

"You still here, Arch?"

Starr never turned around and looked at you when he said something. Always knew you were there. Always knew you were listening.

"Gonna be a blow, sir," Arch said.

"Uh."

"Glass is down to twenty-eight; five."

"Hell with it," Starr said.

Arch stood for a moment and then went out on deck.

Starr felt the age in his bones as he slowly sat up in bed. He shouldn't sleep like this with no covers, he thought. He swung his legs over the side of the bed, making a face as he did so, and adjusted his nightshirt. What if Stella should come barging in here and see him like this? He scratched his head. She had come barging in other times. Starr laughed, at nothing, alone, as men will.

He walked stiffly on his heels to the bathroom and peered at his chin and neck in the mirror. Silver-gray stubble. He didn't want to shave. He stared at the wrinkled old mouth in the mirror. Then he remembered and took his plates out of the jar on the shelf. Holding them in his hand, he made them bite several times with sharp little clicks. He tried to see why they slipped in his mouth but couldn't.

He drank a shot of White Horse from the bottle in the cabinet. He felt a little better, so he drank one more, but that was all. He put his teeth in and walked through his room, still barefoot, to the office. He looked out at the sky through the deadlight. Then he read the weather report on his desk. He went back to his room and began dressing.

When he had dressed Starr went again into the office. He looked at the barometer. Twenty-eight; five, Arch had said. Down to four now. Jesus, what a blow it was going to be! Starr debated whether or not to head out into it. He too felt the heavy stillness of the air. He went out on deck and stood watching the last dribbles of coal rolling off the end of the boom. The hurricane warnings would be up when the boat went out of the river, Starr thought. Arch would stand and look at them without saying anything.

Starr began filling his pipe, carefully tamping the tobacco into the bowl. He wasn't afraid. He had been through the big one in '13, and the *Blackfoot* was a better boat than that other. Wind would come from the southwest, shift around west, Starr calculated. If it got too bad, he could turn back or get in the lee of the west shore. He thought of Arch, a careful man who did the right thing. He and Arch would take her through the storm. Arch would see what it was like not to be afraid. Starr smiled. In a way it would be a test. It might prove that Julius Starr was not yet an old man, with an old man's caution. It could give the lie to Starr's troubled feeling that his own powers were on the wane. He went to the rail above the main deck. "Anchor!" he shouted. Anchor Larson looked up. Starr beckoned, and Anchor left the deck winch and followed Starr to the pilothouse.

Stella Forester heard the short blast of the whistle which meant cast off. She did not get up to watch the boat leave the dock. Stella was too drunk to get off her bed, even to go to the deadlight and look out. She lay on her side, with a bottle and a tumbler. From time to time she poured herself a drink. You're drunk, Stella, she thought. You're what you call dead drunk. She shook her head, trying to clear the moving mist which obscured her vision. Perhaps she should go up in the pilothouse and talk to Julius. Stella didn't want to talk. She was tired, old.

She felt, even in the numbness of the whisky, a nagging

irritability. She was not sure she would be able to repress it, drunk as she was. Therefore it was better not to seek out Julius. She thought too much of Julius to behave like a woman toward him. That bitch of a wife of his gave him enough of that. Such a lady. Stella puckered her lips and made a face. But not say it again to Julius. Never. He knew it all, and loved without hope. She poured another drink. She listened to the sounds of the boat. Winches clanked; men shouted; feet ran heavily on the deck outside. Then there came the slow, bobbing motion as the boat moved. The whistle blew for the bridge, and a low, snarling siren answered.

There was going to be a storm. Stella didn't care. Let it blow its head off. You didn't get seasick when you were drunk. You didn't care, didn't care, didn't care. Now she was getting silly. She simpered at her feet, there at the bottom of the bed. She would be here with Julius. Julius was a man here. That whining little bitch. Stella would be here with him in the storm. Sit home and take your pills, Delilah. I am with your man. Cut his hair when he gets home. I am going into the storm with him. The storm, Delilah. The terrible storm. She began to whimper. Sometimes she couldn't help being afraid. She set the glass on the bedside table and lay back. A quick darkness came, and Stella slept.

Starr watched Arch's face as they passed the light outside Milwaukee. The hurricane flag was flying, whipped to a frenzy by the gusty little breeze which had sprung up. Arch looked a little pale.

"Think it'll blow, Arch?" Starr asked innocently.

Arch did not answer. He looked aft at the smoke coming from the stack. He seemed to be waiting for something. Starr smiled, but the smile disappeared. He realized that he too was waiting for something. Again he thought of turning back. No, not with Arch here. They didn't come strong enough to bother these boats; you didn't get wind like that on the lakes. Starr thought of boats which had gone down. Well, if it got too bad he could head for the lee of the shore or one of the islands and drop the hook. He would not turn back. He watched the iron tower of the light disappear astern. Now he was pacing the pilothouse, just as Arch did. Starr forced himself to sit down in the high chair on the portside. But he did not leave the pilothouse, though they were all clear of the channel now.

"Nor'east by east, three eighths east," he told Anchor.

"Fifteen on your gyro," Arch said.

"Yes sir," Anchor said. He turned the wheel and watched the little numbers clicking across the dial of the gyro compass. Starr always gave you the magnetic course. That was one of the things older men such as Anchor liked about Starr. Anchor looked at the magnetic compass, then at the gyro. Yes, the gyro was right. It was a strange machine, and Anchor didn't quite trust it. He held the boat on her course. Again his mind drifted off into its own secret thoughts. He felt the little pain in his head.

Long, slick combers followed the *Blackfoot.* They swam up under her stern, lifted her, and carried her rapidly forward. A few of them broke over the fantail, but at full speed she managed to keep pretty well ahead of them. They were huge waves. They grew larger and larger, running fast the length of Lake Michigan. Still the wind did not come.

At five o'clock it came. There was a low, moaning sound, far away but coming closer every second with tremendous speed. Then they could see it, suddenly whipping the heavy combers into an impossible wild frenzy. The wind hit the boat with a crash as hard as if she had suddenly piled up sky-high on the rocks. Immediately the hull began to pitch heavily but jerkily, as if it were a small dinghy. In the pilothouse they could feel the shivering crash of the huge waves over the stern. Spray shot up above the after cabin. Now the boat did not ride before the giant combers. Her stern was sucked back into great concave walls of water, as if she were caught in a whirlpool.

Starr's hands were cold. He was master, he told himself. He had brought them all into this. Already it was impossible to turn the boat. If she got in the trough of those waves, with the wind on her beam, Starr knew what would happen. They would have to ride it out before the storm. In '13 it had not been his fault. He had not been master; he had done as he was told. There had been the storm, but not the terror of futile command. Starr felt a great loneliness sweeping over him. He could do nothing to dispel it. No more than he could do about the storm. He looked at Anchor and at Arch. He could not speak to them. Their faces did not show fear, but he knew they were afraid. Starr tried to think of something to say. Words, against a storm. Anything, if only to break the silence here in the pilothouse, the wordless din of the wind outside.

Jonathan Shank shuffled kidney foot back and forth in the galley, putting things away. When the first large wave had crashed over the stern Jonathan had taken the kettles off the stove and dumped their boiling water together with the food into the sink. There would be no hot supper tonight. The galley tilted one way and another. Things began to slide. First a stool fell over. Then the breadbox pitched off the cupboard onto the pantry floor. Jonathan himself was thrown hard against the wall, and his red cook's face twisted angrily. He swore and returned to the job of stowing plates and pans in places where they might not come loose and go flying around. Jonathan hated it when things started flying around. He usually got hit by something, or if he didn't he bumped up against the hot stove. A kettle rolled across the linoleum floor. Jonathan kicked it back under the sink. Then apologetically he picked the kettle up and shut it inside one of the lower cupboards. He'd better see if everything was tight in the officers' mess. He went to the dining room, farthest astern in the after cabin.

"God damn!" Jonathan shouted. Carl, the second cook, woke up in the room they shared just off the dining room. Carl was full of Milwaukee beer.

"What's the matter, Jonathan?" he called. Then he noticed the heavy pitch of the boat. He had to shove hard against the edge of the bunk to keep from rolling out as the stern rose high, higher, higher behind him. Carl wondered how he had managed to stay put here if this had been going on very long.

"Come out here and help me clean up this mess," Jonathan shouted.

"What is it?" Carl asked again. His stomach felt funny.

"Look at your damn floor!" Jonathan shouted. "Hurry up. Come on out here and get a mop and bucket."

Carl looked over the bunk edge at the floor of the room. Six inches of water pitched lazily back and forth, slopping against the wall, then the drawers of the bunk. Carl got up quickly. He was going to be sick. He waded through the cold water to the bathroom, ignoring Jonathan's angry shouts.

In the pilothouse Starr could feel the rattling shake of the screw as it flew free of the water when the stern was forced high in the air by a wave. The engines raced madly; then another wave would approach and crash over the stern; the whole boat would labor heavily as the screw slowed. A little of that and the bearing would be gone. The engine-room telephone rang, and Starr picked up the receiver. "Yes," he said. "Yes, Rodney, I was just going to. Yes, you stay there and look after things. Oh, it is? Well, get the men out of their rooms then. Well, how the hell do I know?" he shouted. "Take 'em all down in the engine room with you. They'll keep you company."

"But the fires, man," MacDougall shouted at the other end of the line, trying to hear Starr above the noise of the engines. "What'll I do if the water gets in the fire hold?"

"Better start the pumps," Starr said. Arch looked quickly at him, then out the window again. Anchor cleared his throat, then held tighter the wheel. Anchor saw this storm in a very personal way. He tried not to think of his sin. . . . Perhaps that was not it. Perhaps it was that woman passenger. She was a Jonah. A Jonah, Anchor repeated to himself, but he knew the storm had come for him. All sailor superstition was gone from him. He was not allowed to enjoy its comforts. Starr clattered the receiver back in its rack and went to the chadburn.

"You're not going to check her?" Arch said. It was the first word he had spoken since they left Milwaukee, a long time ago. His mouth was dry, and his voice cracked a little.

"I've got to. MacDougall says the screw'll shake itself loose if I don't." Starr rang back Half Speed Ahead, and quickly the arrow flipped to position in response.

"My God, sir, she'll swamp herself," Arch said. He looked aft, and now solid water could be seen sweeping over the stern. "Those men in the doghouse. How will they get below?"

"We'll get them down," Starr said. He too watched the afterend of the boat as it sank deep into the trough of each wave then struggled hard to rise again under the great weight of the water which broke over the decks. "God knows how, Arch, but we'll get them down."

It was the moment of indecision when revolt takes place. It was the almost unnoticed, pauseless turning of a tide, so disguised to all that the turbulent motion of the ebb is long mistaken for the advancing swell of flow. In Arch it was no more than a sudden strength of anger which released both needed decision and action. There was not time, nor did there seem cause, to consider implications; who decided, who acted. It did not seem as if there could have been another way. Yet it was a complex new in all its parts. Arch was angry at Julius Starr, but strangely he was more angry at the storm itself, at the lake and the wind. All was instant and done without asides. Arch forgot himself and found himself.

"I'm going aft," Arch said roughly. "I'll get the life line rigged astern from the boom. You don't need me here." Arch was not asking a question.

Starr looked at him, then again at the after cabin as it tried to bury itself in the huge darkness of a wave. "Come back here when you get through," Starr said.

Arch looked wonderingly at him. "What for?" he asked. It was a serious violation of the rules; you do not question the orders of the master. Arch had forgotten that there were rules.

"God damn it, Arch, do what I tell you. Don't you stand there asking me 'what for?' I'm your captain, that's what for," Starr shouted. Arch was impressed, yet not shaken. The tone of voice, the words, did not arouse the old response in Arch. With calm, honest admiration he looked quickly at Starr. The old man was a real captain. There must be a distorted greatness in him, to stand in the midst of storm's fury, face the loss of his ship, ignore the lives of his men, and take time to tell his first mate where to head in. Greatness, yes, and much power, for less of either could not have aroused such jealous might of rage.

"You're going to stay right here with me through the whole damn storm," Starr shouted. "You're going to stay here and do what I say."

"Yes sir," Arch said. He went out of the pilothouse, holding tight to the rails to keep from being blown off the bridge.

Starr paced back and forth across the pilothouse, talking to himself aloud. He looked up at Anchor. "How's she heading, Anchor? Can you hold her on her course?"

"Right on it now, sir," Anchor said. He was steering automatically, but his hands had been doing the right things all the time. He tried to shake off his resignation to this punishment and concentrate on the job of wheeling. It should be a job, Anchor realized. Yet, without thinking about it, he was doing all that any wheelsman could have done. The way that [deckhand had] screamed. Anchor again forgot the wheel, and Starr continued his pacing.

"It ought to shift," Starr said aloud. He was not speaking to Anchor. "It should shift over to the westward, and we'll be in the lee of the land." The boat was following the Wisconsin shore line. Had there been less wind or a lighter sea, Starr knew he could have headed in to Port Washington or Manitowoc. But there was no turning in this sea. They'd have to run before it and hope the wind shifted over farther toward the west. A big wind always went clockwise. *When* was what mattered. When would it start to shift? A thousand possibilities ran through Starr's brain, but none of them could be carried out unless the wind allowed.

He went to the window and watched Arch making his way aft. With a line tied around his waist Arch was crawling on his hands and knees across the hatches. He held tight to the battens and clawed at the tarps when the wind whipped at his body. Once he lost his hold. He rolled toward the side of the ship. His hand clutched one of the tarpaulin clamps, held on. Again he moved slowly toward the after cabin. Starr watched tensely. There was a certain grudging admiration in his face. Finally Arch reached the stanchions of the bunker at the for'ard end of the cabin. He made his way around the starboard side, out of Starr's sight.

Starr looked out at the bridge. "Oh, my God," he said. In his voice was despair and the helpless humor of a badgered man. Burgee was pulling his way up the steps to the pilothouse. It was six o'clock, and Burgee was coming on watch. His old face was stubborn as he lifted the bad foot one step at a time. Burgee wasn't going to be done out of standing his watch, storm or no storm. He came into the pilothouse. Starr had to shut the door for him. Burgee did not have the strength to swing the door shut against the wind.

"Well, Julius," he said, rubbing his hands. "Little party for old Burgee before he gets off, eh?" Burgee considered the storm a deliberate attempt to scare him into accepting his retirement. He had figured it out in his room before he came on watch. He looked innocently out at the lake and watched the huge waves sliding along the shipside. "Reminds me of the 1913 blow," he said. "Only we was over on Lake Huron then."

"Burgee," Starr began. He fought for self-control. He wanted to scream at the old fool right now; ticklish, wild laughter tried to escape his throat. He restrained himself. Burgee's befuddled brain could not understand what was happening. Starr continued more gently, almost coaxing. "Mrs. Forester's all alone down in her room," Starr said. "She's probably scared silly. I got to have a man I can trust to go down there and look after her. Poor woman," he sympathized, "all alone down there in her room. Would you look after her, Burgee? See that there's nothing working loose in her room; get her propped up so she won't knock her brains out?"

"Why, sure, Julius." Burgee smiled. He understood. Julius was very fond of Mrs. Forester. Mrs. Forester would have some whisky. He started toward the door.

"Better go this way," Starr said. He pointed to the inner staircase which led down to his room. "Watch your step now." He stood and watched Burgee slowly descending the steep stairs. By what right have I done this? Starr asked himself harshly. How did I dare? The cannibalism of command. He had no right to endanger even the expiring life of a senile old man.

Stella was scared sober. She sat on the bed with her feet braced, watching the thermos jug roll back and forth across the floor. The woodwork of the room groaned and creaked with the contorting motions of the boat. Stella was afraid she would go mad with fear if this kept up much longer. Slowly the door leading to Starr's office opened. A terrible old hand appeared on the edge of the door. Death, Stella thought. He's come after me. Stella screamed.

Burgee's head appeared quickly around the edge of the door. His eyes were frightened. His shrunken mouth worked absently as he sought for words to say. "Don't be afraid, Mrs. Forester. Julius sent me down to take care of you." He looked about the room. "Nothing big come loose yet." He shook the bureau to make sure its heavy brass hooks were holding it tight to the wall. He bent with difficulty and wedged the thermos jug beneath a lashed-down chair.

"There's a bottle in the top drawer," Stella said. She wanted to laugh but would not let herself. Hysteria would frighten Burgee. The best thing to do was try to get drunk again. "Come and sit here," she said, pointing to the other twin bed. Burgee brought the bottle over, almost falling on Stella as the boat's bow suddenly slanted high in the air.

"I've seen lots worse than this one," Burgee said after they had swallowed three drinks without speaking. "Back in '13 we had a real blow." Stella nodded. This was enough for her. "Thought we were goners. Old man wouldn't beach her. Headed right back out soon as he heard the breakers."

"Do you think we'll get through this one?" Stella asked. She was not sure. Really not sure. She poured Burgee another drink. Her hand was shaking. My God, she thought, get hold of yourself, Stella.

"Sure we will," Burgee said confidently. "Julius'll get us through if anybody can."

Julius, Stella thought. Julius Starr. If anybody can. Drown in cold, burn in hell, something said to Stella. She looked at Burgee, and again she was afraid. There was a wild gleam in the old man's eyes. He leaned back against the wall and waved his arm.

"Blow, winds, and crack your cheeks! rage! blow!" he shouted:

"You cataracts and hurricanoes, spout
Till you have drench'd our steeples, drown'd the cocks!
You sulphurous and thought-executing fires,
Vaunt-couriers to oak-cleaving thunderbolts,
Singe my white head!"

Crazy, Stella thought. He'll kill me if I stay here. He's crazy. She got up and went through into Starr's office.

"Mrs. Forester, come back, be careful," Burgee called after her.

Stella went to the stairway leading from Starr's room to the pilothouse. She scrambled up the steps. "Julius, Julius!" she cried. Starr turned and looked at her. "Are you all right, Stella?"

"Burgee," she said, standing at the head of the stairs. "He's down there in my room. I'm afraid, Julius. Let me stay up here."

"What's he doing?" Starr asked. He scarcely seemed to see

her; his deep-set eyes looked through Stella and saw always the storm.

"Quoting Shakespeare. I think he's going crazy."

"You know he always does that," Starr said calmly. "You go back down there with him. I don't want you up here."

"Julius, please let me stay. I'm afraid of him.

Starr's voice was hard. "You go back down there and take care of Burgee," he said. "You're going to do one useful thing in your life if I have to knock you down those stairs."

Stella turned and descended the stairs. Fear, the useless, womanly surface fear, was gone. It was replaced by a pride, the woman's masochistic pride, somehow greatest when she has been most humbled by a loved man, has been most harshly shown that she is less than all of her man's life. Such is a pride of spirit. Woman's pride in man's spirit. Her small freehold in that spirit becomes at such times sublimely intense, rich, by the force of those endless, stubborn surrounding lands which defy her unconscious, contrary attempts at invasion. Stella was still afraid, but now it was hidden from her face, consigned to the unknown thing which wants to live forever.

And proud, for less than Julius Starr could not have dismissed her in this way. Proud because Stella knew that only Starr, of all the men she had known, could do this; and because he had done it. She must wait below while Julius fought against a storm. A hard, wrong, great man. She must not hold his arms nor ask that he glance at her during the battle. But it was good, and she was proud, to be near him now, fear what he must fear too, feel and hear the fight.

The wind and crashing sounds of the storm could not be heard in the engine room above the constant squealing rhythm of the pistons, the hissing steam. To Sean it was worse not to hear; feel the shaking impact of unseen tons of water; cling to the heavy grating as it slanted and the entire boat shuddered before the surge of giant waves, yet never taste the cold sting of the storm above. He was afraid because it was warm here, because he was with many other men, all lying like himself across the grating, clutching the steel with their hands. Better to face alone the full extent of that which threatened than to huddle helpless beside other bodies, sheltered but waiting.

All things seemed to heighten Sean's fear. The nervous, rapid dance of the engine contrasted to the heavy, unpredictable lurching of the boat. The wheezing, labored stroke of a pump which he could see through the grating below him. Everything that moved, men or engines, made Sean afraid by the quickness and futile weakness of the actions amid the ponderous terror of the storm. The temerity of life alone seemed incredibly out of place, inviting storm's attention and a greater wrath. But to dare action, deliberately infuriate the destroying force by setting puny deeds, machines in its path—this made Sean fear.

Some of the men looked worried, their brows wrinkled with apprehension. Some wore conscious bravery, smiled and joked, but licked nervously at dry lips, glanced about quickly. One seemed to be asleep, but each time a wave shook the boat his eyes opened and he stared at the greasy steel beneath him; always his fingers picked and drummed and clutched for a firmer hold on the grating. Andy's face was pale and sober. He seemed resigned, yet not quite to believe that this was happening. Occasionally he would glance over at Sean, who lay beside him, and Andy would try to grin, but in the uncertain way he reserved for jokes he didn't get.

Sean reached in his pocket for a cigarette, holding to the grating with one hand. As he lighted it Andy squirmed closer on the grating and spoke softly.

"Aren't you scared, Sean?"

"Scared as hell," Sean said quietly. He smiled though, for Andy's face looked very young. It was good to say you were afraid, to know your face did not show all your fear, just as Andy's face must conceal the full depth of fear beneath, and so with the other men.

"So am I," Andy said. "What are you thinking about most, Sean?"

"Oh, I don't know. About Starr some, and about the boat. Hoping they're both good enough. About you and these guys and me. And mostly about something I wanted to do, a friend in Detroit I wanted to see. How about you?"

"You won't laugh?" Andy asked. He looked into Sean's eyes. "You won't kid me about it after?"

"No."

"Well"—Andy looked down through the grating, his face puzzled and poignant—"I was thinking just now about going to school on rainy days. When I was a little kid, I mean. You know"—he looked up at Sean—"how they'd have the lights on in the rooms, and everything smelled wet all day? And your ears kind of buzzed, you were dumb, the teachers were cranky?" Now Andy's face twitched, and his eyes were thoughtful and sad. "I used to sit and shiver all day," he said slowly, "like I was cold. And then it'd be time to go home, and I'd walk through the rain saying something over and over so it wouldn't seem so far. My mother would be waiting for me, watching at the window. She always used to give me hell and make me change my clothes. And our house was warm, you see, Sean? I'd hear my mother going around doing something, and outside it was raining steady; the house was kind of dark—and all of a sudden I'd be all nice and warm again." He looked at Sean, waiting to be understood.

The boat dipped deep into a canyon of water, then shook heavily as she fought to rise again. Heavy, fixed things rattled jerkily with the hull's effort.

"I know," Sean said.

"Hey, down there." All of the men looked up quickly. Arch stood at the head of the starboard stairway, which led directly from the deck into the engine room. "Everybody down below here now?" Arch asked. He did not come down the stairs.

The men looked at each other, and all of them counted or named the men about them.

"The cook ain't," somebody called.

"He'll be down. He sent me on ahead," Carl said. "I brought some coffee down and he told me to stay here."

"He can get down all right," Arch said. His voice seemed to echo through the engine room even with the noise of the engines steadily beating against it. "How about the doghouse? Anybody up there yet?"

Again the men looked about. "Old Tom, he's not here, Arch," a man shouted. "Not on watch either," another added.

Arch wiped a dripping hand across his face and peered down at the men through his fogged glasses. "Sean," he snapped, "Andy, you want to come up with me and take a bath?"

Sean and Andy followed Arch to the deck. Arch had a piece of line. He tied it around each of them. "I'll get hold of the railing down here," Arch said. "Andy, you grab on at the head of the stairs. If Sean slips, haul him in. Hold on tight. Don't breathe if a big one breaks over you." He tested the knots in the line. "Better take a turn around Tom when you get him," he told Sean. "No use doing all this if he washes overboard."

They went out on deck, wading through the fast-moving wash of the last wave. Another one was coming. "Grab hold," Arch shouted. They held onto the rail while the water broke over them, tore at them; at last the wave moved on. This time they made it to the foot of the stairway leading to the upper deck. Again they held on. When they moved up the steps as fast as possible, Arch stayed at the foot. He braced himself between the rail of the steps and the cabin wall. Another wave broke. They could not see Arch below until it was almost time for the next wave. Andy stayed at the top of the steps, braced so that he could hold on either to Sean or to Arch if they slipped. Sean waited his chance, then ran to the doghouse. He tore at the door, trying to open it before the next wave came. The wave broke and drove at his body. For an instant he lost his hold on the slippery, small doorknob. He felt the line tighten around him as Andy drew it taut.

Then the door was open. He was tying the line around Old Tom, hurrying, saying nothing. Tom's face was white. Sean waited at the door until the rushing water was gone for an instant. He dragged Tom after him toward the head of the steps. Tom tried to say something just as another wave broke, and he swallowed too much water. They had to carry him down the stairs. They held their hands over his nose and mouth as each wave broke, to keep him from drowning. Arch led the way back to the door of the engine room.

"All right," Arch said when they stood inside the door. "Take him down there and get some coffee in him." Arch took the rope off himself. "I'm going for'ard again," he said. "Tell the boys to hold onto the grating but for Christ's sake not to get in the road of the engineers." He went out on deck. Arch heard a tearing crash from the stern of the boat. He looked back quickly. Just in time, he thought. The upper deck had torn loose from the thick stanchions which supported it out over the fan-tail. The stanchions hung at crazy angles from the after rail. The heavy steel deck was folded up against the doghouse. As he worked his way midships to the life line the day ended with the quickness of a dropping curtain. The gray light was gone now. It was dark, and you had to feel the big ones coming. Arch was surprised at their silence.

Rodney MacDougall stood at the control levers beside his engines. Over his shoulder he watched the men working at water-soaked Old Tom. Tom tried to sit up and snarl at the men, but they laughed at him. For a moment they forgot their own fears because Tom's showed so plainly in his face however much his quivering lips tried to form the familiar twisted sneer. And with the part of him which was not occupied with the engines or his own fear MacDougall touched lightly the startling fact that a damned agitator like that Tom could look scared and even grateful like anybody else. The pale face there surrounded by other men seemed innocent of threat to anything that mattered. It was a time of fear and repentance for all, including

MacDougall, and he allowed to himself that Old Tom was human even if he was a bolshevik. That didn't mean Mac-Dougall wasn't a Republican though. Not by a damn sight. If he drowned, he drowned a Republican. But drowning, which was hard to imagine, seemed nevertheless a thing he would go through with Old Tom, and it was a worse thing than the election in '32.

Each time the boat rose up from a wave the screw broke free of the water. MacDougall forgot whatever else he was thinking about and slowed the engines tenderly. It was a damn shame to put well-built, faithful engines through a thing like this. The first assistant was down now looking at the propeller bearing. MacDougall was afraid. His wife, the special lamp he had built to read by at home, the children, nights with the boys at lodge, things of a comfortable, prejudiced, harmless life. There must be no show of fear before these strangers from the deck crew. He wished he could go up to his room and sit down for a while. His legs were old and unaccustomed to standing up this long. But this was his place. When anything was wrong this was his place. He looked about the engine room. The captains got you into messes. The engineers got you out of them.

At last Jonathan Shank had reached the end of his patience. He was, he told himself between swearwords, a patient and enduring man. He had mopped up the water in the galley three times. Carl he had sent below with coffee, and the two porters had gone there of their own accord. That had left Shank alone to try to preserve some kind of order in the galley. But there was no use. Jonathan watched the water rushing across the galley floor. He threw down the mop and hurled the galvanized bucket at the messroom door. He had given up the dining room. He had shut the door, but the water just opened it again.

For a moment Jonathan wondered if the boat was going to founder. He shuffled aimlessly through the water, knee-high now in the galley. Well, if they did, they did. He was too mad now to care. He looked once more at the stove, which had hissed cold some time ago. There was nothing more to be done here. He went to the pantry and gathered several loaves of bread. With these under his arm he went to the galley door. He waited his chance and scurried on his bunioned feet to the engine-room doorway.

The wind shifted, but not the right way. Starr could feel the difference immediately. The wind was almost south by east now, instead of heading around into the west. The waves were more terrifying. They grew, piling one on the other, up the entire length of the lake now, and crashed down on the *Black-foot,* taking her on the starboard quarter astern. Starr looked at the chart for the nearest place he could get in the lee of any kind of land. The boat rolled and pitched more madly now than she had before. He had been forced to head out more toward the northeast regardless of the added danger. He didn't want to pile her up on the beach at Pointe Detour. That was where she would go if he ran before the seas.

He peered anxiously ahead for Gull Island light. There wasn't any way of being sure where he was. The chronometer couldn't tell him, nor could the compass. With the wind astern like this he couldn't do anything but watch for a light somewhere. No way either of telling how much leeway she was making.

Starr felt in himself that same incalculable leeway, that drifting away from a course in his own life. You were given many guides, the instruments of man, by which to live. They were not enough. Always the unfelt, dangerous drift remained; you remained ignorant of a part, and helpless. You sought for a light to save you.

No way of telling a damn thing, Starr thought. He stood at the center window watching the blackness outside for Gull Island. Not much water in behind there, but he'd try it anyhow.

As if to taunt him, as if the storm had listened to his thought and set out to make nothing of it, the snow came. Great damp flakes swirled about the boat. They shut out even the steering pole from his sight. Starr opened the window and stood there peering through into the stinging whiteness. It was hopeless, he knew. In the thin chance that the snow might lift for just a second, that he would not have passed the light already, he stood there. Arch handed him a towel, then stood beside him. The two men watched for the faint blink of the light. Starr wrapped the towel about his neck to keep the snow out. On his head the snow gathered white and wet. Around his feet the snow began rapidly to form a small pile. Spray flew up across the bow. Starr did not feel its cold touch on his numbed face. Neither he nor Arch knew how long they stood there. Suddenly, as quickly as it had come, the snow was gone. Anxiously Starr strained his eyes into the far blackness. There was no light.

"We might have passed it," Arch said. He touched Starr on the arm, but Starr did not turn from the window. "Maybe I better try the radio compass."

"No," Starr said. "Closest station is Lansing Shoal. We're nowhere near there yet. You keep an eye out for Gull Island light."

"The light might be blown down," Arch said. "Why not try the compass?"

Starr did not reply nor turn to look at Arch. Again the anger was in Arch. He stood for a moment looking at Starr as if by the eyes alone he could learn why man does not reason in a crisis. Abruptly Arch turned and went to the radio compass. He snapped it on and adjusted the earphones on his head. The directional finder he swung to the approximate location of Lansing Shoal. Static snapped and roared so loud as the compass warmed up that Arch had to shove the phones off his ears and hear with the bones of his head. With a worried, puzzled face Arch swung the finder's turning wheel back and forth. He heard no signals; only the crackling static.

"How's she headed there, Anchor?" Arch called.

Slowly Anchor peered at the magnetic compass. "North-east," he said. He looked at the gyro. "Forty-five on this one."

Again Arch turned the finder, seeking the signals. Both compasses couldn't be wrong.

The wind is the song of dead men, Anchor thought. In the black pilothouse the small light of the compass threw into heavy relief the wrinkles of fear and of resignation on Anchor's face. Terror of death stole quietly through Anchor, but in his brain a voice repeated slowly, "Death you gave freely to another." And Anchor was more afraid of the voice than of the storm.

Starr turned from the window. "Arch, you come away from that God-damn machine," he shouted. "You won't get any thing but static with the wind in the south, you ought to know that. Now come on back here and watch for Gull Island."

"I might get a cross bearing on Detour and Gray's Reef," Arch said. "No signal from Lansing Shoal unless those compasses are shot to hell."

"Course there's no signals," Starr said. "Water's probably got in and fouled the station. Stop fooling around there and watch for that Gull Island light, I tell you. When I get in something like this I trust my eyes a hell of a lot more than I do a machine. Those things never work when you need them, Arch!" Starr shouted, and all of his command was in his voice. He motioned to Arch to return to the window. Starr's fist was clenched and ready to enforce the order.

"I ought to try for that cross bearing," Arch insisted. "We may have passed the island during that snow."

"God damn it, Arch, there's a light on Lansing Shoal too," Starr snarled. "When we see a light we'll try the radio compass on it. Don't be a fool, get back over here."

Arch said nothing. He returned to the window beside Starr and watched the blackness for a light. His teeth were clamped hard together. This was sailing. Rebel if you would; when the captain ordered your eyes to seek, and it was for the ship herself he ordered, you did as you were told. If he were wrong? You died, perhaps, or you became captain yourself. Arch had tried to do what he thought was right. Starr had not allowed it. Starr had better be right himself.

Starr was not right. From the lowest part of the hull there came a loud, shivering scrape which echoed over the entire boat. The *Blackfoot* heeled far over on her side. Starr rushed to the whistle button and blew the distress signal. Short, frightened whistle blasts sounded out in the blackness. They were unheard by any except the men on the boat. Anchor Larson lost his grasp on the wheel when the boat heeled. He fell limply down the steep slope of the pilothouse floor. His head crashed through the plate-glass window on the starboard side. Starr turned to Arch. "All right," he said. "Tell Sparks to send out an SOS."

Arch could not believe it. Though he had argued with Starr for the sake of being sure, he had not thought they were within miles of Lansing Shoal. Perhaps it was an uncharted reef, he thought numbly as he went to the door. No, this was it. The light had been torn down by the waves. He saw Anchor, who lay unconscious, slumped against the side of the pilothouse. Blood streamed down the Swede's face. Arch reached toward him. Suddenly the boat heeled quickly back to port. Arch was thrown against the steering wheel. He saw Anchor's body fly past him. It crunched softly against the newel post of the captain's stairway. Anchor dropped to the floor. The engine-room telephone rang. "I'll take care of Anchor," Starr said. "You have Sparks send that message. Tell them we're up on Lansing Shoal and give the direction of the wind. We'll probably slide off here."

Arch went out and down to the wireless shack just astern of and below the pilothouse. The wireless man was waiting for him. "SOS?" he asked.

Arch nodded. "Lansing Shoal," he said. Starr appeared at the pilothouse door.

"The rudder and screw are gone," Starr bawled above the terrific noise of the wind. "We'll be drifting. Tell 'em for God's sake send help if they can."

"Wind sou'west by west," Arch told the wireless man. The wind had suddenly rat-tailed back to westward again, shortly before they hit the reef. Just a little bit too late. Everything had happened a little bit too late in this storm, Arch thought. "The rudder and propeller were torn off when we struck," Arch said. "Tell them we'll be drifting before the wind." The wireless man began sending out the SOS.

Drifting, or on the bottom, Arch thought. With a hole like that in her, it wouldn't be long. He went back to the pilothouse. Starr was standing over Anchor. "Help me get him down to my room," Starr said. They lifted Anchor and carried him awkwardly down the inner stairway. For a few moments the pilothouse was empty. Then Starr reappeared. Stella had taken charge of Anchor. Arch had started aft again to report on the damage. There was nothing Starr could do here. With the rudder gone, the wheel was useless. The boat was tossed easily by the huge waves. Each time she sank into the trough between two waves there came again that great rending sound of her bursting plates as they hit the rocks below.

The engine-room phone rang again. Starr picked it up. His eyes looked out into the dark water all about the boat. "Yes?" he said.

The boat lurched. She moved now with a sluggish force that made each roll deeper and closer to capsizing than the last. "Water's coming in now where the screw sheared off," Mac-Dougall gasped. "I got the pumps working on it. But there's another hole where the rudder post tore out. Big hole back in the fantail. I can't pump it, Julius. It's running down in here right now. What'll I do?"

"Pray," Starr said. He hung up the receiver.

In the sudden stillness of the engine room they listened to MacDougall speaking to Starr. They watched his strained face as he turned away from the telephone. "He says pray," Mac-Dougall announced. The men did not look at one another. Their faces were pale, and as the boat continued her bucking and rolling they clung unconsciously to the grating. The water sloshed down on them from the flimsy door which had been closed between the engine room and the gangway above. Even in the tense quiet of the dead engines there was not the sound of the wind here. Only the waves as they crashed and echoed through the hull. Waves, and the harsh ripping of rock against reverberating steel.

Arch came down the steps. He glanced at the gangway door, beneath which water poured steadily down into the engine room. His voice was loud in the hissing silence. "Andy, Sean, couple of you other men, come on with me!" he shouted. They got up and went to him there on the landing. "We're going to fix this door," Arch said. The men looked at one another. Behind the thin door they could hear the water sloshing. "Get in as quick as you can so it won't run down here too much. Use planks, boiler plate, anything that's heavy and flat. Lash it all against the door." Arch did not wait. He opened the door and went into the gangway. They followed quickly.

Working waist-deep in the water, they hauled heavy boards through the litter which floated about the gangway. Through the hole which gaped in the fantail they could see more water coming in constantly. They were in danger of being struck by heavy tools from the engineers' workbench. These were tossing from one side to the other, buoyed up by the water as if they were made of wood, thrown by the lurching of the ship. Sean saw an anvil sliding toward him through the water with the grace and quickness of a large fish. He stepped aside. He felt the impact echo in his belly as the heavy steel thudded against the thin steel of the bulkhead. Somehow they found enough boards to cover both of the doorways which led into the engine room. Arch stood by and lashed each board firmly in place. At last he whistled through his teeth that the work was done. They followed him through the water, deeper now, to the stairway on the portside which led to the deck.

Each of the men felt a despairing sense of futility. In the haste of action what they did had not seemed dangerous, but now their knees trembled as they carefully made their way back around the cabin to the starboard side. Their clothes clung wetly to tired bodies, and the physical misery added to their fear and sense of wasted effort. What good to fill one breach when a hundred more would come?

Arch waved the men on to the engine room, beckoning to Sean to follow him for'ard. "You come with me," he said. "I need a man to keep watch on the damage to the forepeak and bow."

Sean looked quickly at Andy. The big boy waved his hand and went with the other men around the edge of the cabin. Sean followed Arch up the deck toward the pilothouse. The boat had slid down off the reef, lifted and carried on the giant seas. She was drifting free now. At times she turned her beam to the waves, a helpless bulk without power or direction. When the great combers broke over her deck broadside Arch and Sean clung to the life line and prayed that it be strong.

Andy sat in the engine room and listened to the sound of the pumps working at full speed. Now that Sean was gone, Andy was more afraid. Things were real. The boat was going to sink, and with it Andy. Alone, far from home, beyond the help of his mother or father, and now even Sean was gone. Andy wanted to cry. To hide his fear did not occur to him, yet he bent his head and stared down at the grating. If he could only be someplace else. If his mother would call him, and it would all be a terrible dream. If she would hold his head against her breast as she had done other times. Somewhere a man was pray-ing aloud. The other men were silent, some with their heads bent in silent prayer joined to the man's spoken words, some whose faces were curious and hesitant, watching the man who prayed. Andy began to pray too, without sound, almost without conscious words. Mother, I am afraid. Mother, come to me, hold me, Mother, for I am afraid.

Sean and Arch descended the dark iron stairs just aft of the forepeak tanks. Below they could hear water sloshing quietly and the heavy pounding of the waves.

"Look at that damn beam," Arch said. His voice was hushed here. A huge steel beam had snapped off. It dangled now from one end, dancing slowly with the delicate movement of a clock's pendulum.

Deeper and deeper into the boat's bowels they went; always it was more quiet. Sean could see the black water below now, in the dim light of the tunnel lamps. Sean wanted to turn and run back up the steps, but Arch kept moving down.

"I can't see a real hole up here," Arch said. "She's all sprung in the plates, but there'd be more water if she had a hole in her." He peered down the long dim tunnel "You can thank God she's a conveyor boat," he said soberly to Sean. "Wasn't for that extra bracing under the hoppers, she'd have broken in half when we hit. An ore boat would have."

They turned and went up the steps again. They were careful when they passed the broken beam.

"You stay up on top with Starr and me," Arch said. "Once in a while I'll want you to come down here and see how much the water rises."

Arch got the medicine chest from his room and carried it up to Starr's room. Stella Forester was standing over Anchor, wiping the blood away as it ran from the cuts in Anchor's face and neck. When Arch and Sean came in she pointed to Anchor's chest. "It's his ribs," she said. "They'll stick into his lungs if we don't tie them up some way."

Arch nodded. He took a bottle of iodine from the chest and began pouring it over the cuts. Anchor moaned and opened his eyes at the stinging pain. Arch took a roll of adhesive tape from the chest. He handed Stella his knife. "Cut his shirt off," he said. When the shirt was off, Arch looked into Anchor's eyes. "Anchor," he said, "can you stand up?"

Anchor shook his head. "I got something I want to say," he whispered weakly. "I got to say something before I die."

Sean and Stella watched silently. Stella's hands picked nervously at her dress. She was very pale. Each time the boat rolled deep or pitched into a wave Stella started and seemed to hold her breath until the sluggish hull righted itself again. Yet she stood ready to help Arch as he worked over Anchor, and Sean saw something in Stella's face that he had never seen there before. He should have known it was there, waiting and ready as were the other womanly traits of Stella, but somehow in any person who is complex, wise, and strange as Stella there is a tendency on the part of others to forget those deepest-rooted forces which she shares fully with her kind, be they ugly or handsome, learned or ignorant. It was an expression Sean had seen in his mother's face and in the faces of many women. And strangely it did not seem incongruous to Stella. It was the frightened, stubborn face of a woman when she nurses the sick or injured. Sean wondered if Anchor knew who stood beside him, who had bathed his bleeding head.

"You're not going to die," Arch told Anchor. "You'll be all right."

"I got to tell somebody," Anchor groaned. "I must confess before, before—" His words broke into a sob of pain.

Confess, Sean thought quickly. Yes, what is it you would confess, Anchor? But Sean did not speak. It was not a time for judging. And in Sean an old suspicion was no longer sharp. It did not seem to matter now, for nothing could be undone by words from Anchor. Perhaps it was wrong, but Sean hoped Anchor would not say the words.

"I must not—" Anchor began again.

"Keep still and stand up," Arch snapped. "Here, Sean." With a surprised, pained look in his eyes Anchor stood up, helped by Sean. Anchor looked wildly at Stella. . . . "Now raise your arms," Arch said.

"I can't, Arch," Anchor said. "Let me die without more pain."

"Raise your arms," Arch repeated. "I'll kill you or cure you." Sweat poured from Anchor as he raised his arms slowly, sometimes letting them drop heavily in Sean's supporting hands as he fought for more strength. "Now grab hold of that curtain rod over the bed there," Arch ordered. "Go on, God damn you, grab it." Anchor's hands slowly raised to the curtain rod. His breathing was slow, at times seeming to catch painfully within his chest.

Quickly Arch ran turn after turn of the tape around Anchor's ribs and chest, making it as tight as he could. He snapped his fingers. Stella handed him another roll, then another, until Anchor was taped from his waist to his neck. "All right, you can lie down again," Arch said. Sean caught Anchor as he fell and laid him down gently on the bed.

Sean followed Arch up the hot, narrow stairway to the pilothouse. When the boat rolled suddenly to starboard they were forced to lie almost flat on the steep stairs to keep from being thrown back to the bottom. Arch was quiet as they shoved open the flat door through the pilothouse floor. Starr did not turn to look at them. Yet Sean felt a tension now, stranger somehow because the conflicts of other men on the boat had been forgotten in the frightening threat of the storm. It was very cold in the pilothouse. The wind tore through the opened for'ard window at which Starr stood, and fought to escape against its own force howling through the blood-specked window where Anchor had fallen.

It was quite dark. Starr was no more than a looming, motionless shadow at the window, darker than the night outside. Sean looked at the wheel. Its polished dark wood gleamed dimly in the single small pattern of the binnacle light. Sean was more afraid than before. The one detail—a wheel without a wheelsman—seemed a more terrible symbol of defeat than all the crashing, shaking assaults the boat had undergone in the storm. Without knowing why he did so, Sean went to the wheel and took hold of its palm-smoothed spokes. His fingers groped for the waxed Turks-head of the midships spoke and turned the wheel until the Turks-head was at the top. What good to turn a rudderless wheel? A man will ask the firing squad to wait while he puffs three times at a cigarette.

Neither Starr nor Arch seemed aware of Sean's presence in the pilothouse. Perhaps it was because he stood at the wheel silently, as a man always stood at the wheel, unnoticed except when an order was given. Starr had turned from the window. He looked into the shadows of Arch's face and waited. Arch had come close to Starr. He held on to the compass housing and peered into Starr's cold, dark eyes as if some softness there, some fear, could plead as words could not; perhaps ask pity, make lighter the stern judgment forcing up to Arch's lips. Starr did not plead.

Sean watched the two men and waited for one to speak. He strained to hear the words that would come, for he knew they would not be loud words, and the shut-in wind here made a constant snarling din. And Sean wondered at, then suddenly understood, the strength of feeling between the two men. When two are driven so far by one shared force that they cannot forget that force even in the face of their own destruction, all distinction between love and hate ceases to exist. By whatever name given their strange need, the two must ever be together. Another foe or friend would not seem worthy.

"I don't think we'll get through this," Arch said softly. "If we don't, there's no use my telling you it was your fault." Still Starr's face did not change. He stared at Arch, taking it. "But if somehow or other we do get through," Arch said, "so help me Christ, Julius Starr, I'll make your name stink up and down these lakes so you'll never show your face within a thousand miles of them again."

"All right," Starr said. "If we get through, you go ahead."

Three men in the pilothouse knew what the words meant. Two were ashamed and afraid to hear them spoken. It was Starr's renunciation of the only god in his life, himself and his command. He offered this, all that he was, as a sacrifice to the demon-god of storm. It was not for his own tired life that he did this. Without power and pride Julius Starr did not care if he lived. But he was still master. He must bring those he ruled through this night storm. If he did, the cost did not matter; Starr would pay with his own soul. Yet three men in the pilothouse knew it was not enough; more than Starr could be offered, but the storm would remain ravenous, unglutted. Each man felt the weakness of himself here in the high-built place of watch and direction, unable to do more than wait and listen.

The boat rose clumsily, crawling sidewise like a crab up the slope of a huge wave, then again she dropped heavily onto the sunken rocks of another reef. Steel rigging of the foremast snapped in the sudden supple twisting of the hull and lashed against the for'ard cabin like a great snake whip. There was the sound of buckling plates from below, then the scrape of the hull against jagged rock. The pilothouse jiggled ridiculously as the foremast began to sway, loosed from its taut stays. Each wave lifted the *Blackfoot* as if to free her, carried her swiftly along, and threw her again onto the ripping rocks. As she struck hard on one particularly large rock, then began sliding off, the foremast gave way. With a sharp, creaking snap it broke off clean about ten feet above the deck just aft of the pilothouse. The upper section fell to the main deck. It bounced as if it were made of rubber hose, beating thick steel plates there into impossibly twisted shapes. Then, as if the storm were sorry for what it had done or wished its mouse to live for more play, another huge comber picked the boat up and threw her again into deeper water.

"Sparks," Starr said. He and Arch went to the starboard door.

"No, he's all right," Arch said. The wireless man had come out of his little room just below the foot of the spar. Arch opened the pilothouse door. "Can you still send without the aerial?" he bawled to the wireless man.

Sparks shook his head. "I'll try to rig up something," he shouted. He turned to his room.

Arch turned to Sean. "You go down and take a look at the plates below. Think there's any use rigging a sea anchor?" he asked Starr.

Starr shook his head. "Won't keep us off the rocks." He returned to the for'ard window. As Sean went down the stairs he saw Arch standing beside Starr. Both men peered out into the night.

Not think of Whitey. Think only of here, of the steps, the door, the wind, more steps wet with broken waves. But not of Whitey; of no shore things. They were gone now, and thoughts made you more afraid. As he descended again into the black depths of the hull Sean wondered what it would be like when the boat sank. It was hard for him to imagine that he must leave the boat, fight with his body the terrible waves. There could not be a time when they would say abandon ship. The ship was solid, big. It would slowly fill with water and sink, but what good to leave it, wrapped in the flimsy bobbing cork of a life jacket? What good to fight with flesh what steel could not withstand? Not of Whitey. Never of Whitey.

The water was higher now. It was fewer steps down until you could hear it; fewer steps until you could see it, mysterious black below. The big beam had broken again, and it lay wedged against other beams, no longer moving in slow dance. Down the tunnel as far aft as he could see, the bracing midships under the hoppers was bent and broken now. The steel plates between tunnel and tanks below were thrown up into ridged waves. Rivets had broken off in plates, and the naked bracing of the tanks had thrust up into the tunnel.

Never of Whitey. Get out of here, and don't think of Whitey. No Arch led the way now. He need not go deeper, closer to that black water there. One hull plate on the starboard side had a large crack in it. Water gushed through an open-lipped hole. The great dark vault hung threatening over Sean.

He looked up, and it was far to the deck. If you abandoned the ship she would follow you. You would look back and up from a water-filled lifeboat, from your mad fight with the water alone. The huge black hull would be lifted ready to descend upon you, borne by the waves to carry you beneath the water. Your bones would lie pinned to deep sands by a great black bulk.

He must not think of Whitey nor of the city nor the things he would have done. A small piece of coal dropped unseen by Sean into the water. He heard the splash and saw the widening circle of ripples on the blackness. Sean ran up the steps as fast as he could. He was afraid.

In the pilothouse Sean reported to Arch. Arch scarcely listened to him; he seemed preoccupied with the sound of the storm. He did no more than nod when Sean had finished. Voices, words seemed out of place now. There was a long silence. At last Arch spoke, softly, as if he hesitated to do so still and had considered the matter carefully for some time.

"You think there's any chance of getting a boat launched in this, Julius?"

"No," Starr said without turning to Arch. "Not a chance. If she goes down, we'll have to try. But listen to that damn wind." They all listened for a moment to the incredible howling outside, a series of sounds in chorus varying in pitch from growling bass to insane soprano. "Small boat wouldn't have a chance," Starr repeated.

Silence fell again upon the three men. They waited, and forgot time because it did not matter. Occasionally, in some strange lull, the ticking of the chronometer could be heard. None of the men went to look at the clock's hands. There was nothing to be said and nothing to be done. Figures set to hours; hours themselves could not measure the storm.

The black night had become a sickly gray when they heard the thundering roar of breakers. The three men looked at one another. Starr opened the door and stood on the bridge listening. Soon they could see the land, a low, sandy blur coming closer every minute.

"Better go aft and get a boat ready," Starr said. Arch motioned to Sean to follow him and started carefully down the steps.

A few small land birds fought the wind to investigate this huge black monster which came to disturb their lonely beach. At last, as Sean and Arch made their way aft by the life line, the *Blackfoot* paused in her swift flight before the storm. There was a gentle, soft, crunching sound as her hull rested in the sand below the waves. As each wave broke over her now she drove deeper and firmer into the bottom. Slowly she swung around until her portside was offered to the waves, her wounded starboard plates protected. At last she no longer moved at all. She had made her landfall.

The men in the engine room felt the stillness. One after the other they came up from below. Each blinked his eyes at the morning light, looked about at the damage done to the ship. Soon the entire crew was lined up along the starboard rail. Faces were pale; some eyes were still red and wet from frightened weeping. Several men were bruised where they had been thrown against the grating below by the boat's violent tossing. All stood there on deck silently. They ignored the cold spray which still flew over the cabin from the portside. Here was a lee—let waves and wind attack to port. Here was light of day, which the men had not hoped to see again. And there, not so far away, good to see, was land. They stared fixedly at the low shore across the water. Andy began to cry. None of the men looked at him. Exhausted, still trembling, the men looked out at security. Each of them wanted to set his feet at once in that sand, to sink down on it and feel the solid texture of land.

Inshore Arch had seen the concrete strip of a highway. They were somewhere west of St. Ignace, he guessed. From Lansing Shoal they must have come over Potter Reef and several of the Miles Coquins reefs. Five times the boat had struck during the long night. There would be a doctor in St. Ignace. Anchor needed a doctor.

"Sean, Andy, Elmer, George, you boys come on with me," Arch said. "Some of you other men come up and help us launch a boat." They went to the upper deck. Some of the men began unlashing the stiff canvas boat cover, and others tugged at the stiff, protesting davits.

Carefully they launched the boat and rowed to shore, keeping in the lee of the *Blackfoot* as much as possible. The lifeboat rode the waves until the bottom grated on the sand. Arch got out and waded through the water to the beach. He did not wait as Sean and the other men hauled the boat as far up as she would go. Arch walked on to the highway.

The four men sat down on the sand to wait for Arch to return. Andy smiled at Sean happily. Like a child the big boy picked up a handful of sand and let it dribble slowly through his strong fingers. Sean too smiled. Then he looked at the sand, resting his head on his knees, and thought of Whitey. Elmer lay flat on his stomach, panting as if he had been running for a long time, and George, a wheelsman, kept digging the heels of his work shoes deeper and deeper into the soft, damp sand. Each of the men sat alone with the reasons for his life, and to each of them the reasons were sufficient. It was good to be here on the land, alive. Good to forget the long night of storm.

Good to be able again to think of promises, Sean thought. To know again, after having denied himself hope in the storm, that he would see Whitey. He would be able to tell Whitey what it had been like to be afraid. And yes, now that it was all over, it seemed good that there had been the storm. He had seen things about men which are not there to see during the calm days. Some things noble, some cowardly, but all were things deep and insistent in men. All of it Sean would tell Whitey. He was impatient to see Whitey. Tell him about Stella Forester and Anchor, and about Andy, and Old Tom. And about Arch and Starr.

Suddenly Sean realized that there was more to come

between Arch and Starr. He remembered the threat last night. It seemed long ago, as if it should now be forgotten. But Sean remembered the words Arch had said. He wondered if Arch would remember. Sean would not answer these things himself. He would take them all to Whitey, save them for wise Whitey. Yet he knew Whitey would not answer them either; he would only listen. A great sense of splendid exuberance filled Sean. It came from such simple things as sand, a friend's image, the stolid joy of saved men.

Julius Starr was alone in his cabin. The storm had not won, Starr thought. The men were alive; the boat was broken but would sail again. The components of Starr's command existed still. But the moment of victory for these things marked too the defeat of Julius Starr. He was not afraid; he could not even be bitter. The price of escape, the ransom of boat and men, had been agreed upon. The fact that Arch, to whom the bargain had been spoken, was one of those saved by the bargain was of no importance. It did not matter that Arch would exact the payment. Starr had no cause to resent Arch's agency in the settlement of a debt owed only to the storm. Arch, he understood, would not take more than he deserved for having been right when Starr was wrong. And Starr knew he had been wrong. For that, if Arch remained ambitious Arch, Starr would pay with his job.

To the storm Starr would pay something more. What was it he would pay? His power, Starr thought. Not power of position, for that power was not his own. Arch could have that. Suddenly Starr saw that the storm had already received what had been promised it. During the night it had collected its fee, Starr's own power as a man, and without other acknowledgment the waves had scornfully thrown the ship upon this solemn beach. Yes, paid in full. For Julius Starr knew that always, in that future he tried confusedly to see, he would stop and think before acting. Caution had come; antidote of power as it had been in Starr; precursor of old age.

Starr sat at the desk in his office. He stared down at the

amorphous imprints of ink upon the blotter. Never again to fight as he had fought this storm. Already to feel the complete truth of man's limitations. To argue that all was not gone, but find himself accepting the minor role of rational, defeated man. An easier way to live, Starr knew. He would come not to blame himself for what nature did to men. Yes, and he would remember being another sort of man.

Pay and be damned. It had all been worth it; he would not have changed with any man. Julius Starr, Master. There was no price too great to pay.

Stella Forester came into the office, but Starr did not heed her. She smoothed his hair, and his head did not move. He does not belong to me, Stella thought. As much to me as to another. I have been with him during a battle, but now he is tired. I cannot have him now; nor was he mine in the storm. He is not for the weak to hold and possess. His love is for the storm. Others may watch but cannot help him. Their peace is not for him; it is a thing of lies and compromise. Stella went back to her room. She tried to soothe Burgee, who was crying weakly for a long-dead mother to come to him. Stella looked down at this old child. Her face was tender, but unrepentant as Starr's.

The doctor was drunk. Arch had hitched a ride in to St. Ignace with a motorist who stopped on the highway to stare at the looming hulk of the *Blackfoot* there near the beach. In town Arch had gone from bar to bar in search of the doctor. At each bar Arch had taken a drink himself. When he found the doctor Arch had the waiter bring black coffee. Arch did not drink any of the coffee himself, but he made the doctor drink it while he tried to explain what he wanted him to do. The doctor thought he was lying or crazy. At last Arch dragged the man by the arm to the street outside and found an old taxicab to drive them back to the boat. Arch felt pretty good. They stopped at the doctor's office for his bag, and Arch had another drink.

On the way back to the boat, cold air warring against the liquor in both men, Arch began to sober up. The doctor at last understood about the boat. He sat blinking his eyes at the cold wind and the sand blown everywhere by the storm, timidly waiting to see the boat. Arch was silent.

At last he had Starr right where he wanted him. Arch knew he could be captain now. He thought of the things he had done during the night. Brave things. Actions without Starr, beyond Starr, better than Starr. It was a good feeling, wasn't it? Arch asked himself. But somehow it wasn't. Arch didn't feel as good as he had before he thought about Starr. Arch had felt what it was to be his own man, and then the old thoughts of Starr had come. But he was entitled to Starr's job, Arch told himself. Starr shouldn't have gone out in such a storm to begin with. A man like Starr shouldn't sail a boat.

Arch thought of Starr's cabin, of his chair with arms in the officers' mess, of many things Starr had which Arch did not have. Then Arch thought of the storm. None of these things had seemed important during the storm. He recalled the unmoving face of Starr as it peered out the window, trying to see through the night, snow gathering on Starr's head, about his feet.

Many thoughts, of Starr and of the storm, filled Arch's mind with the old perplexity, the familiar sense of inner battle between two forces. The liquor made Arch weave slightly as he walked the doctor across the beach to the lifeboat. But Arch did not feel drunk now. He was sober and thoughtful as the men rowed back to the ship, Arch steering, the doctor huddled nervously beside him at the stern. Starr was standing by the after railing watching the lifeboat. The old man's face asked for no pity. Arch could see Starr's hands gripped tight on the rail as the lifeboat swung alongside and the lines were fastened to her. Starr's eyes were cold though, and there was no softness in his face.

And then Arch knew that Julius Starr would not be punished for his mistake. He had beaten Starr, and that was enough. Even as he thought the word "beaten" Arch wondered if he had beaten or only equaled the man on the deck above. The words of revenge meant nothing now. There would not be that scene, planned and carefully awaited during long nights when Arch had nursed ambition alone in his room, that scene in which the inspectors sat sternly behind a long table, hearing Arch give evidence to ruin Starr. Arch would lie for Starr now; he would help the old man out of a tight spot, tell the inspectors anything at all rather than have them punish Starr. Arch was satisfied to have proven himself as much a man as his captain. Inspectors were lappers of spilled milk. Not Arch. He had what he wanted right now. Arch had learned, in the only way a man ever can learn, that he was not a coward.

"Heave away," he called to the men at the davits. The lifeboat rose. As it passed the rail Arch looked at Starr calmly. It was the firm, ungrudging look of one equal in all but command. Arch did not get off at the rail. He rode the boat up to the davits and climbed out on the upper deck.

Bibliography

Bloomfield, Leonard. *Menomini Texts.* Publications of the American Ethnological Society, edited by Franz Boas. New York: G. E. Stechert and Co., 1928.

Braley, Berton. "The Skipper." In *Songs of the Workaday World.* New York: George H. Doran, 1915.

Curwood, James Oliver. "The Fish Pirates." In *Falkner of the Inland Seas,* edited by Dorothea A. Bryant. New York: Books, Inc., 1944.

Eltham, Dean. "Geraniums." *Maclean's Magazine,* March 15, 1929.

Emberg, Ralph A. "Out of the Trough." In *Phantom Caravel.* Boston: Bruce Humphries, 1948.

"The Fisherman *Yankee Brown.*" Ivan H. Walton papers. Michigan Historical Collections, Bentley Library, University of Michigan, Ann Arbor, Michigan.

"The Ghost Ship." *Toronto Telegram,* February, 1931.

Havighurst, Walter. "A Gold-Headed Cane." In *Signature of Time.* New York: Macmillan Company, 1945.

"Helmsmen on Lake Erie." *The Spirit of the Times,* November 1, 1845.

Hurlbut, Frances. "The Fall of the Lighthouse." In *Grandmother's Stories.* Cambridge, Mass.: Privately printed at the Riverside Press, 1889.

Jones, William. *Ojibwa Texts, Collected by William Jones.* Vol. 2, edited by Truman Michelson. New York: G. E. Stechert and Co., 1917–19.

"A Lake Huron Ghost Story." *Saginaw Courier* (Michigan), August 30, 1883.

McCormick, Jay. *November Storm.* New York: Doubleday, Doran and Company, Inc., 1943.

Raine, Norman Reilly. "The Deep Water Mate." *Maclean's Magazine,* October 1, 1928.

Robertson, Morgan. "The Survival of the Fittest." In *The Three Laws and the Golden Rule.* New York: McClure's Magazine, 1898.

Rogers, Stan. "The Lock-keeper." *From Fresh Water.* Hamilton, Ontario: Cole Harbour Music, Ltd., 1984.

Scenes on Lake Huron. New York: Privately printed, 1836.

Schoolcraft, Henry R. "The Origin of the White Fish" and "The Tempest." In *Algic Researches*. New York: Harper and Brothers, 1839.

"The Schooner *Thomas Hulme*." Ivan H. Walton papers. Michigan Historical Collections, Bentley Library, University of Michigan, Ann Arbor, Michigan.

Snider, Charles Henry Jeremiah. "An Anchor in a Graveyard." In *The Story of the Nancy and Other Eighteen-Twelvers*. Toronto: McClelland and Stewart, 1926.

"The Snow Wasset." Ivan H. Walton papers. Michigan Historical Collections, Bentley Library, University of Michigan, Ann Arbor, Michigan.

Vukelich, George. "The Bosun's Chair." *Arts in Society* 1 (Fall 1960): 45–64.

––––––. "The Sturgeon." *University of Kansas City Review* 24 (March, 1958): 163–77.

Woolson, Constance Fenimore. "Ballast Island." *Appleton's Journal* 9 (June, 1873): 833–39.

Biographical Notes

Leonard Bloomfield. 1887–1949. Educated as a linguist at Harvard and the University of Chicago, Professor Bloomfield's innovative approach to teaching languages, documented in *Introduction to the Study of Language* (1914), revolutionized the process of learning a foreign tongue. A prolific writer, he translated and compiled several texts of Native American stories, among them *Menomini Texts* (1928), *Sacred Stories of the Sweet Grass Cree* (1930), and *Plains Cree Texts* (1934). He ended his career as Sterling Professor of Linguistics at Yale University.

James Oliver Curwood. 1878–1927. A popular turn-of-the-century writer from Michigan, Curwood's career was framed by his fiction about the Great Lakes. His first book, written shortly after he left his job as a reporter for the *Detroit News Tribune,* was *The Courage of Captain Plum* (1908) and told of the confrontation between King Strang and a lakes captain on Beaver Island. *Falkner of the Inland Seas* (1944) was a posthumous collection of stories that had appeared in magazines early in the century. Between these two books, Curwood published numerous melodramatic adventure novels and stories, most set in the Canadian wilderness that he popularized as "God's Country."

Dean Eltham. "Dean Eltham" may be a pseudonym for an unknown Canadian writer who published several stories in *Maclean's Magazine* in the 1920s and 1930s. "Geraniums" is his only story set on the Great Lakes.

Ralph Emberg. A writer of travel pieces and a sailor on Canadian Great Lakes ships, Emberg published one short story collection in 1948, *Phantom Caravel.* He was an early collector of lakes sailing folklore and sailor's songs.

Walter Havighurst. 1901–. A well-known writer of Great Lakes fiction and history, Havighurst worked as a deckhand on lakes freighters before attending college at Ohio Wesleyan, the University of Denver, and Columbia University. He later shipped out on salt water in the merchant marine before doing graduate work at King's College, Cambridge. He became a professor of English at Miami University in Ohio in 1928. He is best known for his novels of Lake Erie, *The Quiet Shore* (1937), *The Winds of Spring* (1940), and *Signature of Time* (1949), and for his histories of the Great Lakes, *The Long Ships Passing* (1942), and *The Great Lakes Reader* (1966).

Frances Ward Hurlbut. d. 1892. A member of the Ward shipping family on the Great Lakes, Hurlbut grew up near Detroit, Michigan, graduated from Michigan State Normal School (Michigan State University), and died in Crescent City on North Manitou Island. *Grandmother's Stories* is Hurlbut's only publication.

William Jones. (1871–1909). A highly skilled ethnographer and an American Indian of Fox descent who was born on the reservation, Jones was educated at Harvard and had an extensive command of Indian languages. He collected his Ojibwa materials under the auspices of the Carnegie Foundation between 1903 and 1905 among the tribes living north and west of Lake Superior. He was speared to death in 1909 by members of the Ilongot Tribe in the Philippines while on an anthropological assignment for the Field Museum of Chicago.

Jay McCormick. 1919–. The son of a Great Lakes captain, McCormick grew up in Harbor Beach, Michigan, and spent much of his youth sailing the lakes with his father. He graduated from the University of Michigan in 1942, where he was an editor of the student publications and won several Hopwood Awards for creative writing. *November Storm* won a major Hopwood Award in 1942 and was translated into Portuguese in Brazil in 1944. After a stint as a reporter for the *Detroit News*, he became professor of English at Wayne State University, a position he still holds.

Norman Reilly Raine. 1895–1971. Born in Pennsylvania, Raine began his writing career as a reporter for the *Buffalo Morning Express* in 1912. After World War I service with the Canadian Expeditionary Forces in Europe, he became an editor of *Maclean's Magazine* in Toronto, then a screenwriter in Hollywood, where he won an Oscar for the script of *The Life of Emile Zola* in 1937. He is best known for his Tugboat Annie stories, which ran in the *Saturday Evening Post* and described the rambunctious master of a Puget Sound tug and towing company.

Morgan Robertson. 1861–1915. The son of a Great Lakes captain from Oswego, New York, Robertson went to sea in the merchant service from 1877 to 1886. He attained the rank of first mate, but left the sea to become a jeweler. When his eyesight failed he turned to writing, producing more than two hundred stories and several novels during his career, most set on salt water. Sinful Peck, his most famous character, is a lakes sailor who terrorizes ocean-going captains with his bravery and intelligence, much as Melville's Steelkilt did in *Moby-Dick*. Robertson was not a good businessman, however, and he found writing difficult because of his poor education. Despite his early success and accolades from writers such as Joseph Conrad, he died nearly destitute in an Atlantic City hotel.

Henry Rowe Schoolcraft. 1793–1864. Educated at Union College and Middlebury, Schoolcraft became Indian agent for the Lake Superior tribes in 1822 and later Superintendent of Indian Affairs for Michigan from 1836 to 1841. He did extensive research on Indian subjects and produced some of the first systematic Native American ethnological studies in the United States. In 1823 he married Jane Johnston, a daughter of John Johnston, "the patriarch of the Sault," and Oaha-guscoday-way-quay. Jane's maternal grandfather was Waub Ojeeg, a powerful Chippewa Chief and a legendary storyteller. The tales and myths Schoolcraft heard from his wife's family and others found their way into all his works, the most famous of which is *Algic Researches* (1839).

C. H. J. Snider. 1879–1971. Charles Henry Jeremiah Snider went sailing on the lakes when he was eleven and that voyage, in a timber drogher from St. Catharines, Ontario, to Fairhaven, New York, wedded him to the lakes and to sailing craft forever. By the end of his life he calculated he was personally acquainted with 1,500 vessels, and as the author of a dozen books about sailing craft on the lakes and the column "Schooner days" in the *Toronto Telegram*, he had written about many more. He is the lakes' foremost writer about sailing craft in the War of 1812, describing them with the entertaining mixture of fact and fiction that marked his newspaper columns.

George Vukelich. 1927–. A newspaper columnist in Madison, Wisconsin, and host of Wisconsin Public Radio's "North Country Notebook," Vukelich has published poems and stories in numerous periodicals, including the *Beloit Poetry Journal*, *Sign*, the *Atlantic*, *Poems Out of Wisconsin*, and *Botteghe Oscure* of Rome, Italy. *North Country Notebook*, his collection of environmental essays, was published in 1987. He sailed the lakes as a merchant seaman on the *Norman B. Ream* and the *D. M. Clemson* and is the author of a novel about the fishing industry, *Fisherman's Beach*, published in 1962.

Ivan H. Walton. 1893–1968. The maritime folksong and folklore of the Great Lakes was Professor Walton's lifelong interest. During his tenure as a professor of English in the School of Engineering at the University of Michigan from 1919 to 1962, he dedicated himself to collecting and preserving the folklore of the schooner age on the lakes in interviews and recordings. He founded the Michigan Folklore Society, and the archive of his work, including his notes, articles, books, and recordings, is at the Bentley Historical Library at the University of Michigan.

Constance Fenimore Woolson. 1840–1894. Born in New York, the grandniece of James Fenimore Cooper, Woolson was raised in Cleveland and spent her summers on Mackinac Island. She was the first woman to write maritime fiction about the lakes, and her 1882 novel, *Anne,* set partially on Mackinac Island, was a best seller that inspired any number of sentimental pilgrimages to the island. A pioneer of post–Civil War realism, she created strong female characters who anticipated twentieth-century writing by many years. She moved permanently to Europe in 1879, and despite a successful career, she fell or threw herself to her death from her bedroom window in Venice. She was buried in the Protestant Cemetery in Rome by her friend of many years, Henry James.